THE
CHAKRA BIBLE

THE
CHAKRA BIBLE

THE DEFINITIVE GUIDE TO WORKING WITH CHAKRAS

Patricia Mercier

STERLING
New York

An Hachette Livre UK Company

First published in Great Britain in 2007
by Godsfield Press, a division of
Octopus Publishing Group Ltd
Carmelite House, 50 Victoria Embankment
London EC4Y 0DZ

Published by Sterling Publishing Co., Inc.
1166 Avenue of the Americas, New York, NY 10036

Distributed in Canada by Sterling Publishing Co., Inc.
c/o Canadian Manda Group, 664 Annette Street,
Toronto, Ontario, Canada M6S 2C8

This book is not intended as an alternative to personal medical advice. The reader should consult
a physician in all matters relating to health and particularly in respect of any symptoms which may
require diagnosis or medical attention. While the advice and information are believed to be accurate
and true at the time of going to press, neither the author nor the publisher can accept any legal
responsibility or liability for any errors or omissions that may have been made.

Patricia Mercier asserts the moral right to be identified as the author of this work.

16 18 20 19 17

Manufactured in China

ISBN 978-1-4027-5224-7

CONTENTS

WHAT ARE CHAKRAS?

○ ○ ○ ○ ○ ○ ○

In Chapter 1 the chakras are introduced and the concept of "subtle energy" is explained, both in relation to other therapies and in the way it affects our bodies, minds and spirits.

the flow of subtle energy in our bodies

We are not just physical bodies—remarkable though that is—for around us is a pulsating electromagnetic energy field that is described either as a rainbow-like aura or as a luminous light body. This "subtle-energy" field interacts with our physical body by flowing through concentrated spirals of energy. In yoga practice these spiralling energy centers are known as chakras, a Sanskrit word meaning "wheels of light."

There are seven main chakras (plus a number of smaller ones) that interact with the body's ductless endocrine glands and lymphatic system by feeding in good energy and disposing of unwanted energy. It is vitally important for our general health and the prevention of illness or "disease" that we nourish our chakras in the correct way.

how this book works

This book begins by introducing you to the chakras and the subtle bio-energies in and around our bodies, usually referred to as the "layers" of the aura (Part 1). It continues with in-depth information about each of the seven main chakras, their correspondences in the physical body and how you can use breathing and visualization exercises to balance your life-force energy (Parts 2–8). The origins of chakras in the Indian tradition are explored and linked to the present-day practice of yoga.

Chakras are fundamental to an understanding of holistic healing, and these seven sections of the book offer easy-to-use instructions for utilizing crystals, color, sound, aromatherapy and a number of other effective self-heal methods, giving a broad-based understanding for beginners, healers and practitioners alike.

The later sections of the book explore the newly discovered chakras: the Earth Star, Hara/Navel and Causal Chakras, the Soul Star and Stellar Gateway, and the Sun, Moon and cosmic chakras (Part 9). The chakras as a whole are placed within the context of other traditions, such as Taoism, the Kabbalah, Sufism, Inca and Mayan teachings and shamanism, and the Earth and Planetary chakras are introduced (Part 10). Culminating with a section on chakras and healing, the book explains how to give healing to recipients (Part 11).

An aura may be seen by clairvoyants and by Kirlian photography.

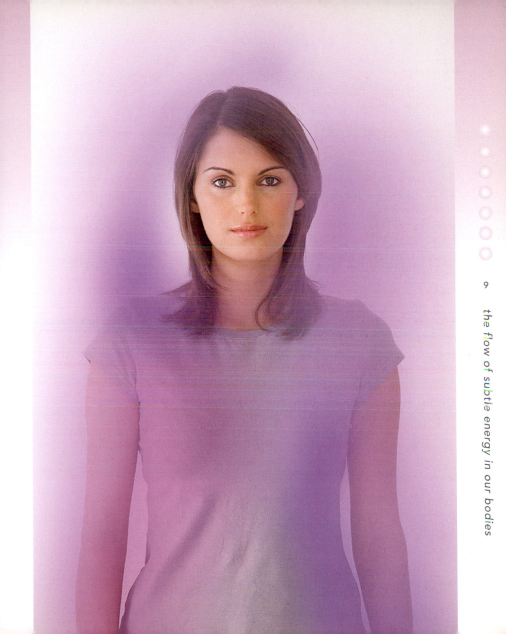

the flow of subtle energy in our bodies

the aura and the chakras

The body's external subtle-energy field can best be described as an aura—a rainbow of light surrounding the body. Those sensitive people who can see delicate bio-energies say that the colors within the aura are constantly changing, depending on our state of health, emotions and spiritual development. Each time we glimpse a rainbow, it is always in front of us and our back is to the Sun; since no two people can ever be in exactly the same place at the same time, each person sees a slightly different rainbow. In the same way we each see people's auras differently, because we are looking through our own perception at their auric field.

perceiving the human aura

Seeing the human aura is an ability that we have either had since childhood or can achieve through intense spiritual discipline. Like a rainbow, the aura is made of "drops" of energy that vibrate on different frequencies to produce colored light.

When looking for subtle energies, we are often limited by cultural conditioning. As children we probably had a greater chance of seeing colored light energies around people, but as we grew older were told that it is not possible to perceive auras, fairies or angels. However, those who retain a healthy regard for the natural world often excel at seeing energies. Fortunately, there are ways to train the rest of us. First of all, try to detect the energies around trees. They usually have a huge energy field, which can be seen if you

The primary rainbow shows colors violet to red, this is reversed on the secondary rainbow.

look *beyond* the trees without straining your eyes (see pages 280–281). Another way is to ask a friend to stand about 10 ft. (3 m) away against a plain wall in dim light—again look *beyond* them, and have no expectations.

the chakras as a blueprint

In the same way that the body has organs, the chakras are the organs of the luminous energy field. They are pulsating discs of focused energy with particular color affinities. The spiral of each chakra narrows as it nears the physical body, and the seven major chakras "hook" directly into the spine.

Chakras transmit information from the aura and represent a "blueprint" of the body; they also hold information of past pain and trauma, as imprints in the auric field. These affect our emotional and physical health through their connection to the endocrine glands that regulate human behavior (see pages 40–41).

what does the aura look like?

Scientists can measure the electromagnetic field close to our skin, which is often seen in dim light conditions as a fine golden glow around a person. An even finer field of energy—the human aura or luminous body—extends outwards, sometimes as far as 30 ft. (9 m) in faster and higher frequencies, penetrated by the swirling chakras. Esoteric teachings usually assign this energy field a number of layers (see pages 14–15), each of which corresponds with a color and a quality. These colors progress through the aura like those of the light spectrum, from red to violet.

the aura in history

Throughout the ages people have been aware of the human energy field, in diverse cultures worldwide, from ancient Egypt, Greece and China to India, Persia and the Americas. In Hindu tradition it was called prana; in China, ch'i; while in ancient Greece Pythagoras wrote of "vital energy" being perceived as a luminous body.

During the 1930s to 1950s scientific research by Dr. Wilhelm Reich enabled healers to show not only the existence of the auric field, but also its correlation with chakras, as intense energy vortices within it.

Many researchers now agree that the human energy field provides an energy matrix upon which physical cells grow. This means that the energy exists *before* the physical body. They have shown that disturbances in the auric field eventually manifest as disease in the physical body, meaning that healing any imbalance in the aura will assist the body to resist illness.

the light spectrum

As humans, we exist within the 49th Octave of Vibration of the electromagnetic light spectrum. Below this range are barely visible radiant heat, then invisible infrared, television and radio waves, sound and brain waves; above it is barely visible ultraviolet, then the invisible frequencies of chemicals and perfumes, followed by X-rays, gamma rays, radium rays and unknown cosmic rays. If you remember that you are a Being of Light in a physical body, you will be open to understanding how chakras are vital to all interactions of life on Earth.

Our auric field and subltle energies are "colored" by our personal strengths/weaknesses, health/sickness, happiness/sadness, love/hate and the degree to which we commune with our spiritual life.

The halo of a saint or Christ is usually shown as an auric glow around their Crown Chakra.

sensing the layers of the aura

The human energy field takes on an egg-like (or cocoon) shape around the body. Spiritual healers can discern that it comprises a number of layers blending together in a magical way. Generally the energy becomes faster and finer as it moves further away from the body.

When seen together, as one rainbow mix of swirling light, the luminous auric field of a spiritually advanced person will merge into the pure, clear white Light of Spirit (written with a capital L, to distinguish it from light in the visible spectrum).

what are chakras?

THE AURA'S SEVEN LAYERS

These start with the layer (Energy Body) closest to the physical body.

Name of layer	Main color
1 Etheric Body (or lower etheric)	Red
2 Emotional Body (lower emotional aspect)	Orange
3 Mental Body (lower mental aspect) These three "bodies" are within the *physical plane*	Yellow
4 Higher Mental Body This "body" is within the "astral plane"	Green
5 Spiritual Body (etheric template)	Turquoise
6 Causal Body (celestial body)	Deep blue
7 Ketheric Body/True Self (higher mental aspect) These three "bodies" are within the *spiritual plane*	Violet

auric qualities

- **Etheric Body** This is associated with touch/feeling. If this level is strong, you will have a healthy body and enjoy all the pleasures of your five senses (taste, touch, sight, sound and smell).
- **Emotional Body** This is either light and bright or swirling with dirty clouds of energy. Negative issues, such as unresolved emotional "baggage," can stagnate here; conversely, if you feel happy at a core level, your first and second energy bodies will display clear, bright colors.
- **Mental Body** This is concerned with mental concepts in the rational world. It pulsates at a very fine level when you have an active, lively mind.
- **Higher Mental Body** This is where our auras merge and interact with other people, plants, animals, surroundings and the cosmos. Here we feel the love of relationships, since it is strongly associated with the Heart Chakra.

- **Spiritual Body** This is associated with Divine Will and acts as an etheric template for the first level (Etheric Body).
- **Causal Body** This is where we experience the spirit world, its influence and what it "causes" in our lives.
- **Ketheric Body** This links us to Divine Mind, our higher truth, our super-consciousness.

A simplified diagram of a glowing human aura showing colors of the seven layers.

subtle energy in other traditions

Central to many therapies and disciplines (particularly those originating in the East) is an understanding about different types of energy flow; for example, acupuncture, shiatsu, tai chi and chi kung concentrate mainly on balancing energy pathways—the body's meridians. Aromatherapy, sound therapy, mantras, color/light therapies, radionics, gem/crystal therapy, flower essences, Reiki, hands-on spiritual healing and psychic surgery (among others) work with subtle energy in general to bring wholeness and health to our bodies.

traditional chinese medicine

Acupuncture is traditionally believed to work by normalizing the free flow of subtle energy (or ch'i) in the body. The earliest known written text of Traditional Chinese Medicine—the *Nei Ching*—is thought to have been written between 2697 and 2596 BCE. It provides evidence of the continual use of acupuncture by emperors and common people for 4,500 years. In more recent years, researchers have found provable evidence of the effectiveness of acupuncture, particularly in the treatment of pain.

Ch'i (or qi) is regarded in Traditional Chinese Medicine as a unique energetic substance that flows from the environment into the body (in India this is referred to as prana). In the Chinese system ch'i is absorbed into the body through the skin at particular portals of entry formed by the acupuncture points. These points connect to meridians, or lines of energy within the body, and each pair of meridians is associated with a specific body organ or function.

Another key aspect of Traditional Chinese Medicine is Yin and Yang: the positive and negative creative forces of the universe that complement one another when your health and body are in a dynamic equilibrium. Yin is regarded as the female principle, represented by these keywords: passive, destructive, moon, darkness, death. Yang is the male principle, represented by these keywords: active, generative, sun, light, creation of life. Tied in with this principle is Five Element Theory, which relates energy and the internal organs of the body to the five elements of Fire, Earth, Metal, Water and Wood.

An acupuncturist's teaching "dummy" showing meridians and treatment points.

what are chakras?

homeopathy

Homeopathy is a complex system of treating many body imbalances and "diseases," and was developed by Samuel Hahnemann (1755–1843), a brilliant German physician, using the principle of "like cures like" (that is, giving diluted remedies that, in large amounts in healthy people, would produce symptoms similar to those being treated). This principle was found in earlier Greek writings and can be considered one of the first really holistic treatments.

During the course of his medical research with homeopathic preparations, Hahnemann discovered—to his surprise—that the greater the dilution, the more effective the medication was. In this process of "potentization" he found that his medicines became so diluted that not a single molecule of the original herb or substance was present, leaving only a vibrational pattern or "signature" to treat the disturbance in the patient's "vital force" and bring about healing.

Keep homeopathic preparations in a cool and dark place, taking care to avoid bottles touching one another or handling contents with your fingers.

crystal essences and flower essences

Crystal essences are explored later in this book in connection with the relevant chakras and can easily be made at home

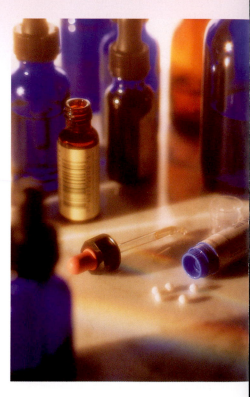

(see pages 70–71 and 150–151). They are valuable to use on the physical symptoms of chakra imbalances. They hold the memory of the crystal in the water from which they were prepared and focus the body on healing itself at bio-molecular level.

Some people describe flower essences as tinctures of "liquid consciousness." They enhance our emotional and our spiritual balance. For example, flower essences that target the Crown Chakra and subtle bodies also weaken all the miasms (disease-causing energy traces) so that they can be eliminated from deep cellular levels and passed out through the chakras and aura. The action of flower essences upon chakra energies is complex, and it is recommended that you consult a trained practitioner.

radionics

Radionics was developed more than one hundred years ago from the work of Theosophist Alice Bailey (see pages 26–27). It is based upon unity, wholeness and an interactive universe of vibrational energy. Because it uses the Earth's energy field, treatment can be given effectively from a distance and may be used on any living person, animal, plant or on the Earth. A

number of radionic instruments are available that enable a practitioner to diagnose and treat a range of energetic imbalances. The instruments themselves are passive devices, which rely entirely upon the subtle-energetic perceptions of the practitioner.

Erica cinerea is used as a flower essence to give us inner strength and resistance to stress.

sources of chakra knowledge: the upanishads

The concept of the chakras originated in Hindu culture and they are therefore rich in associations with the Hindu religion. The term *Hindu* means "of the Indus" and refers to the river running from the Tibetan Himalayas through Kashmir and along the length of modern-day Pakistan. The history of the Hindu people stretches back more than 5,000 years and has given rise to one of the most profound spiritual traditions in the world.

the four collections

The information we have about the chakras comes principally from the Upanishads, sacred writings that form part of the Hindu scriptures known collectively as the Vedas. The word *Veda* means "knowledge," and the four collections or earliest texts—the Rig, Sama, Yajur and Atharva Vedas—are referred to as *sruit*, knowledge that was revealed to the great seers. It is a difficult to put a date on the Vedas because they are assumed to have been passed down orally for nearly a thousand years before they were first written down between 1200 and 900 BCE.

The earliest Upanishads were written in the 7th century BCE. In total there are 108, although most commentators identify 13 key texts within that group. The term *Upanishad* literally means "those who sit near" and suggests the practice of listening closely to the secret doctrines of a spiritual teacher.

key upanishad texts

The main message of the Upanishads is that enlightenment (and even immortality) can be achieved by meditating with the awareness that your soul is at one with all creation. The soul is identified with what is real and immortal, and with the life-breath or *prana*. The texts also explore the concept of karma and reincarnation. The two key Upanishads for chakra teaching are the Brahma Upanishad and the Yogatattva Upanishad.

The Brahma Upanishad This describes four places occupied by the soul (the navel, heart, throat and head) and says that each place is characterized by a particular state of consciousness: the navel or the eye is the

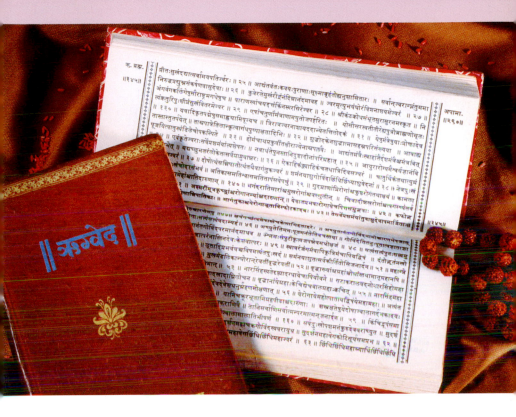

Indian Vedas (Riga, Yajur, Sama, Atharva) are sacred texts written in Sanskrit.

waking consciousness; the heart is dreamless sleep; the throat is dreaming; and the head is the transcendent state.

The Yogatattva Upanishad This relates five body parts to the cosmic elements: earth, water, fire, air and space. Each element corresponds to a particular mantra (or mystical syllable) causing an internal vibration and to a deity. The text refers to the *siddhis*— super-normal powers attained through the mastery of yoga and of different elements.

shakta theory

The original models of the chakras from the Brahma and Yogatattva Upanishads were adapted in Tibetan Buddhism as Vajrayana theory and as the Tantric Shakta theory.

Vajrayana Buddhism aims to assist the student in achieving full enlightenment or Buddhahood through perhaps just a single lifetime. Using techniques based on ancient scriptures known as the Tantras, the practitioner tries to identify with and practice the enlightened ways of the Buddha. Tantric techniques include the repetition of mantras, the use of breath control, healing mudras (or hand positions) and the use of mandalas (circular symbols of the universe) for meditation. In the Tibetan Buddhism tradition only five chakras are identified.

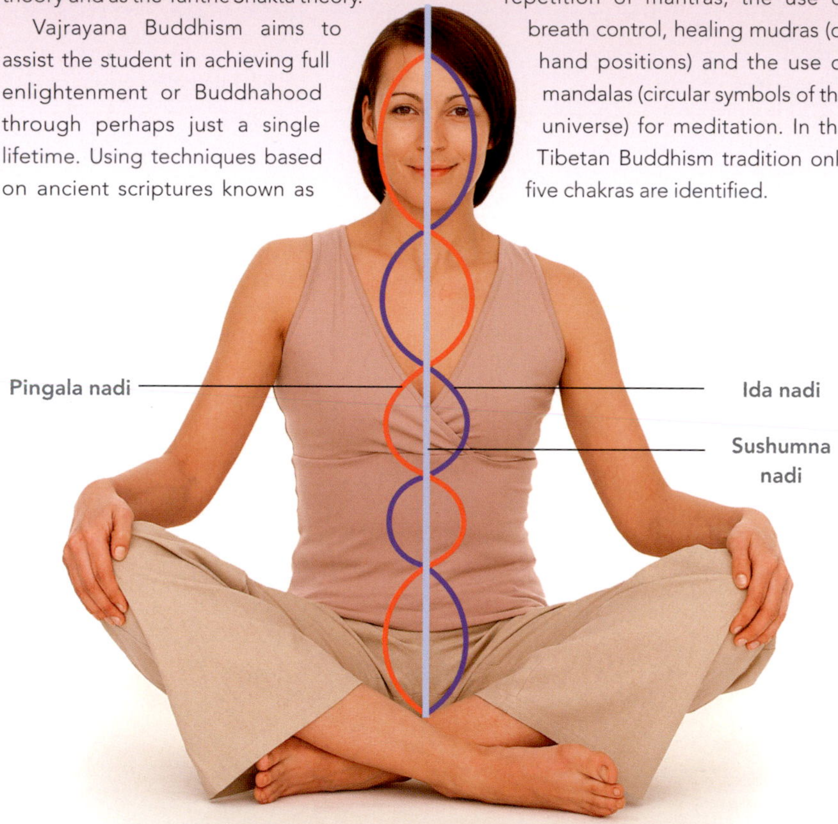

what are chakras?

Pingala nadi

Ida nadi

Sushumna nadi

Shaktism arose as an organized sect in India in the 5th century CE, and it is this sect's interpretation of the chakras that has most influenced the Western understanding of them. Shaktism describes the seven major chakras that we recognize today. In Shakta theory the chakras are viewed as centers of pure consciousness and are focal points for meditation. Shakta theory firmly established symbolic associations and correspondences for each chakra: its element, visual symbol, mantric sound, deity, color and animal. The Shakta way also teaches us about kundalini energy: the energy that was unleashed during the creation of the world; Tantric practice focuses our attention on awakening this energy at the base of the spine for a specific purpose.

the nadis

The Tantric texts refer to the nadis (or channels) of vital life-force (or prana), which thread throughout the body and link with the chakras. According to Shakta theory, the seven chakras are strung along the primary nadi in the body—the sushumna nadi—like pearls or jewels. It is also believed that there are two secondary nadis on either side of the sushumna: ida on the left (containing descending life-force or vitality); and pingala on the right (containing ascending vitality). The aim is to direct the energy of each secondary nadi into the central nadi, where it then ascends through each chakra in turn. When kundalini energy reaches the highest chakra (the Crown Chakra), the yogi (or master of yoga who has achieved a high level of spiritual insight) achieves a state of oneness with God.

This understanding of the chakras was popularized by Sir John Woodroffe, who wrote under the pseudonym Arthur Avalon, in a book entitled *The Serpent Power*, first published in 1919.

Of the estimated 72,000 nadis, three main ones are activated.

sir john woodroffe and carl jung

Born in 1865 in England, Woodroffe traveled to India, where he practiced law. He became Advocate-General of Bengal and then Chief Justice at the Calcutta High Court in 1915.

Throughout his life he was fascinated by Sanskrit and Hindu philosophy, becoming the first Western student of Tantra and, with the help of Indian colleagues, translating into English nearly 20 original Sanskrit texts. A prolific translator and lecturer, he did much to popularize Indian philosophy in the West.

Woodroffe translated some key texts on the study of chakras, although he is probably most famous for his book *The Serpent Power—The Secrets of Tantric and Shaktic Yoga*, which provides a guide to kundalini practice (the raising of the energy that lies dormant at the Base Chakra). Woodroffe used the term "serpent power" as being the closest English description of kundalini.

carl jung and kundalini energy

The eminent Swiss psychologist Carl Jung (1875–1961) also did much to develop the Western understanding of kundalini. He presented a seminar on kundalini yoga to the Psychological Club in Zurich in 1932, which has subsequently been recognized as a highly significant moment in the appreciation of Eastern thought by the West.

For Jung, kundalini yoga was a model for the development of higher consciousness. In order to undergo profound personal growth, Jung believed that the individual must be open to the parts of himself beyond his own ego. He was interested in the techniques of Tantra and believed they gave insight into the unconscious mind. For Jung, gaining access to the unconscious was essential for spiritual growth as well as personal harmony.

Jung was fascinated by many other aspects of Eastern thought, and in particular made popular to the Western mind the study of mandalas and yantras (geometric devices used as an aid in meditation) as a means of accessing the unconscious. He regarded the mandala as a universal archetype, a symbol of universal themes found in every individual. Over many years he discovered that drawing and coloring mandalas helped him bypass rational thought and access the images and energy of his unconscious mind. In the context of kundalini energy, Jung saw another means to access the power of the unconscious and attain self-realization.

Carl Jung, founder of analytical psychology,
spent much of his life exploring other realms.

theosophy and the chakras

The Western understanding of chakras also owes much to Theosophy, the school of mystical thought established by Madame Blatvatsky in 1875. In his books *The Inner Life* and *The Chakras* (1927), C.W. Leadbeater was the first person to explore some of the key ideas we now hold about the chakras.

Charles Webster Leadbeater was born in 1854 and was ordained as an Anglican priest in 1879. He joined the Theosophical Society in 1883 and, after meeting Madame Blavatsky, abandoned the Church and followed her to India in 1884. Returning to England in 1889, he began to study past

lives and explore his spiritual powers. Leadbeater was perhaps most famous for discovering Jiddu Krishnamurti, an Indian mystic who became a famous world speaker on peace and developing awareness.

leadbeater's interpretation of the chakras

Working mainly through his own intuition, Leadbeater established the idea that chakras could be seen through psychic vision—an idea not found in Indian traditions. If you are sufficiently clairvoyant, he argued, you will be able to perceive the chakras as rotating discs or wheels. He also observed that chakras were energy vortices. Thus the idea developed that subtle energies of many kinds are centered in, and moved via, the chakras. By contrast, in some Indian, Tibetan and other traditions they are simply seen as centers of consciousness that a practitioner can access, and from which increased awareness develops.

Jiddu Krishnamurti lectures to a crowd of people. Krishnamurti (1895-1986) was an Indian philosopher who believed that God must be experienced directly in order to be known.

Leadbeater was also the first person to suggest that the chakras are energy transformers, linking the various subtle layers of the aura, such as the etheric, the astral and the mental. This idea has now become a central aspect of our understanding of chakras, which are seen to play a crucial role in helping us to maintain a healthy flow of energy. Ensuring that the chakras are open, clear and rotating correctly has become a major focus for everyone working with them.

the chakras and the endocrine glands

Theosophist Society founder Alice Bailey, along with Leadbeater, was among the first to associate the chakras with particular endocrine glands and the sympathetic nervous system (see pages 40–41). There is no evidence that Indian mystics made this association, although the pioneering work of Theophilus Gimbel on light and color for healing led him, among others, to note that the traditional position of the chakras corresponds to the positions and functions of the glands of the endocrine system and to the positions of the nerve ganglia along the spinal column.

major and minor chakras

major chakras

Within the main Indian yogic teachings, seven major chakras are assigned specific qualities, all the minor chakras also have an important role to play, not least in regulating the flow of energy.

THE MAJOR CHAKRAS

Chakra	Color of influence	Element	Body sense	Endocrine gland
Base/ Muladhara	Red	Earth	Smell	Testes/ovaries
Sacral/ Svadisthana	Orange	Water	Taste	Adrenals
Solar Plexus/ Manipura	Yellow	Fire	Sight	Pancreas
Heart/ Anahata	Green/Pink	Air	Touch	Thymus
Throat/ Vishuddha	Turquoise	Ether/Akasha	Hearing	Thyroid/ parathyroids
Brow/Ajna	Deep blue	Spirit	Extra-sensory perception	Pituitary
Crown/ Sahasrara	Violet/gold	Spirit	All the senses	Pineal

Crown
(Sahasrara)

Brow
(Anja)

Throat
(Vishuddha)

Heart
(Anahata)

Solar plexus
(Manipura)

Sacral
(Svadisthana)

Base
(Muladhara)

minor chakras

The minor chakras are concerned with vital body functions. Located in key points, they receive and discharge subtle energy to keep the body healthy. Those on the soles of our feet and knees maintain our connection or "groundedness" to the Earth. The gonad chakras interact with our sexual functions aided by the Base and Sacral Chakras. Stomach, liver and spleen chakras interact with the Solar Plexus Chakra. Thymus chakra supports the Heart Chakra. Breast and clavicle chakras can affect the lymphatic system. Eye and temple chakras feed the brain but can develop to detect extra-sensory information or send healing to others. Hand chakras give and receive the gift of touch to express our heart love.

alta major

Another vitally important chakra—the Alta Major, situated at the base of the back of the skull—is the energy point for race memory and survival patterns inherited from our ancestors, as well as for distant memory, possibly involving past-life recall.

THE MINOR CHAKRAS

Twenty-one minor chakras are normally identified:

- One on the sole of each foot
- One behind each knee
- One for each gonad
- Two for the spleen
- One for the stomach
- One near the liver
- One for the palm of each hand
- One on each breast
- One on each side of the clavicle
- One for each eye
- One on each temple
- One for the thymus gland (center of the chest)

Thymus Chakra

Although this is classified as a "minor chakra," it has an increasingly important role to play in modern life (see pages 208–209).

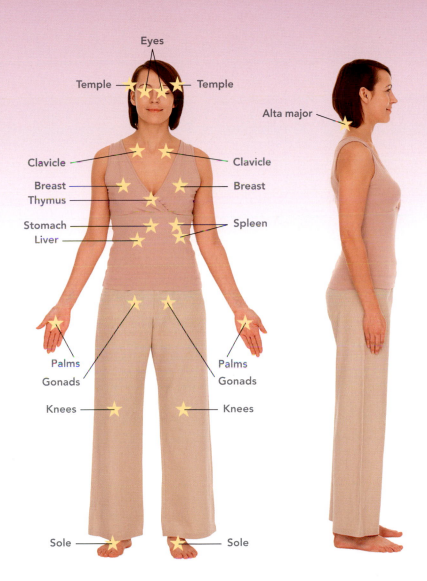

Eyes

Temple — Temple

Clavicle — Clavicle

Breast — Breast
Thymus —

Stomach — Spleen
Liver —

Alta major

Palms — Palms
Gonads — Gonads

Knees — Knees

Sole — Sole

major and minor chakras

chakras as part of the matrix of life

The minor chakras can be thought of as subtle-energy "defenders" of the body. The seven major chakras, which play an important role in our biochemical balance, are considered "initiators" of key body functions. Together, the major and minor chakras, the auric field and crossing/interpenetrating energy lines throughout the physical body and energy fields form the matrix of all human life.

While we cannot always see these forms of energy in the auric field and in the chakras, healers throughout the ages have informed us of their existence. Russian scientist Semyon Kirlian discovered a new type of photographic image, which was named Kirlian photography after him, in the 1940s. It now provides us with evidence that living objects display an electrical-corona discharge phenomenon close to the skin. An advancement of this technique, electronography, enables images of the whole body and internal organs to be seen. Interpreting the patterns on Kirlian photographs gives a healer or practitioner indications of a person's bio-electric energy (chi or prana) and therefore of their body's health.

As science has developed, researchers have discovered that even finer and more subtle energies are at play within us, as scientific instruments are created that can register them. Physicist David Bohm suggests that higher levels of order and information may be holographically embedded into the fabric of space and matter/energy. In the future we will come to learn more about how parts of our DNA are switched on by interfacing with this holographic information level.

the importance of balance

Each chakra has a role in balancing some aspect of the subtle life-force energies that enter through the aura and in transducing that energy into a nature that is acceptable to the body. As it does so, it comes into a harmony or resonance with adjacent chakras. Additionally each chakra gives out energy messages through the aura to our immediate and wider environment. These messages, in the form of minute subtle electromagnetic impulses, are affected by a number of factors, including our emotions. Through our auric field and our chakras we are interconnected with our environment, time, colors, sounds, objects and the cosmos. The way we experience other Beings of Light—people—is that they have come within the range of influence of our aura. Often we experience an instant attraction or rejection—not necessarily

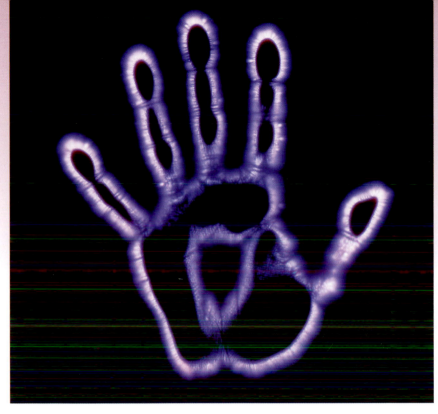

Kirlian photograph showing electrical corona discharge around the outline of the hand.

because of apparent likes or dislikes at an everyday level, but because we naturally feel better in the presence of another harmonious energy field.

As you read this book you will begin to see patterns of behavior or of health within yourself. In this way the book will act as a mirror, enabling you to "diagnose" your subtle-energy levels and, if you wish, bring your own auric energy field and chakras into a state of balance. In the next few pages we look at the importance of being in balance; how to better understand and care for your physical body and emotions.

chakra balancing

As you read this book you will discover various ways to bring the chakras into balance, as you learn how color, light, aromatherapy, reflexology, food, crystals, color breathing, yoga as well as other techniques are used.

understanding the condition of the chakras

To balance the chakras, you must first be clear about the condition of individual chakras and interpret this in terms of energy flow through these "wheels of

CHAKRA QUALITIES

- **Active** The chakra is functioning as intended, showing a healthy input and output of energy. The person in question will normally be fit and healthy. Different parts of their energy field—the emotional, mental and spiritual bodies—will be vibrant as well.

- **Underactive** The particular chakra needs some type of stimulation, perhaps in order to cope with adverse conditions in the physical body or in the energy field.

- **Passive/balanced** The chakra energies are either "at rest" or in a harmonious balance of input and output.

- **Overactive** The chakra is overstimulated, possibly because it is trying to eliminate imbalances in the physical body. According to deep shamanic practices, our luminous bodies can have a range of undesirable energies attached to them. Overactivity of certain chakras may be due to them trying to eliminate long-held imprints that are detrimental to our well-being (such as the imprints of addiction or abuse).

light." People who can see the luminous auric field perceive chakras as vortices of swirling lights, spiralling into contact with the physical body at key points corresponding to particular parts of the body, both front and back. The exceptions are the Crown Chakra, which opens upward above the head, and the Base Chakra, which opens downward from the perineum. Some people describe chakras as being "open" or "closed," but better descriptions are given opposite.

exercise to balance the chakras

Here is a simple exercise to help you begin to balance someone else's chakras.

1 Ask them to sit on a hard chair or stool and then stand behind them.
2 Use your right hand to *gently* stretch the back of their neck, by placing your hand just under the occipital bone at the base of the skull and giving a little pull, as you support their forehead with your left hand. This has the effect of bringing all the seven main chakras into a central vertical alignment. Unfortunately it is not a technique you can practice on yourself.

chakra awareness

Analyzing what is happening with your chakras can be a powerful way of tuning into your mind, body and spirit. To do this you should observe which chakras react noticeably when you are in stressful situations. Perhaps you have recurring problems or illnesses, and should ask yourself if you are going backward, instead of forward, in your life. For example:

- If your Base Chakra is not strong, you may feel unhappy with your body size or shape, or may have a feeling that you are not in control of your life. On the other hand, if your Base Chakra is overactive, you may explode angrily at the slightest provocation.
- Low energy flow through the Sacral Chakra will cause you not to have any joyful moments in your life. If it is hyperactive, you may experience tears of frustration.
- Inactivity of the Solar Plexus Chakra will cause you to feel powerless when you are under pressure and to develop a queasy feeling, or "butterflies" in your stomach. Overactivity will make you domineering and a "control freak."
- If you feel that your "heart has missed a beat," it may indicate a weak Heart Chakra as well as a weak physical heart. If you redden or your pulse races in stressful situations, your Heart Chakra may be overactive.
- A weak Throat Chakra will make you unable to speak your truth, or you may stutter or shake. An overactive Throat Chakra will cause you to speak before you think—sometimes with hurtful words.
- If you cannot visualize and organize your life very well, then your Brow Chakra is underactive. If you experience nightmares, it may have become hyperactive.
- An inability to think clearly when under stress means that your Crown Chakra is weak. If you want to eat all the fruits of spiritual attainment before you have learned how to plant, water and grow them, then your Crown Chakra is unbalanced.

Later in this book we will look in depth at each chakra in turn.

No one can think clearly when they are under severe stress.

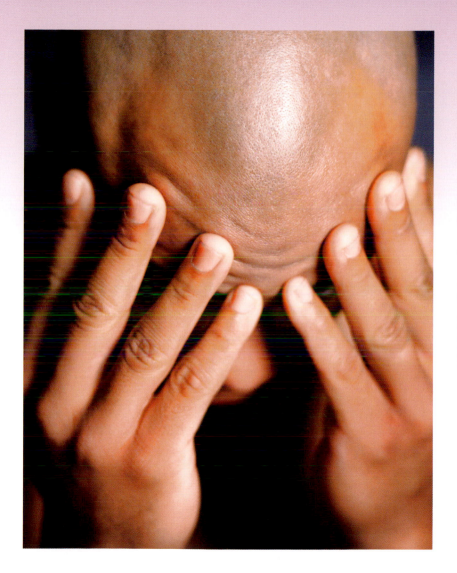

how chakras affect the physical body

From Mother Earth you receive all your sustenance: the air that you breathe, the water that you drink, the food that you eat. These fill you with prana, the vital life-force that can be absorbed into your body through your chakras.

Your body is unique in its requirements for health, so it is vital to understand the energies at play both within your body and within your energy field. For many reasons, you can block the interconnecting auric pathways of light, and "disease" will result. Chakra healing helps clear the pathways, so that positive energy can pass through the auric filaments and nurture your physical body. A good way to imagine this is that the pathways are like golden, glowing spiders" webs that integrate all aspects of you: body, mind, soul and spirit. When your body complex is fully in harmony with life, a larger central line of energy, called the Sushumna/Hara Line, extends down through your auric field right into the Earth's core—this is your "umbilical cord" to Mother Earth! Take a quiet moment to "ground yourself," picturing your central energy line like a strong root that pierces through all the crystals and layers of Earth. Breathe deeply and relax.

connecting with nature and with your body

When you are distanced from healthy food, air and water, a separation begins that damages or even cuts this central line of energy, and disharmony results. We all know that we feel better in a natural environment, so try to spend as much time as possible in Nature: walk outside sometimes, go to the park at lunchtime, or enjoy the energy of beautiful green plants in your home or office: they give you a beneficial charge of negative ions; conversely, it is positive ions (present in large concentrations in polluted city air) that do *not* benefit your health.

Now you can begin to see the complexity of the influences upon us. We each need to find strategies to keep ourselves healthy when modern living starts to compromise our immune system. Perhaps you enjoy an alcoholic drink or two that stretches to more on the weekend, or you need strong coffee to keep you awake at work. On the weekend

Take long walks to enjoy the beauty of the natural world. Breathe in its beneficial essences as you walk.

maybe you smoke or take recreational drugs. You sit in front of the television and forget to take the dog for a walk. You eat snacks because you are too tired to prepare a healthy meal. Think about how sluggish your body is: your chakras are no longer vibrant "wheels of light"; your auric field is closing in. Next week you will go to the doctor with fatigue, headaches, or a pain in your chest—*wake up*!

chakras and the endocrine system

The endocrine system is a complex part of the human body and is still in the process of being fully understood. The ductless glands of the endocrine system provide a chemical communication network that controls a huge number of physiological processes. Theosophist writers (see pages 26–27) were the first to observe that the position of the chakras on the body parallels that of the glands of the endocrine system.

how the endocrine system works

Hormones are produced by the glands of the endocrine system and act as chemical messengers in the blood, affecting the functioning of cells. Only certain cells in the body, known as target cells, are receptive to particular hormones.

Hormone receptors are found either exposed on the surface of the cell or within it, depending on the type of hormone. The binding of hormone to receptor triggers a cascade of reactions within the cell that affects virtually every function of the body.

A simplified interpretation of endocrine gland functions.

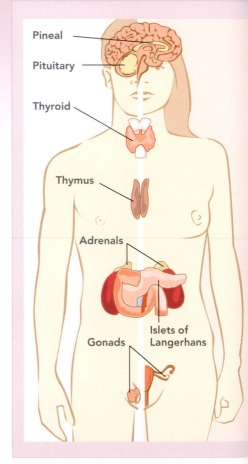

Pineal

Pituitary

Thyroid

Thymus

Adrenals

Islets of Langerhans

Gonads

THE MAIN ENDOCRINE GLANDS

Each gland influences the production of particular hormones:

- **The pineal gland** secretes a hormone that may help regulate patterns of sleeping and waking.

- **The pituitary gland**, often called the "master gland," makes hormones that control several other endocrine glands.

- **The thyroid (and parathyroid) gland** hormones control the rate at which cells burn fuel from food in order to produce energy.

- **The thymus gland** plays an important part in the development of the immune system in early life.

- **The adrenal glands** play a large role in regulating the body's response to stress, balancing the immune system and metabolism.

- **The gonads** (testes in men and ovaries in women) secrete the sex hormones testosterone in men and estrogen and progesterone in women, which control sexual development, sex drive and fertility.

- **The islets of Langerhans**, specialized cells in the pancreas, function as endocrine glands. They secrete the insulin needed for the metabolism of sugar.

The hormones secreted by each of these glands have a dramatic effect on human psychology, and imbalances in them can cause both physical and emotional problems.

chakras and the endocrine system

how chakras respond to our emotions

Chakras respond to our own emotions—and to those of other people, which they try to "dump" on us. It is up to each of us to keep our own auric field clear and to understand that no one else can do so—you are the only one who can "empty your recycling bin"; you are responsible for your own emotions. When you live with this responsibility, you can never say, "He hurt me emotionally," "She hates me" or the classic "You have made me feel bad." Be positive, open and willing to change.

EMOTIONS AND CHAKRA IMBALANCES

Clairvoyants can see various emotions in the auric fields and the chakras, as well as the imbalances they may cause:

Emotion	Symptom	Chakra imbalance
Anger	Flashes of red	Solar Plexus
Defensiveness	Cords or armoring	Solar Plexus and Brow
Resentment	Cloudy/dull colors	Heart and Solar Plexus
Sadness	Cloud	Above the head and around the Heart
Jealousy	Hooks of energy	Heart and Brow or Solar Plexus
Hysteria	Fragmentation	Whole of auric field and numerous chakras

Note that negative emotions are often centered around the Solar Plexus Chakra.

rebalancing the emotions

When a couple are in love, all their chakras complement one another, their inner auric fields become as one, and their outer field merges into a beautiful golden heart shape. Conversely we talk of having "a broken heart" if a relationship ends; the Heart Chakra, once open in reciprocating love to a partner, has now become so depleted in energy flow that it is underactive. This results in heartache and deep emotional states that cause us to neglect the body, hunch our shoulders and breathe inadequately; it is quite likely that serious heart or lung health issues may result. In these circumstances you can do a lot to help yourself, but a trained chakra healer will be able to beneficially rebalance the energies,

When we are in a loving relationship, the Heart Chakra is open and full of energy.

probably using a number of methods described in this book.

One time-honored way to calm agitation is with the breath. Say to yourself, "STOP, stop whatever is running through my head." Breathe deeply three times. Relax your face, shoulders and hands, then continue what you were doing *slowly*—the anger having now left you. Overleaf is a relaxation technique that will calm many emotions, including anger, sadness, irrational fears and anxiety, and will release the stresses that build up at chakra level or are a result of imprints of these emotions.

relaxation technique

This exercise releases stress and helps to balance the chakras naturally, bringing you to a state of harmony. You can practice it every day if you wish. Even if your body is sick, try to do this relaxation because eventually it will increase your energy levels.

1 Arrange that you will not be disturbed for about 30 minutes. Spread a blanket on the floor and lie flat on your back with your feet slightly apart. Use cushions to support parts of your body, if necessary. If you wish, you can record these instructions to play back to yourself or play some beautiful soft music.

2 Close your eyes. Take three deep breaths, and breathe out any feelings of stress, pain and tightness in your body.

3 Now you are going on a journey through your body, beginning with your right foot. Let it relax, then focus the relaxation up your right leg to the knee, then to the hip, relaxing each part, muscle by muscle.

4 Do the same with your left foot and leg.

5 Relax your buttocks, sexual organs, pelvis and lower back. Relax deep inside your body: your solar plexus, heart and lungs. Feel the relaxation as a softness and warmth spreading through your body.

6 Visualize all the vertebrae in your spine like the notes of a piano keyboard: beginning at the bottom, let every vertebra soften into a relaxed position as if you were gently touching a note on the keyboard with your fingers. Travel right up to your neck and experience waves of relaxation washing over you. You may begin to see colors swirling within your inner vision.

7 Feel your arms and hands becoming limp and heavy as you relax even more.

8 Move your head gently from side to side to release any long-held tension in the neck.

9 Relax all the muscles of your face and scalp, and let the activity in your brain slow down.

10 Enjoy the soft music or taped words, but try not to go to sleep. Maintain a state of relaxed awareness for around 20 minutes.

11 Slowly start to breathe more deeply, then take one very deep breath, visualizing it full of a healing golden light that touches every part of your body—inside and out.

12 Stretch your legs and arms, roll onto one side and sit up slowly.

13 Appreciate the new you, with chakras balanced and body relaxed.

relaxation technique

chakras and healing: food

Your body needs a variety of fresh unprocessed foods to be healthy, because denatured foods lack prana. Chemical additives (such as monosodium glutamate) and sugar substitutes, which are often labeled "sweeteners" (saccharin and aspartamine), have been proven to be detrimental to health—as is fluoride, which is commonly added to water supplies and toothpaste. They must be avoided if you value your long-term health. Remember to read the labels on any food or cosmetics that you buy, to avoid chemical-based food substances that will compromise your well-being. If you don't understand the ingredients and labeling of food and cosmetics, don't buy them.

There is evidence that the color pigmentation in natural foods (such as beta-carotene in carrots, many vegetables and algae) has a vital role to play in balancing us at many levels. Cutting-edge research suggests that digested food is changed into color light impulses, creating a level of vibrational energy in our blood that individual cells can absorb. To keep us in peak condition we require fresh food whose natural colors mirror the colors of the chakras. In the picture shown here, the colors of the higher chakras and Solar Plexus Chakra are represented by fruits and vegetables. To activate or balance a particular chakra, eat foods in its own color; to calm overactivity, eat foods in its complementary (opposite) color.

the importance of balance

An increasing number of people are now eating only raw foods, and while this is a good way to cleanse the body, it may not suit everyone. What you need to achieve is balance. Remember Yin and Yang (see pages 16–17).

Eggplant, red cabbage, purple kale, blueberries and blackberries are examples of blue/purple foods.

FOOD COLORS AND THEIR BENEFITS

- **Red foods**: An underactive Base Chakra may be restored by eating red-colored fruits and vegetables. If it is overactive, you may have skin conditions such as angry red eczema or psoriasis; in these cases red-skinned vegetables (particularly hot red chilli peppers and spices) must be avoided.

- **Yellow foods**: Yellow citrus fruits are acidic and stimulate excretion on both physical and psychological levels. If you want to calm your Solar Plexus Chakra, eat bananas (in moderation) or make them into "smoothie" drinks.

- **Green foods**: Green salad vegetables and lightly cooked greens (such as cabbage and spinach) cleanse and balance the whole body.

- **Blue foods**: Blue/purple fruits and vegetables have perhaps evolved on a higher level and bring balance to the higher chakras.

Oranges, carrots, Sharon fruit, pumpkin and peaches bring color balance to Sacral Chakra functions and nourish the body.

Foods can be classified as Yin and Yang too. For example, whole grains, milk, most vegetables and vegetable protein are Yin, whereas processed food, denatured grains, meat and strong spicy seasonings are Yang. Drawing upon general macrobiotic principles, 50 percent of your daily food intake should comprise whole cooked grains.

In Indian Ayurvedic practice, food is also classified into certain types according to the three attributes or gunas:

- Inertia/darkness (tamas)
- Energy/restlessness (rajas)
- Order (sattva).

Thus tamasic food is salty, bad or denatured; rajastic food comprises meat protein and rich flavors; sattvic food consists of nourishing bland milk products, most fresh fruits and vegetable protein, and is considered to hold the most life-force. From a yogic perspective, high protein (meat) diets, garlic and onions "set the body on fire" detrimentally. Traditionally, bland and fatty milk products are taken by a yogi to improve the transmission of pranic energy through the nervous system and subtle nadis of the body.

Hot chili peppers (extreme Yang/rajastic) are avoided by some yoga ascetes.

The first three chakras are concerned with maintaining the physical body and with the way we perceive food—Base Chakra: smell; Sacral Chakra: taste; Solar Plexus Chakra: sight.

Don't become obsessive about your food; simply listen to what your body needs at any one time, because overindulgence is just as harmful as a bad diet. Balance and variety are the keywords in a healthy diet for a radiant body and chakras.

Cabbage and leafy green vegetables (extreme Yin/sattvic) are beneficial body cleansers.

chakras and healing: reflexology

Reflexology is a development of an ancient healing technique suggesting that the soles of our feet and the palms of our hands mirror our whole body. It uses fingertip pressure on the feet or hands to relieve pain or energetic blockages in various parts of the body. Reflexology demonstrates that pranic energy circulates in our physical body. It is an effective technique because energy terminates in the feet or hands, where the reflexes are found. If the energy circulation is blocked in any way, it shows up in the reflex as pain or soreness when that area of the foot or hand is treated by a reflexologist.

In reflexology the body is divided up into ten zones that correspond to specific parts of the soles of the feet (and the hands). There are a few reflexes on the top of the feet. The most important treatment area for maintaining chakra balance is the spinal reflex, which runs right along the arch of the foot from the heel (calcaneus) to the top of the big toe. If treating yourself; press each foot reflex firmly for around 30 seconds. At the same time visualize the body chakra and associated color. It is important to work on all reflexes to bring balance. Repeat on the other foot.

CHAKRA REFLEXES ON THE FOOT

- **The Base Chakra** is toward the back of the calcaneus bone of the heel, relating to gonads (testes and ovaries).

- **The Sacral Chakra** is where the calcaneus and navicular bones join, relating to the adrenal glands.

- **The Solar Plexus Chakra** is at the back of the cuneiform bone, relating to the pancreas.

- **The Heart Chakra** is in the center of the metatarsal bone, relating to the thymus gland.

- **The Throat Chakra** is where the phalanges (toe bones) meet the metatarsal, relating to the thyroid and parathyroid glands.

- **The Brow Chakra** is where the first and second phalanges meet, relating to the pituitary gland.

- **The Crown Chakra** is at the top of the first phalange (big toe), relating to the pineal gland.

A reflexologist will often use pressure on these individual chakra reflexes, as well as treating the more usual ones relating to the physical body. It is a very efficient way to bring a chakra into a state of balance and is something that you can learn to do yourself quite easily.

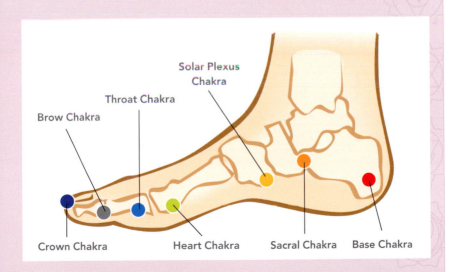

Brow Chakra

Throat Chakra

Solar Plexus Chakra

Crown Chakra

Heart Chakra

Sacral Chakra

Base Chakra

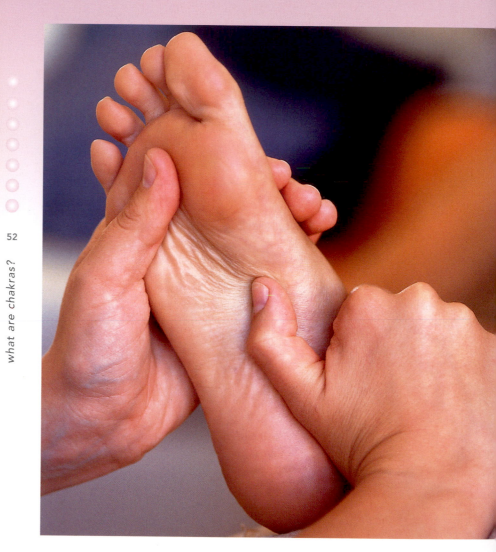

self-treatment on the chakras

Here is an example of how to treat your own Throat Chakra using reflexology.

1 Observe the condition and shape of your feet—they mirror your whole body. From a reflexology perspective, if they are painful or deformed, this indicates that your body is not functioning properly and you should consult a health professional.

2 Soak your feet for ten minutes in warm water with three drops of peppermint essential oil added.

3 Refer to the chart for the Throat Chakra reflex, identifying it on your right foot. Then find the base of the big toe in the area of the second phalange—the neck reflex is a little below this. The thyroid reflex is on the lower half of the second phalange, while parathyroid reflexes are on the top and bottom.

4 Note any tenderness in the aforementioned regions as you apply firm fingertip pressure for a few minutes. Reflexology always treats the whole foot; however, you may finish by massaging away any stiffness in the relevant area.

5 Remove any unwanted energy using light, sweeping strokes with both hands from shin to toes.

6 Shake your hands vigorously before moving to your left foot and repeating the procedure.

chakra reflexes and color

One way to give color to the chakra reflexes is to strongly visualize the color, channeling it to them as you hold the feet. You do not necessarily need healer training to do this—just ask that you will be a pure channel through which healing energy will flow. Alternatively, use a clear quartz crystal with a natural point (about 2 in./5 cm long is ideal): hold the point of the crystal against the chakra reflex and again channel the color through.

When you use crystals in any reflexology treatment, always ensure that you cleanse them before and after use, by placing them in a bowl of clear water or using some other appropriate method, as shown later.

The best way to massage your own foot is to sit with it resting on the opposite thigh.

chakras and healing: kinesiology

Kinesiology is a diagnostic and healing method. The most well-known mode is known as applied kinesiology, in which professionals use muscle-testing to help define what is going wrong in the body or what imbalances are present. Today many kinesiology practitioners are trained chiropractors, osteopaths, doctors and dentists with a medical background. Kinesiology focuses substantially on the physical aspects of the body and the nervous system.

One modern technique is assimilation kinesiology, which works with the subtle-energy properties of essential oils and crystals, based on the concept that the health of the etheric bodies and chakras controls the health of the physical body, the emotions and mind. Another form is energetic kinesiology, which identifies and corrects imbalances within the muscle/meridian/organ matrix, using the ancient Chinese knowledge of energy flow through the acupuncture meridians.

muscle-testing the chakras

Muscle-testing is one technique that "diagnoses" chakra imbalance. While you need to visit a qualified practitioner to benefit from kinesiology, you can practice a simple form of muscle-testing with the assistance of a friend.

1 Stretch one arm in front of you at shoulder level.
2 Establish your strong response by thinking of something pleasurable while your friend tries to push your arm down to your side. Your arm should test strong.
3 Check your weak response by thinking of something traumatic. Your arm should test weak when your friend pushes it down.
4 Place one hand on the appropriate chakra area, with your other arm stretched out in front at shoulder level. Now ask your friend to try to push your arm down again.
5 If it drops easily, the chakra is weak; if it remains strong, the chakra is functioning in a positive mode.

A kinesiology practitioner using one of the many ways to muscle-test a client prior to treatment.

Another way to muscle-test your chakras is to touch a chakra point on your body with the middle finger of your dominant hand (the one you write with). Then, thinking strongly of the location and condition of the chakra, bring the thumb and first finger of each hand into an O shape and lock them together. Now ask, "Does this chakra need balancing?" and pull the fingers and thumbs apart. With a little practice you will be able to feel some resistance, indicating that the chakra is strong; or you will easily pull them apart, indicating that the chakra is weak.

Always identify the lowest chakra that tests weak and work on that one, since that is the root of the problem.

chakras and healing: aromatherapy

Aromatherapy is the use of volatile liquid plant materials (known as essential oils) and other aromatic plant compounds to enhance mood and health. Massage techniques using essential oils can benefit the chakras by clearing them of unwanted energies and rebalancing them.

Lavendula spica *(shown here)*, Lavendula officinalis *and* Lavendula vera *have been used therapeutically for thousands of years.*

chakra massage

A well-trained aromatherapist will be aware of which essential oils have a sympathetic resonance with individual chakras. If you are treating yourself or a friend, look at the boxed text to establish which oils to use. Then place a 5 ml teaspoon of base carrier oil into a saucer and add one or two drops of your chosen concentrated essential oil.

If you are giving aromatherapy to another person, it is best to get some training or to follow carefully the instructions in a comprehensive book such as *The Aromatherapy Bible* by Gill Farrer-Halls (2005). Auric and chakra massage is done to another person when they are fully clothed.

1 Put just one drop of your combined essential and carrier oil into the palms of your hands, then rub them together.
2 Working within the auric field, and not on the actual body, slowly sweep the palms of your hands down the front and back of the recipient. Do this until you perceive a change in their energy levels.
3 Alternatively, concentrate on one chakra area in the auric field, allowing your hands to move in a relaxed way in a spiralling pattern. Normally chakras

what are chakras?

are cleared of unwanted energies by spiralling counterclockwise and are returned to balance by spiralling clockwise.

4 Always wash your hands in cool water after cleansing or healing another person, in order to remove unwanted energies from your own auric field.

Caution: Never take essential oils orally. For massage on the skin always dilute them with base carrier oils. If your skin is sensitive, do a simple skin test first: make up the mix in the recommended dilution and apply a few drops to the inside crease of your elbow. Wait 24 hours to see if any irritant reaction occurs.

Note: During pregnancy, or for children under the age of 12, do not use essential oils (or ingest herbs) at all, except under the recommendation and supervision of a professional.

OILS FOR MASSAGE

Essential oils are extremely strong and are always mixed with a base or "carrier" oil when used for massage. Always use high-quality extra-virgin cold-pressed oils as a base oil, and the best essential oils that you can buy from a specialist company. Never use baby oil, since most types are made from a petro-chemical mineral oil that is not compatible with the skin. For massage on dry skin, use sweet almond oil with the addition of 10 percent wheatgerm (check for nut and wheat allergies first) or avocado oil. The word "natural" on a label is not sufficient: you need to be really sure you are getting "pure essential oil." Cheap oils sold for "burners" or vaporizers must never be used on the skin.

When used in massage, essential oils are always diluted. For adults a general rule is 2.5 percent essential oil to 97.5 percent base oil. To ascertain this, measure your base oil in milliliters and divide by two; the answer gives the number of drops of essential oil that you should add—for example, 20 ml of base oil requires a maximum of ten drops.

chakras and healing: aromatherapy

APPROPRIATE ESSENTIAL OILS FOR CHAKRA MASSAGE

Chakra	Chakra qualities	Essential oils
Base Chakra	Grounding/stabilizing Earth energy	Patchouli, myrrh, cedarwood
Sacral Chakra	Transmuting sexual energy	Sandalwood, jasmine, rose, ylang-ylang, champaca
Solar Plexus Chakra	Transducing solar and pranic energy	Sage, juniper, geranium
Heart Chakra	Flow of unconditional love	Rose, melissa, neroli
Throat Chakra	Self-expression, communication, will	Chamomile, lavender, rosemary, thyme
Brow Chakra	Balancing the higher and lower selves, ESP	Frankincense, basil
Crown Chakra	Divine love and super-consciousness	Ylang-ylang, rosewood, linden

what are chakras?

oil diffusers

You can combine essential oils" beautiful aromas with the power of heat and light by using an oil diffuser/vaporizer. Put a little water into the reservoir, add up to five drops of neat essential oil and light a "tea light" underneath. Place it in a safe place and, as the water evaporates, your room will be filled with a wonderful aroma. Alternatively, put a few drops of neat essential oil in a saucer of water on top of a radiator.

The aroma can be chosen to produce a relaxing, therapeutic, stimulating or sensual atmosphere. During illness an oil diffuser used with some of the more herbal-smelling oils—for example, sage, thyme, rosemary, tea tree or pine, in combination with lavender—can inhibit common airborne bacteria such as cold and influenza viruses. It may also help people who have difficulty breathing, but for severe conditions always take medical advice.

Burning oil in a diffuser can fill a room with wonderful aromas.

chakras and healing: reiki

Reiki is a form of spiritual healing using the hands as channels of energy. It was "rediscovered" in Japan by Dr. Mikao Usui (born in 1865), who originally trained as a Buddhist monk. He traveled all over Japan, China and Europe studying a number of spiritual disciplines, at a time when Japan was just opening up to the Western world.

In March 1922, during a long retreat on a mountainside, Dr. Usui had a great spiritual revelation as an intense Divine Light came into the top of his head. His awareness was greatly expanded and a number of healing symbols were transmitted to him as light images. Thus began a period of him giving healing, using the symbols he had received, to the most needy—especially among the thousands of victims of the great Kanto earthquake—until his death in 1926.

ki, the life-force energy

In Japan, ki (life-force energy) is seen as having seven different constituents. The seventh is Reiki, which organizes all the other forms. It can be translated as "soul force" or a spiritual power with the ability to promote all life processes. Divine ki (from which all types of ki come) enters the body at the Crown Chakra and proceeds through the Brow Chakra.

Reiki transmits ki from master to student in initiatory stages that are known as "degrees." During these initiations, Reiki energy is passed to all the seven major chakras, as well as to the hands. Reiki is now a popular method of spiritual healing, though few people realize that when it was first transmitted by Dr. Usui to potential teachers, it was essentially a path of personal enlightenment.

the hands as channels of energy

As taught in modern times, the Reiki hand positions that are used to give healing are (almost without exception) on, or over, the chakra locations. Students are taught that Reiki passes through their Crown Chakra and subsequently to the minor chakras in the palms of their hands. A healer then becomes a channel through which Reiki healing energy can flow, as she or he places their hands within the auric field or upon the body of the recipient. Healers are trained not to direct this energy, but simply to let it flow where it is needed, as intended by the Reiki masters.

Reiki is a beautiful gentle energy—to give
or to receive.

chakras and healing: reiki

chakra balancing with reiki

If you have received Reiki initiation, you can balance all seven chakras of the recipient using the following technique, as you channel Reiki energy. You may have special ways to prepare yourself to give healing; Reiki training usually advises that you are in a calm and peaceful mode, have washed your hands and psychically cleansed the space in which you are working. Then, with your eyes closed, place your hands into Kanji One position in front of your Heart Chakra, saying a prayer or dedication if you wish. Then "bring in" your alignment with the Reiki masters (by calling their name/s, out loud or silently, and asking them to be present) and ask them to guide you in the healing that follows. "Bring in" any other beings who come in a good way to assist you. Now open your eyes and move to the recipient's head.

1 Place both hands upon the recipient's crown, asking for Divine Light to flow through you to their head.
2 Move to their left side and place your right hand at the Brow Chakra and your left hand at Base Chakra. Hold this position for one or two minutes.
3 Lift (don't slide) the hands to put the right hand at the Throat Chakra and the left hand at the Sacral Chakra. Hold this position for one or two minutes.
4 Again lift (don't slide) the hands to put the right hand at the Heart Chakra and the left hand at the Solar Plexus Chakra. Hold this position for one or two minutes.
5 Move to the recipient's feet and hold the palms of your hands flat against the soles of their feet. Hold this position for one or two minutes.
6 Remove your hands. Return them to Kanji One position in front of your Heart Chakra, saying a prayer or words of thanks to the Reiki masters and other beings that you may have asked for guidance during the healing.
7 Leave the recipient to relax while you wash your hands and forearms in cold water, then help them to sit up. Offer them a glass of water and make sure that they are grounded (see page 111) before they leave.

Note: This chakra balancing may form part of a longer Reiki healing session.

chakras and yoga

Yoga is a branch of Indian philosophy that is concerned with the union of the individual together with the universal consciousness. Our knowledge of yoga is based on the Yoga Sutras, ancient Indian texts that describe the philosophy and practices of yoga. They were written sometime during the period from the 5th century BCE to the 2nd century CE, and define an eight-limbed path (ashtanga) that must be followed in order to reach samadhi, where the spirit is liberated and joins the Universal Spirit.

types of hatha yoga

Within Hatha yoga there are many styles, such as Ananda, Ashtanga (or Power), Iyengar and Sivananda.

Ananda yoga This style uses gentle postures designed to move the energy up to the brain and prepare the body for meditation. Classes also focus on proper body alignment and controlled breathing.

Ashtanga (or Astanga/Power) yoga This form comprises a challenging series of poses that focus on strength and flexibility, by synchronizing movement with the breath.

Iyengar yoga Practitioners of this style hold each pose for a longer amount of time, and props such as straps, blankets and wooden blocks are often used in classes. Iyengar yoga focuses on body alignment.

THE SIX MAIN YOGA PATHS

The term "yoga" actually describes a number of different paths, not all of which are based on physical practices. The six main paths are:

- **Jnana yoga:** Where the practitioner pursues enlightenment via the path of knowledge, using study and meditation.

- **Bhakti yoga:** A path of devotion based on worshipping a god or guru.

- **Karma yoga:** A path to enlightenment based on selfless action.

- **Mantra yoga:** A path based on the repetition of sacred sound.

- **Raja yoga:** An eight-step path to enlightenment based on posture, breath control, meditation and the withdrawal of the senses.

- **Hatha yoga:** This is the type of yoga with which most people in the West are familiar—it is based on physical postures, breathing exercises, cleansing and mindful awareness.

Sivananda yoga This traditional type of yoga concentrates on connecting the body to the Solar Plexus, where an enormous amount of energy is stored. A typical class will combine postures, breathing, dietary restrictions, chanting and meditation.

A yoga practitioner performing a simple "tree" posture.

how yoga practice can help balance the chakras

Yoga practice is of specific benefit to the chakras because the postures (asanas) assist in freeing up prana. As you perform the bending, stretching and twisting poses, you help prana to flow freely throughout the energy channels, or nadi, of your body. Yoga is particularly helpful for the release of kundalini energy (see pages 96–97), helping

ACTIVE AND PASSIVE ASANAS FOR EACH CHAKRA

Active asanas
1 Begin standing in balance
  Pranamasana (prayer pose)
2 Base Chakra
  Virabhadrasana 1 (warrior)
3 Sacral Chakra
  Parivrtta Trikonasana
  (twisting triangle)
4 Solar Plexus Chakra
  Gomukasana (cow pose)
5 Heart Chakra
  Bhujangasana (cobra pose)
6 Throat Chakra
  Dhanurasana (bow pose)
7 Third Eye Chakra
  Adho Mukha Avanasana
  (dog face-down pose)
8 Crown Chakra
  Salamba Sirhasana 1 (headstand)

Passive asanas
9 Crown Chakra
  Salamba Sarvangasana 1
  (shoulder stand)
10 Third Eye Chakra
  Halasana (plough pose)
11 Throat Chakra
  Paschimottanasana
  (sitting forward bend)

12 Heart Chakra
  Janusirsasana (head-to-knee pose)
13 Solar Plexus Chakra
  Ustrasana (camel pose)
14 Sacral Chakra
  Natarajasana (pose of Shiva)
15 Base Chakra
  Garudasana (eagle pose)
16 End sitting in balance
  Lotus pose or simpler asana

For a full yoga session to balance every chakra, work through all the asanas from 1 to 16. Alternatively, refer to the relevant section of this book and select asanas for a specific chakra. However, you should always begin with a standing balance (1) and end with a sitting or balancing asana, such as the lotus (16). Instructions for each asana are given in the relevant chakra section. Asana positions are never forced—only stretch to your own comfortable level. If in doubt, join a yoga class or consult a qualified teacher.

Note: If you have a medical condition, do not attempt extreme asanas unless you have taken medical advice and are working with a qualified yoga teacher.

what are chakras?

it rise up through each chakra one by one, ascending up the spine to the crown.

Kundalini energy can fail to rise if the bandhas, or body locks, are not in place (see pages 100–101). It also fails to rise if one or more of the chakras are blocked, but the regular practice of kundalini yoga can help to unblock the chakras.

The best way to practice yoga is by joining a reputable school and working progressively through each class. In this book we show the asanas that can be particularly beneficial for each chakra, but remember that it is important to warm up the body first, and always take medical advice if you have an existing health condition or have not performed physical exercise for some time.

Active asanas clear excess/negative energies from the whole body and auric field by ascending from Base to Crown. Passive asanas then draw prana into deep core level, harmonizing our energies as we descend back down the chakras from Crown to Base.

A student preparing to move gently into Halasana (plough) posture.

chakras and healing: crystals

Healers observe that most disease is caused by an energy imbalance, usually a reduced flow of pranic life-force throughout the chakras. Crystals and gems help to realign, rebalance and energize the chakras into appropriate functions. Apart from pain, anger, sexual imbalances and some psychotic states, it is unusual to find too much energy present in a chakra, but levels of energy can be ascertained clairvoyantly or by dowsing with a pendulum (see pages 374–375).

Our chakras have a sympathetic resonance with crystals, and researchers have now developed instruments that can measure an instantaneous fluctuation of electrical energy when a crystal (particularly quartz) comes near a chakra. If you are unsure which crystals to use, you can always be effective with clear quartz, since it channels all the rainbow colors of the spectrum through its crystalline matrix. Learn to love the crystals you are using, and the inner Light within them will offer itself to you.

how to choose crystals

Let your intuition guide you when you are collecting crystals, and try to have some idea what you want to do with them. For example, do you want them to look attractive in your room, change the energies in the room, or do you wish to use them for healing purposes?

Crystals do not have to be large or expensive to be effective. It is a good idea to get together a selection of crystal pebbles (tumbled stones) in the seven colors of the spectrum, together with two clear quartz "points" about 2 in. (5 cm) in length. Ideally, keep them wrapped in red silk, and cleanse their auric field before and after use.

how to cleanse crystals

All hard crystals can safely be cleansed in clear water, or in water with a small pinch of salt in it. Then either put them into sunshine or moonlight to energize them. Other cleansing methods to try are: the smoke of incense, flower remedies, sound, meditation, Reiki healing or placing the crystal in the earth—ensure that each time you have love in your heart as you handle the crystals.

Relaxing and chakra balancing with crystal pebbles (tumbled stones) can help increase pranic life-force flow through the chakras.

how to dedicate crystals

When a crystal first comes into your guardianship, hold it and get to know it, then cleanse and meditate with it. Then make a dedication. For example, you might say:

*May this crystal work only with the power of Unconditional Love and Light For the highest universal purpose of … ***

* Here you can add "clearing the auric field" or any other appropriate dedication.

Making a crystal essence by the indirect method.

how to use crystals

After you have cleansed and dedicated a crystal, you are ready to use it in healing work, such as calming or balancing the chakras.

1 Hold it in your non-dominant hand close to the chakra in question, preferably against your skin, bringing it into contact with the body. Leave it there for some minutes.
2 Now move your hand away from your body by 2 in. (5 cm). Wait some minutes.
3 Move your hand farther away by 6 in. (15 cm). Wait some minutes.
4 Move your hand 12 in. (30 cm) away. Wait some minutes.
5 Move your hand an arm's length away from your body. Wait some minutes.
6 Each time you move your hand farther away, imagine that you are linked to the crystal with a golden cord of light.
7 Finally move your hand and crystal in and out of your auric field over the chakra. You will find the position that feels most effective. Wait for some minutes, really "connecting" to the crystal.
8 When you have finished, thank the crystal and cleanse it, ready for reuse.

making a crystal essence by the indirect method

You can add crystal essences to bath water, or slowly sip seven drops of the essence three times a day. The indirect method means that the crystal itself does not come into direct contact with water—only its vibration is transferred to the "memory" of the water.

1 Clean any dust or dirt from your crystal with a soft feather. Cleanse it psychically by intention, or with sound or incense.
2 Place the crystal in a clear glass jar, then stand the jar in a glass bowl of pure spring water. Put the bowl in sunlight for 12 hours to transfer the vibration of the crystal to the water. Alternatively, place a minimum of four large quartz crystal points around the outside of the bowl of water, pointing in toward the center.
3 If you wish to keep the essence for more than a few days, you need to preserve it in a solution of 50 percent brandy/vodka to 50 percent essence. All crystal essences should be kept in the cool and dark, away from strong smells, with the bottles not touching one another.

chakras and healing: color

We have already seen how each of the major chakras has been assigned a color, starting with red at Base Chakra and progressing through the spectrum to violet at the Crown Chakra (see page 28), and have explained that these colors actually mingle together in a complex way, rather as the colors of a rainbow merge together.

When we come to color therapy, we find that not only do we treat a chakra with the predominant color, but we also use the complementary color from the opposite side of the color wheel to induce a state of balance in the chakra. In the eight-section color wheel, we can see that the complementary color of red is turquoise; the complementary of orange is blue; the complementary of yellow is violet; and the complementary of green is magenta. In addition, other colors may be appropriate in certain circumstances.

color therapy

In common with other forms of vibrational healing, color therapy treats an energy imbalance that may cause disease in the body—and *not* the disease itself. Color treatment is ideally given in the form of light (see boxed text page 74), not as a pigment.

For someone who is new to awareness of color, it is best to limit any application of color to the specific chakra and not to overdose on it.

There are numerous ways to take color therapy, but one of the easiest is to obtain glass bottles of the desired color and fill them with 8 fl. oz. (250 ml) of pure spring water. You stand the bottles in sunshine for a minimum of three hours, then sip the water, which now holds the energetic imprint of that color, over the course of a day.

If you are drawn to using color therapy seriously, you will find that it is based on a fascinating combination of ancient wisdom and cutting-edge research, and you would be wise to study with a teacher or to read one of the excellent books by the late Theophilus Gimbel, the pioneer of color therapy and the international teacher of light therapy in the UK.

Pouring water into a colored bottle prior to placing it in the sunshine.

QUALITIES OF DIFFERENT-COLORED LIGHTS

- **Red light** is stimulating, in particular increasing energy to aid blood circulation. It is not used if there is anxiety or emotional disturbances—here the complementary turquoise is best.

- **Orange light** aids the action of the Sacral Chakra and spleen, where prana is split up into all the colors of the spectrum and flows to the other chakras. It is also used to treat imbalances of energy in the kidneys.

- **Yellow light** represents the intellect and solar energy. Nerves become activated with yellow, and for this reason it is used to stimulate energy flow through them and through the muscles. It also benefits the skin and plays a part in the energetic metabolism of calcium.

- **Green light** is regarded as a cleansing/detoxing color. It is used for all manner of imbalances in the physical body and acts like an antiseptic.

- **Turquoise light**, in combination with its complementary red, helps clear the energy of acute infections.

- **Blue light** is calming; it therefore reduces pain, can enhance spiritual growth and balance sleep patterns.

- **Violet light** is appropriate for the eyes and the stagnating energy of nerve-related problems. Violet in the aura indicates inspiration, insight and development of one's higher self or spiritual attainment.

- **Magenta light**, used in color therapy, is really only attainable with light, not pigment or dye. Just below the frequency of ultraviolet it can be seen as a soft glow at sunset. Magenta light activates additional chakras above the crown. At bio-energetic level it releases imbalances that can manifest as serious disease. At an emotional level it allows us to let go of old relationships; on a physical level, it helps us to clear out "clutter" from our lives.

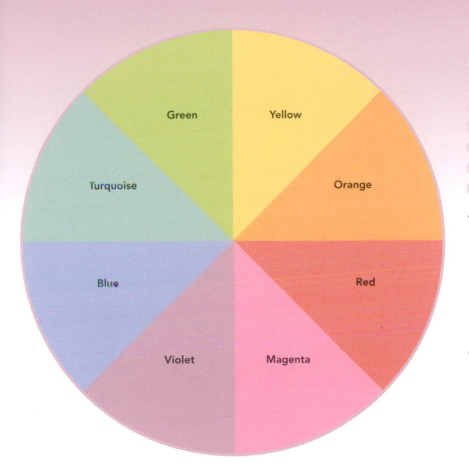

This color wheel is often used in color-light healing to show complementary colors.

chakras and the spirit: yantras

The yantras are symbols that are used to represent each chakra and can be a useful meditation tool. They are the yogi equivalent of the Buddhist mandala: visual symbols of complex spiritual concepts.

Each chakra yantra is based on a lotus, the traditional symbol of enlightenment in Hindu and Buddhist thought. The increasing number of lotus petals in each chakra, as we ascend the ladder, suggests the rising energy or vibrational frequencies of the respective chakras—each functioning as a transformer of energies from one potency to another. The yantra for each chakra also contains specific symbols relevant to that chakra. We will explore these in greater detail in the sections devoted to individual chakras.

how to use yantras

If you are using yantras in meditation, place them so that you can see them on the level and can focus upon them comfortably. Traditionally a yantra is considered to be more powerful than a picture of a god, which, to be energized, requires a yantra to be affixed at its base or back and used together with a mantra.

It is generally recommended that a drawing or print of a yantra is placed in the north/northwest direction of a room, facing the south/southeast direction. However, the special Sri Yantra, considered to be the "mother" form of all yantras, is traditionally placed in the east, facing west.

yantras as a centering device

Yantras are powerful "centering" devices for harnessing divine energies. Centering means that you draw all your inner and outer focus to a still point at the center of your mind. If you are centered, you will not be disturbed by events in your everyday life. However, centering comes into its own when you use it as a preliminary focus before meditation.

It is said that our mind is like a troupe of monkeys leaping from branch to branch, feeding on the tastiest fruits and chattering all the time. Our task is to stop them leaping about, find a stillness and satisfaction in deep silence, and bring our attention to a fixed point. This could be an external object, such as a yantra, a candle flame or an inner perception (such as turning our closed eyes upward toward the Brow Chakra). To gain the skill of centering, constantly but gently draw your awareness away from disturbing thoughts and toward the center of your focus.

Yogis practice Tratakam (concentration, without eyes blinking) on the Shri Yantra.

chakras and the spirit: sound

Our energy field responds to sound. Not surprisingly, our aura tightens when we hear dissonant sounds and expands joyfully when we hear sounds that we find satisfying. Our chakras "flower," too: their symbolic petals open when they are given harmonious sounds, either sweet songs or music. Because we respond so well to sound, chakras have been associated for thousands of years with special devotional chants that bring the qualities of the Divine into everyday life.

sacred OM

OM or AUM is the symbol of the Absolute—it is the essence of Hinduism. It means oneness and a merging of our physical body with our spiritual being. It is regarded as the most sacred syllable, the first sound from which emerges each and every other sound, whether of music or of language. It is a mystic sound that is the basis for mantras (chants); it is the sound of origination and dissolution containing past, present and future. A famous mantra, the Gayatri, begins: "OM, Bhur, Bhavah, Svah"—which represents Earth, Atmosphere and Sky.

When you sing or use OM in a mantra, you begin the sound AHH in the back of the throat, bringing the sound forward in the mouth to OOO and MMM with the lips closed—this is why it is sometimes written AUM. You may chant OM silently or out loud, repeatedly, to benefit your whole luminous energy field.

In the Upanishads, the sacred Hindu writings, OM represents the triad of gods: Brahma, Vishnu and Shiva. It is said that Shiva's drum produced this sound and through it came the notes of the octave: SA, RI, GA, MA, PA, DHA, NI. By this sound Shiva creates and re-creates the universe. OM is also the sound form of Atman, the life principle of the universe and our individual soul.

Musically, OM or AUM is made up of three base notes—"A," "U," "M"—or the basic SA PA of the fundamental scale and again SA (the base note) of the immediately higher scale. When you sound these three notes continuously, all the basic notes from SA to NI also sound.

Practicing OM firstly clears blockages in the vocal cords and the Throat Chakra, then begins to clear the whole of the physical body, other chakras and the auric field. For this reason, nearly all the Vedic mantras and prayers have OM or AUM at the beginning.

*The sacred OM should resonate and vibrate
throughout your head and chest.*

"bija" mantras

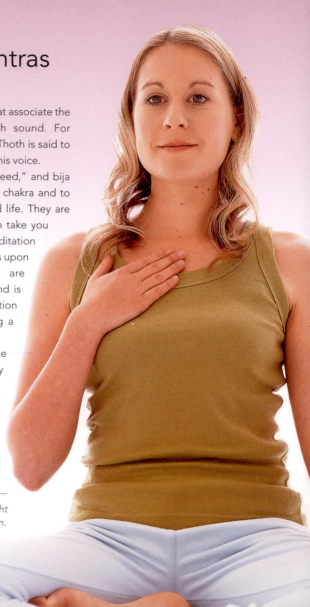

Many cultures have myths that associate the creation of the world with sound. For example, the Egyptian god Thoth is said to have created the world with his voice.

Bija means "jewel" or "seed," and bija mantras connect us to each chakra and to the source of all manifested life. They are like precious jewels that can take you into an inward focus. In meditation they are used silently to focus upon each chakra. When they are sounded out loud, the sound is extended so that each repetition runs into the next, creating a continuous drone of sound.

Because chakras resonate with vibrations on many levels, sound, singing, toning, chanting and music are highly beneficial when they are used with right intent. You really do shine like a "jewel" when you sing!

Practice chanting with a straight spine and comfortable position.

BIJA MANTRAS AND THEIR ASSOCIATED CHAKRAS

Chakra	Bija mantra	Note	Sound
Base/Muladhara	LAM	Note of deep C	Sounding like "larm"
Sacral/Svadisthana	VAM	Note of D	Sounding like "varm"
Solar Plexus/Manipura	RAM	Note of E	Sounding like "rarm"
Heart/Anahata	YAM	Note of F	Sounding like "yarm"
Throat/Vishuddha	HAM	Note of G	Sounding like "harm"
Brow/Ajna	OM	Note of A	See pages 78–79
Crown/Sahasrara	OM	Note of B	See pages 78–79

bija mantras and yoga

During yoga practice a number of techniques greatly improve its effectiveness. Among them is correct breathing (pranayama), visualization of the color assigned to the chakra and associated with the posture (asana), and the sounding of the bija mantra associated with the chakra (see boxed text). Because it would be difficult to recite a lengthy mantra while holding a posture, the short, repetitive bija mantras are more appropriate, for they increase your focus and the power build-up in your body. So during the period of holding the yoga posture, chant the bija mantra repeatedly out loud. Feel the sound vibration and "push" it into a chakra area.

If you find it difficult to know which note you are sounding, try to use the bija mantras intuitively in an ascending scale, and trust that you will be giving yourself a healing balancing sound.

hindu deities and the chakras

Shakta theory (see pages 22–23) finally determined the Hindu deities and animals associated with each chakra, and in each section of this book devoted to a specific chakra we will provide more detailed information on these. Meditating on the significance of the appropriate deity can greatly enhance your chakra awareness. But first let us explore in greater detail the Hindu pantheon.

Today there are four major forms of Hinduism: Saivism, Shaktism, Vaishnavism and Smarthism. In Smarta Hinduism a variety of forms of God are seen as aspects of the one universal spirit, Brahma; while Saivism, Shaktism and Vaishnavism tend to focus on Vishnu. A key concept in Hinduism is that of trimurti, also known as the Hindu trinity, which describes the three aspects of God, in the form of Brahma, known as the creator; Vishnu, the maintainer or preserver; and Shiva, the destroyer.

brahma

Brahma is the creator and giver of boons. As he meditates, Brahma emits from himself both the material elements of the universe and the philosophical concepts that enable us to understand our material world.

vishnu

Vishnu is a benevolent god, willing and able to bestow favors on his worshippers. His consort Shri (also known as Lakshmi) is the goddess of prosperity and good fortune.

VISHNU'S INCARNATIONS

Ten animals and human figures have been identified as incarnations of Vishnu in the world. They appear successively when the world is in danger from evil. They are:

1   Matsya: the fish
2   Kurma: the tortoise
3   Varaha: the boar
4   Narasimha: the man-lion
5   Vamana: the dwarf
6   Parashurama: a Brahman
7/8 Rama and Krishna: Rama is the hero of the Hindu epic, the Ramayana
9   The Buddha: the ninth avatar
10 Kalkin: the tenth and future avatar who will establish a new era

what are chakras?

83

hindu deities and the chakrashindu deities and the chakras

shiva

Shiva is a wrathful avenger as well as a herdsmen of souls. He is linked with yoga and asceticism, but is also a figure of erotic power and is worshipped in the form of a lingam, or sacred phallus. His wife appears as Sati, Uma or Parvati, and he is also sometimes paired with Durga and the dark goddess, Kali. Shiva is also lord of the dance, the source of all movement in the

Wonderful sculptures of gods and goddesses grace Hindu temples.

universe. His dancing steps are intended to relieve by enlightenment the sufferings of his devotees.

Shiva's children by Parvati are also important deities: Skanda and Ganesha, the elephant-headed god.

indian astrology and the chakras

Indian astrology is called Jyotirvidya, which means "to have knowledge of the cosmic Light." Indian astrological traditions only work with seven planets—the Sun, Moon, Mars, Mercury, Jupiter, Venus and Saturn—those that can be seen with the naked eye and were discovered by ancient star-watchers before the other planets in our solar system (Uranus, Neptune and Pluto). Two imaginary points, formed by the intersection of the paths of the Earth and the Moon—the two nodes named Rahu and Ketu—are also included.

In Hindu religion and mythology, these nine "planets" have nine deities assigned to them, which are known as the Navagraha. Because they have an impact on the lives of individuals, Hindus honor these deities so that they bring peace and harmony into their lives.

Each of the planets is thought to bestow a particular boon on humans. In addition the planets are believed to influence historical events, the fate of entire nations and Earth herself. Consulting astrological influences is an important part of life in India, the great culture that has given the world the wisdom of yoga and the chakras.

chakra associations with Indian astrology

We can see correspondences between Indian astrology and the planets and chakras if we place our understanding in the context of the three qualities used in Ayurvedic teachings. These are classified as rajastic (active), tamasic (inert) and sattvic (balanced) (see pages 46–49). Using this

The goddess Durga holding symbols of her power. (Rajasthani folk art painting.)

THE PLANETS AND THEIR DEITIES

Planet	Ruling deity	Over-ruler	Crystal
Surya/ Sun	Agni, god of fire	Shiva	Red ruby
Soma/Moon	Apas, water goddess	Parvati	Moonstone, natural pearls
Mangal/Mars	Bhumi, earth goddess	Skanda	Red coral
Budha/Mercury	Vishnu, the preserver	Vishnu	Emerald
Brihaspati/Jupiter	Indra, king of the gods	Brahma	Yellow sapphire, yellow topaz
Sukra/Venus	Indrani, queen of the gods	Indra	Diamond
Shani/Saturn	Yama, god of death	Prajapati	Blue sapphire, black stones
Rahu/The Dragon's Head (north lunar node)	Durga, goddess of power	Sarpa	Honey-colored hessonite
Ketu/The Dragon's Tail (south lunar node)	Chitragupta, god of karma	Brahma	Cat's eye

system, the following chakras are associated with the "planets" used in Indian astrology:

- The Sun and Moon with the Brow Chakra
- Mercury with the Throat Chakra
- Venus with the Heart Chakra
- Mars with the Solar Plexus Chakra
- Jupiter with the Sacral Chakra
- Saturn with the Base Chakra.

chakras and the seven-year cycles

Yoga teaching links the seven major chakras to seven-year time periods. They commence, as might be imagined, at birth in the Base Chakra and work successively through each of the chakras. Thus there are 49 years (7 x 7) of unique experiences, each year "colored" by a particular chakra. In our fiftieth year we begin a new seven-year cycle, starting again at the Base Chakra—but at a higher frequency of energy. This gives us another type of life experience as we begin the next seven-year cycle.

how to use the seven-year chart

For a child in year 13—that is, they have just had the 12th anniversary of their birth—they are under the *overall* influence of the Sacral Chakra as puberty develops from year 8 to 14. As you can see from the keywords, they begin to explore their sexuality and creativity and start planning at that time how to break away from the influence of their parents.

Now look at an elder in their 98th year. They have experienced 14 times seven-year cycles and are currently in the Crown Chakra overall cycle, a period of unity and enlightenment.

There is also a one-year cycle of chakra associations, whereby each year of life is linked to a particular energy and its own keywords. This can give rise to conflicts between the seven-year and one-year cycle, which can shed further light on an individual's actions and behavior at a particular time.

what are chakras?

Family relationships and personal growth can be understood through seven-year cycles.

BASIC UNDERSTANDINGS WITHIN EACH SEVEN-YEAR CYCLE

Year	Chakra cycle	Keywords
0–7 and 50–56	First/Base	Life-force energy; connection to the Earth and material world; stability; initiating new beginnings
8–14 and 57–63	Second/Sacral	Sensuality; creativity; enthusiasm; exploring creativity and boundaries
15–21 and 64–70	Third/Solar Plexus	Development of personality and feelings; wisdom; expansion and limitless possibilities
22–28 and 71–77	Fourth/Heart	Love; compassion; selflessness; development of healing skills in self and others; working to heal the Earth
29–35 and 78–84	Fifth/Throat	Communication; self-expression; inspiration; independence; openness to higher development; speaking with wisdom
36–42 and 85–91	Sixth/Brow	Realization of inner senses, such as clairvoyance, intuition; responsibility; deepening life experiences
43–49 and 92–98	Seventh/Crown	Time of inner work; unity; enlightenment; inner spiritual transition, contemplation and meditation

Chapter 2

THE BASE CHAKRA: MULADHARA

• • • • • • •

Chapters 2–8 present the seven major chakras in depth, with a range of exercises to help balance your life-force energy. Wisdom is drawn from Tantric yoga sources and from modern interpretations.

muladhara chakra

The Base Chakra, or Muladhara, is also known as the root, adhara, mula, padma, brahma padma or bhumi chakra. It is the first of the seven major chakras and associated with the element of Earth, symbolizing the densest grade of manifestation and the basis of life.

In the kundalini yoga system of Shaktism, the Muladhara center is described as having four lotus petals, blood-red in color, each corresponding to the psychological states of greatest joy, natural pleasure, delight in controlling passions, and blissfulness in concentration, leading to meditation.

the functions of muladhara

In terms of energetics, this chakra channels Earth energy upward through the feet and legs to process and stabilize it. It then moves the energy on, up the spine, now transmuted into a form that the body recognizes as signals, to balance the endocrine system (the gonads: ovaries and testes) through the release of hormones. When we do not get the full flow of this Earth energy, imbalances in our physical body result.

"Grounding" or "rooting" us is the main function of Muladhara. When we are grounded, we are at one with life and Muladhara functions as intended. We enter into a sympathetic vibration with the electromagnetic frequency of the Earth, coming into tune with the beat of "her" heart.

Muladhara is also closely associated with returning karma—the sum of our experiences from previous existences. This is sometimes referred to as "good" or "bad" karma, but all karma is there for us to learn from, and we are fortunate if we believe that we get more than one chance at life!

The first and second chakras also act as the energetic recycling bin of the auric field. They change negative emotional energies into power and light, and return to Earth any "toxic waste" that the other chakras cannot deal with, thus keeping the rainbow purity of the aura. If our Muladhara chakra is disassociated from the Earth, we cannot expel these waste emotions.

MAIN CHARACTERISTICS AT A GLANCE

Color	Red
Key issues	Sexuality, lust, obsession
Physical location	Between the anus and genitals, opening downward
Associated spinal area	Fourth sacral vertebra
Physiological system	Reproductive
Endocrine gland	Gonads
Nerve plexus	Sacral-coccygeal
Inner aspect	Grounding spiritual energies
Physical action	Sexuality
Mental action	Stability
Emotional action	Sensuality
Spiritual action	Security

health issues and muladhara

Muladhara means "the support of the root," "the keeper of the beginning" or the "bearer of the foundation." First-chakra needs are instinctual: we need shelter and food. The compulsion to overeat or hoard material items and money is a negative expression of our instinct for survival. If we can never get enough food, money, goods and sex to satisfy us, then Muladhara is dysfunctioning and we are seriously disconnected from the Earth. But the chakras are our teachers and can lead us gently to higher realizations. As you will see later (see page 96), the primal power of kundalini is coiled here like a snake, ready to awaken us to our true spiritual selves. This is one of the goals of Tantric yoga.

The positive attributes of Muladhara give us remarkable abilities to survive under extreme conditions. They also urge us to procreate and express love to our partners and children, spurred on by the feminine urge of the primal kundalini serpent, the Earth Mother energy lying dormant within us.

associated body system

This chakra is connected to minor chakras on feet, ankles, knees and groin that support the upward flow of energy from the Earth. When we deny our connection to Earth wisdom, our bodies react and disorders manifest, affecting the sacrum, spine, excretion and sexual organs. If the Muladhara chakra is blocked, you will not experience a very fulfilling sex life. Conversely those who try to suppress sexual urges may have hidden fears and end up with diseases associated with imbalances in their approach to sexuality.

Holistic practitioners always treat the *energy* associated with a disease, rather than the disease itself. They look for underlying causes and dysfunctions. If they are trained in color therapy, they will use red light to stimulate sexual dysfunction and blue light to calm and balance.

associated endocrine gland

The Base Chakra is linked to the endocrine glands. In women these are the ovaries, which produce the hormones estrogen and progesterone. Estrogen promotes secondary female characteristics and menstrual cycles, and can also be found in the placenta, adrenals and male testes; progesterone prepares the uterus for a fertilized egg. In men, these are the testes, which produce the hormone testosterone, which develops and maintains male characteristics and produces sperm.

the base chakra: muladhara

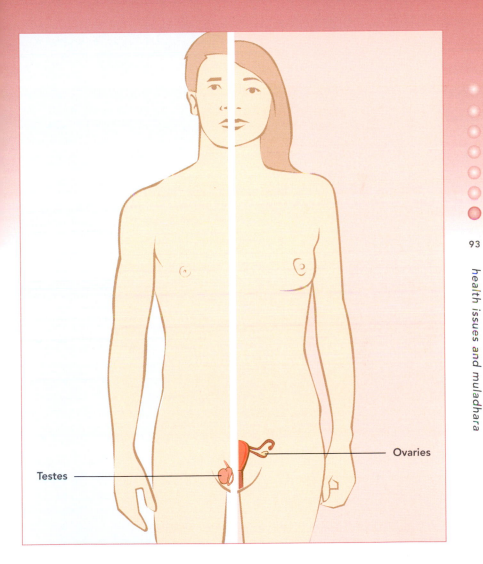

Testes

Ovaries

mental, emotional and spiritual issues

Because Muladhara is located between the legs, the actual point of body contact of this chakra is the sacral-coccyx joint, which is associated with the position of our body in time and space, how we move and the tactile sense of touch. From this you can see its importance during love-making.

All of the major chakras are situated in a vertical line ascending from the base of the spine to the head, making a core line for the flow of radiant energy. It is controlling this core radiance that leads to transformation of the sexual urge into spiritual enlightenment during Tantric yoga. A "spin-off" of fulfilling sex is the resulting secretion of beneficial hormones that are needed to revitalize us and keep us young.

transmuting the emotions

We can all understand hormonal imbalances at puberty and menopause. During these times we often go through extremes of emotion. The hint that we receive from Tantric yoga is that we can transmute these emotions if we move energies upward through the chakras—concentrating not just on base sexual desires, but on a wholesome, vibrant body and fulfilling spiritual life. At menopause it is vital that women complete

the upward movement of energy, for neglect may develop disease in the womb and breasts. Men at this point in the same cycle may end up with testicular disease or, quite literally, "heart-break."

stability and security

Muladhara is the foundation of life. Confidence in who we are and whom we trust are functions of the Base Chakra. If our early life felt safe and protected, then trust in the world is normally well-established. If, on the other hand, our conception was traumatic, or the environment of our mother's womb and our childhood was disruptive, then the stresses in the first chakra tend to make us see the world—and other humans—as frightening.

When this first chakra is flowing fully, it has been described as a beautiful red lotus flower with an intense golden center. The lotus starts life in muddy water at the bottom of a lake or river and grows upward to blossom in the light. For this reason it symbolizes human potential and growth from our beginnings, through mastering our emotions, to blossoming in the Light of Spirit. This is why the chakras are often depicted as lotuses.

In Tantric yoga, control of radiant energy between the chakras leads to transformation of the sexual urge into spiritual enlightenment.

kundalini energy

In Tantric yoga teachings the colors of blood-red, yellow and gold are traditionally associated with Muladhara. Surprisingly, despite being the lowest and first of the seven major chakras, this is the bliss center for our physical body. In Muladhara we experience joy, pleasure, passions and blissfulness in concentration; above all, this center leads us to the bliss of realizing the Divine in the physical body through

sexuality. The highest forms of spirituality in the majority of cultures do not reject the body, but see it as a medium for the transmutation of body and spirit together.

body electrics

We have bodies that are wired for bliss. We have a subtle electrical energy grid of meridians (as understood in acupuncture) and channels of energy called nadis (in the yoga tradition) already in place. However, the grid sometimes gets blocked and the energy that flows through it reduced. Yoga and aesthetic practices purify the grid's energy lines so that a radiant light flows as intended.

As always, the simplest methods are often the best. Notice what you think, say, eat, drink and breathe. How do you move, sit and stand, dance and sing? It's not so much what you *do* that is important as how you *feel*, and with what sentiments you act. For anyone, the first step in the right direction is simply recognizing that you are a spiritual being, born with a potential for growth into the limitless Light of Spirit.

According to Shakta Tantric doctrine, Muladhara is the place where kundalini—a latent cosmic energy—resides in every living human being. When this latent power is activated through Hatha yoga practices (pranayama, purification of the nadis, and so on), it rises through each of the spinal chakras in turn and up through the top of the head, to the Sahasrara/Crown Chakra, or "Thousand-petalled Lotus," above. There it unites with its opposite polarity, the Paramashiva or Supreme Godhead Consciousness, and the yogi attains total liberation from everyday reality. Put more simply, kundalini is the feminine Shakti power of the eternal goddess, who wants to unite with her Lord Shiva at your Crown Chakra. She desires him and becomes impatient to unite with him; she needs to rise up your spine, surging through the chakras in ecstatic bursts of infinite Light and Power, and shimmer in your head.

Tantric Yoga teaches the right use of kundalini energy and how to be full of joy in every moment.

kundalini energy and the nadis

Kundalini energy can be awakened through a combination of Hatha yoga postures, bandhas (body locks), pranayama (correct breathing), mudras (hand gestures), mantra chanting, meditation, and visualization techniques. During this process our latent kundalini energy works with the nervous system to achieve a profoundly new level of consciousness.

This dormant energy rises through the nadis. According to an ancient Tantric text, there are 14 main nadis. The three most important are the ida, pingala and sushumna nadis (see pages 22–3). The Base Chakra is where all three meet. From Muladhara,

the subtle energy from ida and pingala ascends, alternating at each chakra. If kundalini flows through sushumna to its full destination, soul realization is consciously achieved.

awakening kundalini energy

The key processes for awakening kundalini energy are purifying mind and body. Purifying the body eliminates accumulated toxins, and whatever purifies the body will also purify the mind. According to Ayurvedic medicine, fasting is one of the most effective methods of detoxing the body. Other methods include pranayama and bodily cleansing.

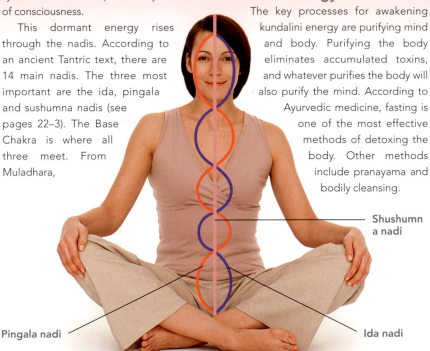

Shushumna nadi

Pingala nadi

Ida nadi

THE EIGHT "LIMBS" OF PATANJALI

In the 2nd century BCE the great Indian sage Patanjali compiled a collection of yoga writings called the *Sutras of Patanjali*. Composed of eight "limbs," they proceed in sequential order:

1 **Yamas** In Sanskrit this means "restraint" and is a code of conduct. There are ten yamas: non-violence, truth, honesty, sexual continence, forbearance, fortitude, kindness, straightforwardness, moderation in diet, and avoiding impurity in body, mind and speech.

2 **Niyamas** There are ten niyamas, or observances: austerity, contentment, belief in God, charity, worship of God, listening to explanations of doctrines, modesty, a discerning mind, repetition of prayers and sacrifice.

3 **Asana** These are yoga postures. When you achieve correct posture, the body's forces are balanced, the breathing is slowed and meditation is facilitated.

4 **Pranayama** Control of prana. Slowing the breathing so that your breath is held between inhaling and exhaling is the secret of pranayama.

5 **Pratyahara** Withdrawing from the distractions of the sensory world through deep concentration.

6 **Dharana** Stilling the mind. Concentrating on each chakra in turn is an excellent way to develop dharana.

7 **Dhyana** Uninterrupted meditation in which there is no fixed point (such as a chakra) to meditate on. It is a state of profound calmness, where the experience of bliss begins.

8 **Samadhi** The state of complete equilibrium and self-realization where one becomes free of awareness of the self, time or space.

kundalini energy and the nadis

With the body seated motionless and at ease in a cross-legged or Lotus posture, practice of Pranayama and Pratyahara can begin.

the bandhas

The bandhas, or "body locks" (see pages 66–67), are vital in activating the sushumna nadi and awakening kundalini. Because of the way they block or channel pranic energy in specific ways, they must not be attempted except under the supervision of a competent teacher. If performed in the wrong way, bandhas put considerable strain on a number of physical organs, including the heart, lungs and eyes. Most bandhas are initially learned while practicing certain asanas. As can be seen from Patanjali's eight "limbs" (see pages 98–99), the practice of pranayama comes once the asanas have been mastered. Subsequently pranayama breathing techniques, and their effects on the body and mind, are modified by the use of bandhas.

The following three bandhas are the ones generally practiced. Below is a brief résumé of their function, the order in which they are learned and when they are used.

1 jalandhara bandha or neck lock

This lock aligns the cervical and thoracic vertebrae so that prana can flow freely into the cranial area. From an energetic perspective, performing this bandha holds powerful but subtle energy within the spine and, coupled with a tongue lock, is used during the raising of kundalini. It is learned while in Sarvangasana (shoulder stand), when it prevents excessive blood flow to the brain and strain upon the eyes and ears.

2 uddiyana bandha or diaphragm lock

Uddiyana in Sanskrit means "flying up," and this lock is performed so that prana will fly up through sushumna, the central energy channel. It is learned during basic pranayama practice.

3 mula bandha or root lock

Mula bandha concentrates on the first three chakras. It is learned during advanced pranayama practice. By contracting the anal sphincter and the sex organs, the apana, downward-moving energy that resides in the lower organs and lower three chakras and prevents prana

An advanced Yoga practitioner using the neck and root locks.

the base chakra: muladhara

from escaping downward, is reversed and forced to flow up. As apana and prana fuse, they create the force needed to activate kundalini energy. While applying this bandha the expert practitioner will achieve restraint of the mind (manas), intellect (buddhi) and ego (ahankara).

4 maha bandha or great lock

This describes the application of all three previous locks at the same time. Maha bandha is used during pranayama, meditation and especially with Raja yoga and Tantric practices. It harmonizes the nervous system and the glandular systems. Ojas or subtle seminal fluid is also beneficially reabsorbed into the body and sexual energy is channeled sequentially through the whole chakra system.

the bandhas

the granthis

According to Tantric texts, the granthis (or knots) are energy blocks or psychic hurdles that we must cross to raise more energy in the sushumna nadi. They can potentially obstruct the path of kundalini energy as it undertakes its ascent to the higher centers. Generally Western culture suffers from a kundalini dysfunction that holds us at first- or second-chakra level. Such a blockage stops us from feeling in touch with our whole body or from sensing our spiritual potential. We all need kundalini in order to survive in our physical bodies. When we have an ecstatic "raising" of kundalini, the increased potency and higher vibrational quality allow us to actually *feel its power*.

brahma granthi

This is the first knot to overcome and is also known as the perineal knot. It is located in Muladhara (some texts locate it at the navel). Known as the knot of names and forms, the world of ambitions and desires, it is called "Brahma's knot" because the god Brahma is the creator of the sensory world. By being trapped in the world of the senses, sexuality, physicality and a restless focus on earthly attachments, we become unable consciously to raise our kundalini past this point.

Practicing the yamas and niyamas (see pages 98–99) is one way to begin to undo this knot. Withdrawing from the world of the senses and practicing visualization and meditation can also help to refocus the mind. When kundalini passes through the knot of Brahma, images and distractions from the sensory world will no longer interrupt the meditation path.

vishnu granthi

This is located in the Heart Chakra and is named after the god Vishnu, the lord of preservation. It creates a desire to preserve ancient knowledge, traditions, spiritual orders and institutions. This attachment is made stronger by the compassion that characterizes the Heart Chakra. However, only by the attainment of true discrimination and wisdom can one discover the will of God and be freed from illusory attachments.

rudra granthi

This knot is situated in the area of the Brow Chakra. In Tantric scriptures it is stated that when awakened rising kundalini reaches this point, and the power to see past, present and future as the omniscient nature of consciousness can be achieved.

the base chakra: muladhara

However, the rudra granthi becomes an obstacle to complete full enlightenment, because the yogi may become lost in his desire to achieve paranormal powers and visions.

Brahma the Supreme Being, is the first deity of the Hindu Trinity, the cause and all-pervading spirit of the Universe. He is rarely portrayed in the sculptural adornment of temples.

muladhara yantra

*In this lotus is the square of Earth,
surrounded by eight shining spears.
It is shining yellow and beautiful
like lightning, as the seed-sound
Lam, which is within.*

Sat Cakra Nirupana, a Sanskrit text written
c.1577, which describes the chakras and
kundalini energy

description of the yantra

Number of petals Four, symbolizing the
four directions and four qualities of bliss.
Color Red petals surrounding a yellow
square (Earth)—the element associated
with this chakra.
White elephant Airavata reminds us of our
instinctive animal nature. An elephant is
strong and intelligent, but has destructive
tendencies, a dilemma that often confronts
us in Muladhara. Airavata has seven trunks,
which symbolize the elements that are
essential for physical life (see box).
Trikona A triangular shape that represents
Shakti (female) energy.
Lingam, or phallus Represents male, Shiva
energy. Kundalini energy is shown as a
serpent wrapped around the lingam.
Crescent moon Crowns the lingam,
symbolizing the Divine source of all energy.

the bija mantra

Muladhara's bija mantra (see pages 80–81) is
LAM and, when sounded, it creates a block
against our energy descending beneath our
foundations, and encourages concentration.

THE ELEPHANT

Each chakra has a magical teaching
story woven around it, starring Hindu
deities (see pages 106–107) and real
or mythic animals. In representations
of Muladhara, the elephant is often
to be seen. This animal is revered in
India, and is a symbol of earthly
abundance and good fortune; it is
sacred to Indra, that aspect of nature
governing the natural laws of Mother
Earth. Its seven trunks indicate that
the strength of the elephant is
supporting all seven major chakras;
they also represent the seven
elements that comprise the human
body: earth (Raja), fluids (Rasa),
blood (Rakta), flesh, nerves and
tissue (Mansa), fat (Medba), bones
(Asthi) and bone marrow (Majjan).

muladhara yantra

deities associated with muladhara

brahma

Brahma, the Lord of Creation, is depicted as having four heads, to symbolize the fact that he is all-knowing and can see in four directions at once. Each of his heads also represents the four forms of human consciousness: the physical self; the rational self; the emotional self; and the intuitive self.

Brahma is shown as having four arms, in each of which is generally held:

- Upper left hand: a lotus flower, the traditional Hindu symbol of purity
- Lower left hand: the sacred Hindu scriptures
- Lower right hand: a vase containing amrita, the fluid of vital potency
- Upper right hand: this hand is raised in the mudra (hand gesture) of granting fearlessness.

Brahma is shown as a child, reflecting the relative immaturity of the consciousness at this level. He appears during the hours of dusk and sunrise. Meditating on Brahma helps to develop peacefulness and stillness.

dakini

Dakini is Brahma's consort and combines the forces of the Creator, the Preserver and the Destroyer. She embodies the revelation of Divine knowledge and the nectar of life (Amrita). Sometimes she is depicted riding upon a fierce lion representing the lower human nature. She too holds several symbolic items:

- Lower left hand: a trident, which symbolizes her destructive energies
- Upper left hand: a skull, symbolic of detachment from the fear of death— a common psychological block in the first chakra
- Upper right hand: a sword, representing the power to overcome fear and difficulties
- Lower right hand: a shield for protection against problems that could sway us from our spiritual path.

creating an altar

Finding ways to honor our connection to the Earth is as old as humanity. All ancient cultures knew that their lives depended on maintaining a strong bond to what many called Mother Earth. It helps us to feel this connection if we take time to walk in Nature, enjoy her gifts and give thanks for them.

Making an altar is not necessarily either a religious act or a pagan ritual, but is a positive action in the 21st century that is of benefit to our health and our body–mind–spirit connection. By connecting to the Earth, we bring our Base Chakra into balance. Here are some suggestions for your altar:

- Find a quiet place indoors, or outside in Nature, and place a red cloth on the ground to form the basis of your altar. This color honors your blood and body, representing your Muladhara chakra and your grounding to the Earth.
- During your walks in Nature, keep your eyes open for any gifts that she offers you: for example, unusual-shaped seeds, feathers, shells or stones. You can place these on your altar.
- Make a collection of all the things that represent your childhood—your beginnings of life. Whatever they are, honor them as being a part of you.

However, if the memories are painful, ceremonially burn the objects.
- Gather wild flowers or herbs to place on your altar.
- Light candles and position them on your altar.
- Find poems to celebrate Nature or sexuality, and read them out loud.
- Bake yourself a loaf of bread (baking puts your own energy into the bread) and, together with some wine or red fruit juice, have a ceremonial meal at your altar.
- Draw some pictures or mandalas (circular meditational symbols), and place them on your altar. Alternatively, find photos of those who inspire you and put them there.
- Spend time each day at your altar, using it as a special space where you can meditate and nurture yourself.
- Best of all, share your altar-making with friends, and sing, dance, read poems and give loving inspirational thoughts to one another.

Elemental energies are represented on this altar to remind us of our bond with Nature.

crystals to calm muladhara

Recommended gemstone crystals for calming the Base Chakra are small, uncut pieces of emerald or blue sapphire. To achieve clarity about spiritual matters, use blue sapphire to enable a connection to be made with your spiritual origins, ancestral roots and cosmic origins.

Uncut gemstones, such as these sapphires, are reasonably priced.

emerald

Emerald, when used on the Base Chakra, will calm it by bringing you into a deeper resonance with Mother Earth. Emerald helps to ground us, so that we feel much more at peace with our lives on Earth. It is vital that we are all grounded through our Base Chakra, since unless we are, the other chakras will not be fully in alignment with our soul purpose.

In addition, the Base Chakra is the place where kundalini energy "sleeps" curled up. Kundalini is none other than our life urge—our desire to be here in a physical body. When the Base Chakra and kundalini are wildly out of balance, we may succumb to our basest sexual actions. If we are the victim of sexual abuse, it is possible that emerald, of all the gemstones (in combination with professional treatment), will calm our shattered emotions and violated auric field. People who demonstrate great anger (whether of a sexual nature or not) will have a disturbed Base Chakra. Until it is balanced, no amount of treatment will remedy it. When anger is held at Muladhara, it completely blocks the energetic Earth connection and we are unable to experience the beauty of kundalini rising through the chakra system.

using emerald to ground yourself

Arrange not to be disturbed for 30 minutes (turn off your telephone!).

1   In a cross-legged meditation pose, sit on the floor on your emerald (if you don't want to actually sit on it, hold it in your non-dominant hand at your Base Chakra). If you sense that you need a lot of grounding, put a dense stone under each foot as well.
2   Now relax, but keep your spine straight, visualizing roots growing out from under your feet: first a strong "tap root," then smaller roots in a network of finer and finer filaments, working their way through the earth, rocks and stones. Your roots are so powerful that they can pass around any obstacles and eventually connect to the crystalline heart of Mother Earth at the center of the planet.
3   Come slowly back to everyday awareness.

An expensive sparkling cut emerald and uncut pieces that are equally effective.

crystals to balance muladhara

A popular New Age myth is that a set of seven "chakra stones" of different colors will balance your chakras. They might be effective, but healers who specialize in using crystals use different crystals for specific purposes.

This book recommends precious gemstones to activate or calm each chakra. In addition we suggest a number of less precious stones to balance out the energies and bring harmony—these stones can be "tumble-polished" so that they end up looking like smooth pebbles.

A healer will generally only work on one or two chakras at a time: you should never overload someone's body or auric field with the power of crystals. Far better to ascertain the lowest chakra that is out of balance and work upon it. Check that it is balanced to optimum levels before proceeding to the next chakra. When all the chakras are balanced, they come into a state called "harmonization."

To check the state of your chakras, try the following techniques:

- Sensing them with your hands
- Visualizing the condition of the chakra in your mind's eye
- Using a pendulum
- Muscle-testing (kinesiology, see pages 54–55)
- Clairvoyantly seeing the chakra (if you are gifted in this way).

Keep healing crystals, such as the carnelian shown here, wrapped in red silk.

carnelian

A small carnelian pebble/tumbled stone (or black tourmaline) is ideal for balancing Muladhara. And, provided you have consulted a doctor about any acutely painful condition, you can use a flat, polished carnelian, taped into position over the problem area, for pain reduction. Remove the carnelian at least three times a day and cleanse it by washing.

using carnelian to balance yourself

Create a quiet and clear sacred space around yourself, then begin.

Polished or uncut carnelian has a special affinity to Base Chakra energies.

1 Sit quietly in a chair with a straight back and your bare feet flat on the floor. Have your carnelian ready cleansed (see page 68) and close by.

2 Let your breath flow deeply into your body, and ground yourself (see page 111).

3 Close your eyes and visualize the condition of each chakra in turn, working upward. Notice what colors and energies you see. Are the energies still or moving? Now return to the Base Chakra: this is the one you are going to balance with the carnelian.

4 Holding the carnelian in your non-dominant hand, visualize the Base Chakra again. Ask for it to come into balance. You can even talk to it—and thank it when it seems balanced.

5 Come back slowly to everyday awareness.

visualization using crystals

For this visualization you ideally need three small pieces of black tourmaline, although one will do. You are going to root yourself into the collective unconscious mind of humanity.

1 Turn off your phone and make sure you will not be disturbed. Allow about 30 minutes for this exercise.

2 Sit in an upright chair, in a cross-legged yoga posture or lie down. Take your shoes and socks off.

3 Your tourmaline should already be cleansed (see page 68). Place one piece underneath your spine and sit on it (if you have only one tourmaline, put it here); rest the other pieces in the palm of each hand.

4 Begin to breathe deeply. Do this for some minutes.

5 Be aware of the ground beneath you, and start to visualize a strong root growing from the bottom of your spine out through the soles of your feet.

6 Imagine that you are a tiny seed full of life-force energy. Tiny rootlets are growing from your spinal root, seeking nourishment in the Earth. They are looking for water. Your task is to see the network of roots taking up water,

passing it into your body through the Base Chakra.

7 Now see your spine as the trunk of a tree. Check that your body is finely balanced on either side of your spine.

8 Visualize your head in the element of air. Now you can see yourself fully as a tree with roots, trunk and branches.

9 Look closely at the branches: What type of leaves do they have? Do they have flowers or fruit on them? Accept whatever you see.

10 Now focus inwardly, realizing that you draw nourishment from the Earth, just like a tree. In the world of energy vibration, nothing is separate: you and the tree are one.

11 When you are ready to finish, breathe more deeply. Let go of the tree visualization. Reach down to your feet and rub them, then rub your legs.

12 Hold all your crystals in the palms of your hands and, breathing on them, thank them for their energy.

13 Stretch your body, remembering that you are a tree reaching up to the light.

You may find it helpful to keep notes of your experience or make a drawing of your tree.

*Black tourmaline counters
negativity, grounds the Base Chakra
and brings all into alignment.*

aromatherapy and muladhara

Our sense of smell is acute and can distinguish between those smells that we call bad or offensive and those that give us pleasure. Perfumed oils have been used since the earliest times: by 3500 BCE priestesses in Egyptian temples were burning tree gums and resins such as frankincense to clear the air and mind; ancient Greeks and the Egyptians were skilled at blending all manner of herbs in fatty-paste pomanders for the treatment of wounds and cosmetics; and the Romans used fragrant oils for massage.

It was brilliant Arab physicians who were among the first to build up the most comprehensive knowledge of the therapeutic properties of plants. By the 12th century the "perfumes of Arabia" were being brought back to Europe by knight crusaders, although the knowledge

BASE CHAKRA ESSENTIAL OILS

Essential oils that have a sympathetic resonance with Muladhara are:

- **Cedarwood**: This comes from steam distillation of the wood. It is antiseptic, anti-seborrhoeic, astringent, diuretic, emmenagogic, expectorant, sedative and an insecticide.

- **Patchouli**: This oil is steam-distilled from dried, fermented leaves and is very popular in India and the Far East. It acts as an anti-depressant, anti-inflammatory, anti-microbial, antiseptic, aphrodisiac, deodorant, sedative and an excellent insecticide.

- **Myrrh**: This is derived from a shrubby tree that produces a brown resin from the bark. It is anti-inflammatory, antiseptic, astringent, carminative, emmenagogic, expectorant, fungicidal and sedative.

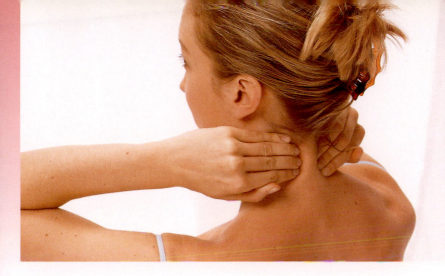

of how to distill them remained unknown in Europe for many more centuries.

In the first years of the 20th century a French chemist, René Maurice Gattefosse, and Dr. Jean Valnet began to make essential oils. During World War I, Valnet used them to successfully treat severe burns, battle injuries and psychiatric problems.

Caution: Essential oils should not be used on babies and children under 12 years. During pregnancy their use is limited to a few safe oils, which an aromatherapist can recommend.

simple aromatherapy massage

This massage is easy to perform on yourself.

1   Refer to page 57 for instructions on mixing essential oils with a base oil. Sit on the floor comfortably, covered with a towel. Remove all clothing from your upper body and expose your neck.
2   Put a little oil on your hands and massage over your neck and shoulders, gradually increasing the pressure.
3   Work the muscles of each shoulder firmly, making small friction circles wherever you feel deep-seated tension.
4   Put your fingertips behind your head on either side of your neck, then make friction circles up and down the neck muscles.

yoga asanas for muladhara

As we have seen (pages 64–67), you start a yoga session by balancing the chakras with a standing balanced asana (posture) such as Pranamasana (prayer pose). This is simply standing straight with the spine lifted, as if a cord is pulling it up from the crown of your head, and placing your hands together in the prayer position. You then proceed, undertaking the recommended asanas, and end your yoga session with a balanced sitting asana, such as Sirhasana (simple sitting posture), Siddhasana or Padmasana (lotus posture), or lying down in Savasana (corpse/relaxation pose).

active: virabhadrasana 1 (warrior)

This strong standing asana makes a firm connection with the prana coming into your Base Chakra. Physically it strengthens your legs and benefits your back. It also helps to discharge excessive

1

sexual energies through the Base Chakra, while foot chakras and reflexology reflexes benefit by receiving the energies of Earth. In addition, the upstretched arms remind you of your connection to a higher source. The state of consciousness associated with Muladhara is annamayakosha (deep sleep), which is experienced through the physical body. As you use your breath to move you in a light, fluid way into this asana, visualize it being red in color.

1 Stand with your feet about 3 ft. (1 m) apart. Turn your right foot to the right, and bend your right knee until it is in line with your ankle.

2 Keeping your back straight, stretch both arms above your head, bringing the palms of your hands together. Repeat on the other side.

2

active: trikonasana (triangle)

The strong triangle shape of the legs in this pose is symbolic of the movement of Earth energy upward through the chakras, which begins with the Base Chakra. It complements the downward-pointed triangle of cosmic energy depicted in the yantra. Thus you start a journey to understand the symbolism of the interlocking triangle that you will encounter at the Heart Chakra. The physical and subtle-energy benefits of this pose are similar to those of Virabhadrasana 1.

1

1 Stand with your legs wider than your shoulders, making an equilateral triangle with the floor. Raise both arms to your sides, level with your shoulders.

2 Turn your left foot out, slowly bend to the left and take a firm hold of your left ankle with your left hand. Your neck should be relaxed, with your head falling sideways. Your right arm should be stretched over your head, parallel with the floor. Repeat on the other side.

yoga asanas for muladhara

2

passive: garudasana (eagle)

Garudasana is the penultimate asana (number 15) in the sequence of asanas to benefit the energies of the chakras, and demonstrates that you have come to a state of inner stillness and balance through the practice of the other asanas. It benefits the knees, ankles and shoulders, and helps to prevent cramp in the calf muscles. A gentle and peaceful type of energy is now locked within the sexual organs as you maintain this balance to complete your yoga practice.

1 Stand upright with your feet together and your hands at your sides. Bend your right knee, bringing it over the left knee and tucking the right foot behind the left calf. Balance.

2 Now bend your elbows in front of you and entwine your arms, so that the right elbow rests on the front of the left arm's inner elbow. Join the palms of your hands together. Maintain your balance. Repeat with the other leg and arm.

2

Chapter 3

THE SACRAL CHAKRA: SVADISTHANA

svadisthana chakra

The Sacral Chakra, or Svadisthana, is also known as the spleen and navel center, adhishthana, bhima, shatpatra, skaddala padma, wari-chakra and medhra. In the Indian Tantric tradition, Svadisthana can be translated as "one's sweetest abode" or "one's own place."

In the kundalini yoga system of Shaktism, Svadisthana is described as having six lotus petals, shown variously as white, saffron or orange in color, that symbolize its secret connection with the high Sixth State of Consciousness into which we are evolving. The petals are associated with: affection, pitilessness, a feeling of all-destructiveness, delusion, disdain and suspicion on the path to the Sixth State. Svadisthana has a crescent in the center, the tattwa (truth) of water. This second chakra corresponds to the element of Water and is traditionally associated with sexual energy. It does not correspond with the sex organs (these are the function or Muhadhara), but to the original life-sustaining energy behind sexual impulse. The crescent moon is also symbolic of the mysterious powers hiding within the unconscious mind and relates to the pre-rational dream state of consciousness.

the functions of Svadisthana

Indian teachings place a great deal of emphasis on celibacy, in order to raise and transmute powerful sexual energy, passing it to the brain (or, more correctly, the Upper Tan Tien Center, to use the Taoist paradigm) and thereby increasing higher consciousness. This is actually the basic principle behind celibacy in all religions (including Catholicism). In practice, though, this noble ideal often flounders, because someone who is not ready to renounce physical sex may become psychologically unbalanced and full of guilt, or turn to pedophilia or other unnatural forms of sex.

When Svadisthana is fully developed, it produces the necessary radiance to unite in a bond of love with another soul and fuels the growth of consciousness to enlightenment. Because this chakra is concerned with assimilation—of sexual expression and food, as well as ideas and creativity—it is often referred to as the center of self-expression and joy.

MAIN CHARACTERISTICS AT A GLANCE

Color	Orange
Key issues	Relationships, violence, addictions
Physical location	Upper part of the sacrum below the navel
Associated spinal area	First lumbar vertebra
Physiological system	Genitourinary
Endocrine gland	Adrenals
Nerve plexus	Sacral
Inner aspect	Feeling
Physical action	Reproduction
Mental action	Creativity
Emotional action	Joy
Spiritual action	Enthusiasm

health issues and svadisthana

Svadisthana is closely linked to the adrenal glands. The first chakra, Muladhara, guards and protects the physical form and reacts to stress by preparing the body for "fight or flight" when it is in danger or threatened. This message is passed on to Svadisthana, triggering the release of adrenaline and then starting a complex hormonal change in the body. This is a normal reaction, but when stress is constant or unnaturally prolonged, it becomes our enemy. Then the body no longer knows how to switch off the freely flowing excess of hormonal secretions, and chronic stress conditions may result. There are many major illnesses that are now medically associated with chronic stress.

Any negative emotions held at the Sacral Chakra, such as anger and fear, can eventually cause illness. Nowadays we are told to face our fears, but this is not always appropriate; instead, use those fears as a warning and start to change your patterns of behavior so that you learn from what once stressed you or caused you fear. People in life-threatening situations have sometimes found that their fear is transformed by sending their aggressors unconditional love.

associated body systems

Sexually this is the pleasure chakra that "turns us on." It is deeply concerned with our relationship to others, our motivations for our relationships and how much joy we bring to them. It follows then that imbalanced sexual encounters—perhaps eventually leading to disease of the sexual organs—are associated with this chakra. Being part of the urinary system linked to the kidneys, Svadisthana is also closely connected to the way we process water in our bodies. Other illnesses resulting from dysfunction of this chakra include colitis, irritable bowel syndrome, bladder tumors, malabsorption diseases of the small intestine, and unexplained lower back pain.

associated endocrine glands

The Sacral Chakra is linked to the adrenal glands that lie above each kidney. They are concerned with the production of adrenaline, cortisol and aldosterone. Adrenaline activates the body when we are stressed or frightened by rapidly raising the heart rate and blood pressure. Cortisol reacts against inflammation and affects the digestion of carbohydrates and protein and aldosterone acts on the kidneys, retaining water and sodium.

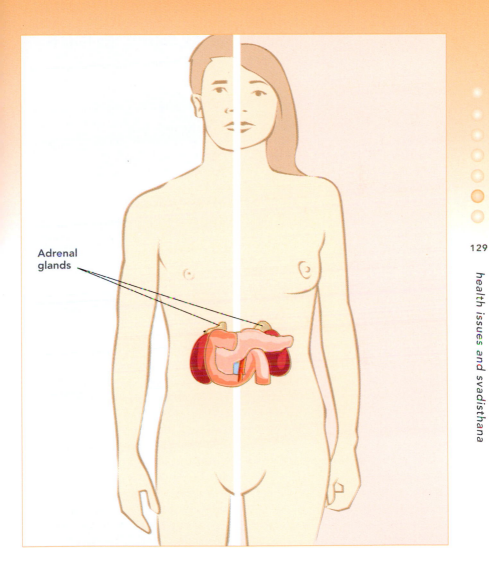

Adrenal
glands

emotional issues and svadisthana

This chakra has developed its imprints and subsequent responses to the birth of our consciousness of feelings. When it is stressed in adults, this may be the result of our early years in which we learned how to understand our self in relationship to our mother. In the seven-year cycles, it is appropriately linked to the years 8–14 (see the chart on pages 84–85).

sexual problems

Stress to this chakra causes us to put up defences to avoid our true feelings, especially concerning someone of the opposite sex. During love-making, as kundalini energy rises from the first chakra to the second, it may hit a wall of blockages, and a real feeling of bliss will not be able to arise through the subsequent chakras. So stress in this area may cause us to go from one lover to another, seeking satisfaction and a deep longing to unite with the other half of our soul. Alternatively, we may provide a phantom lover for ourselves or for our sexual fantasies.

When the radiance of Svadisthana begins to flow more freely, the ability to feel both pain and pleasure increases—sometimes in bittersweet love affairs. This can make it a real test of courage to move beyond our defenses, regain our true self and experience loving intimacy. It is necessary to let go of past fears, disillusionments and disappointed romantic expectations—all unneeded energy imprints held in this chakra.

If we are unaware of our Sacral Chakra energies, we unwittingly fuel feelings of rigid control, overprotectiveness, jealousy, anger and the inability to receive love. Svadisthana is associated with addictions of all kinds, and with a desperate need for approval. Shamans and some spiritual healers are able to drain toxic waste from a negative imprint in this chakra and then dissolve the imprint itself.

Conversely, when we are fully aware of the positive energies of Svadisthana, we create the right conditions for our subtle and physical abilities to unite with another person. This can take us into a blissful flowering of the soul on a path of enlightenment. Such a state requires a beautiful, tender type of love that we give and receive *unconditionally*. Unconditional love has no rules, no expectations, no payback—it is the type of love a mother naturally gives to her child, and can be found in mature loving partnerships.

Stress to the Sacral Chakra can lead to jealousy or the inability to receive love.

activating your prana

This exercise activates prana and stores it at the Hara/Lower Tan Tien/Sacral Chakra, which are situated so close to one another that we can think of them as one center located between the navel and the pubic bone. The Hara (in Japanese) or Tan Tien (in Chinese) is a highly significant energy store. When we increase the pranic flow in our auric field, we strengthen our whole body–mind complex, and this visualization of a ball of silver energy at the Hara/Tan Tien also purifies the breath.

the sacral chakra: svadisthana

1 Stand with your legs shoulder-width apart, your feet pointing forward and your knees comfortably bent, as if you are sitting down in the posture.
2 Practice seven deep breaths to relax yourself.
3 Bring your hands to your navel, with your palms facing each other and 8 in. (20 cm) apart.
4 Visualize that you are holding a ball of sparkling, silver light energy—prana—between them.
5 As you inhale slowly, expand the ball by moving your hands away from each other.

6 As you exhale slowly, bring your hands closer together to concentrate the silver energy. You should start to feel the energy held between your hands.
7 Do seven inhalations and exhalations in this way, then bring the ball of silver energy close to your navel and "push" it into your body.
8 Now hold your hands against your navel and, taking seven more deep breaths, feel the expansion and contraction of your abdomen, and the energy ball inside you increasing and decreasing in intensity.
9 Finally relax and move your body a little.

Note: In Tibetan Buddhism, which was influenced by Indian Tantra, the navel center (which is a little above the Lower Tan Tien) constitutes the "Fire" center.

This exercise to activate pranic flow in the auric field will help strengthen the body–mind complex.

making friends

We have already seen that wholeness in the second chakra is concerned with our ability to give and receive love—knowing that we are lovable and loved. These basic human emotions establish a positive identity for us at a deep core level of our being. When we know that we can give and receive love unconditionally, we can give emotional support to others—again without condition.

This chakra is therefore also about friendship—our ability to relate to others on a deeper-than-everyday level. How do you see your friendships?

- Does your friendship require a "payback" from the other person?
- Are you judgmental about them?
- Or bitchy behind their back?
- Do you sometimes feel envious of them?
- How often have you felt jealous of them?
- Do you use your friends because they have influence with others?
- Do you like to be seen with the "in crowd"?
- Are you too busy at work to make friends?
- Do you have friends of different ages and from different religions and backgrounds?
- Do you always try to keep in touch with them, even if they live many miles away?
- Do you make an effort to help friends?
- Do you take pleasure in seeing your friends happy?
- Are you genuinely pleased they have all the things you don't have?
- Do you share what you have with them?
- Do you devote time to nourishing your friendships?
- Can you dance or sing with your friends?
- Can you sit with them in silence and feel comfortable?

Perhaps you don't have *any* friends? Ask yourself why?

In friendship it is not necessary to persuade people, nor is it necessary to hasten change. Just hold one another in the highest regard and change, if needed in your relationship, will naturally unfold.

Talk to one another but never put on another what you do not wish on yourself.

the sacral chakra: svadisthana

creativity and svadisthana

As we have seen, the creative life impulse arises from Mother Earth and is received in the first chakra, then moves to Svadisthana. The color generally assigned to this chakra is orange—always described as a happy color. In India orange is worn to indicate that an initiate, a monk or a sannyasin (someone who has given up the material life to integrate into the spiritual world) has achieved a degree of enlightenment from sexual desires. He or she has risen beyond the raw, generative, fiery energy of Muladhara and is in the process of going beyond interpersonal feelings of love, developing a love of the Divine in whatever aspect he or she is studying.

"This is fine if you want to live in some kind of spiritual isolation, like a monk or nun," I can hear you saying. But what of the ordinary person who wants to live in the world and experience life to the full?

The answer is that moving beyond the sexual connotations of this chakra brings you to creativity in its many forms:

- **Dance** Traditionally offered to the god/goddess as a sacred celebration
- **Singing** Originating from praising the Divine
- **Yoga** Controlling the activities of mind
- **Painting/drawing** Celebrating self-awareness.

the chakras and creativity

Each person finds their own ways to move with creativity. Perhaps you are creative when cooking, sewing or writing; while gardening; or in your work. Whenever you do creative actions, you have a beneficial effect upon your subtle-energy bodies and your physical body. For example, when singing or chanting, Svadisthana energies are raised and expressed through the Throat Chakra.

Creativity is a precious accomplishment for humans—animals are not able to express themselves in the same way. Often it is expressed through our hands: there are chakras in the center of the palms (that are energetically linked with energy flow from the Heart Chakra) and acupuncture meridian lines end at the fingertips. It has been demonstrated that when the hands are brought together into the traditional position of prayer (palm against palm), the effectiveness of prayer increases. Interestingly, a Muslim will often greet you by shaking hands, then touching his heart. In many spiritual practices the hands are folded across the heart, and in yoga and Indian dance the mudras (hand gestures) are a whole science that alters the energy flowing through the hands in specific ways.

Taking time for inner focus is very beneficial before beginning any creative pursuit.

dance and svadisthana

Indian dance is particularly associated with the creative energies of Svadisthana. It is a complex traditional form, blending nritta (the rhythmic element) with nritya (the combination of rhythm and expression) and natya (the dramatic element).

- Nritta is the rhythmic movement of the body in pure dance. It does not express any emotion.

- Nritya is usually expressed through the eyes, hands and facial movements. It comprises abhinaya, depicting rasa (sentiment) and bhava (mood).
- Nritya combined with nritta makes up the usual dance program.

Indian dancers in Rajasthan expressing joy in the "dance of life."

To appreciate natya, or dance drama, you have to understand and appreciate Indian legends. Most Indian dances take their themes from Mother India's rich mythology and folk legends. In classical dances the Hindu gods and goddesses, such as Vishnu and Lakshmi, Rama and Sita, Krishna and Radha, are all colorful characters. Each dance form also draws inspiration from stories that have been handed down through the ages, vibrantly depicting the life, ethics and beliefs of the Indian people.

Throughout the world traditional dances carry the soul of the people and express a deep-felt need to use the human body to celebrate the great universal truths of life. Indian dance does just that in a sacred (but usually lively) form. It is an excellent way to begin to understand India's rich ethos and traditions. Dance not only delights the onlooker, but also imparts great truths within its forms.

the dance of life

Watching Indian dance can create an almost hypnotic fascination. Close your eyes for a moment and transport yourself to a Hindu temple, hearing the music of the sitar (a kind of lute) and tabla drums; imagine female dancers in bright-hued clothes twirling in a spiral formation, with silvery bells on their ankles, following the complex rhythms. Perhaps it will impel you to jump up, play some music and create your own dance to honor the life-force flowing through your chakras.

dancing your chakras awake

A beautiful way to balance your chakras is using music or dance. It is best to do the following intuitive dance exercise in the dark of the evening and to light some candles, all of the same color, in your room. Begin by playing a specially chosen piece of music (classical or otherwise) that inspires you.

1 **Forget** everything you have ever learned about dance steps and sequences.

2 **Stand** very still and get in touch with your inner energies. Then, breathing deeply, imagine that you are inhaling the color of the candles you have chosen to light.

3 **Visualize** the music bringing colors into the parts of your body where it is most needed.

4 **Move** and let the music inspire you, especially in those areas of your body where you sense that you need the color. Let your feet—not your mind—direct the dance.

5 **Flow** allowing the music to flow into the rest of your body. Loosen your movements and dance with abandon, so that you use all the space in the room. Perhaps you spin, circle around, jump or feel a stillness as you hold a particular position. Let the music take you onto the floor, where you can move and stretch as much as you wish.

6 **Conclude** as the music ends; your dance will come to a natural conclusion. As you finish, enter fully into the silence and stillness around you.

7 **Lie** down for some minutes. All your chakras will now feel recharged, refreshed and harmonized.

Shiva, Lord of the Cosmic Dance, is said to have revealed 8,400,000 bodily positions to humankind. His dance symbolizes Divine movement. We, too, can dance with ecstatic movement to balance our chakras.

dancing your chakras awake

the wisdom of svadisthana

Bhagwan Shree Rajneesh (now called Osho) was a controversial but enlightened character during the 1970s and 1980s, who had a worldwide following of devotees known as sannyasins, whose orange clothing made them easily distinguishable. One of his teachings was that Life is a Mystery.

Humanity presently lives upon a planet of choices: each of us can live our lives in the way we choose: in joy or despair. Our life is not ready-made, but something we have created. Bhagwan pointed out that a Jew creates a Jewish life, a Christian a Christian life, a Muslim an Islamic life, and so on. That is what people have been doing through the ages. But now is the time to change this, because these types of lives keep us in limitation and do not let us come into contact with life "as it is." When we overlay life with religion or philosophy, it distorts life, giving it a particular color. We are then unable to see life in its purity. Bhagwan taught that the tiniest blade of grass, the smallest leaf, is as significant as the biggest star. The smallest thing is also the biggest, because all is oneness.

living life "as it is"

When asked, "How does one live a life that is free?" he answered, "My message is very simple; Live life as dangerously as possible. Live life totally, intensely, passionately, because except for life there is no other God." He said he was not denying God, but was for the first time bringing God into real perspective, making him alive, bringing him closer to you, closer than your heart—because he is your very being, where nothing is separate, but here and now. Through exploration of sexuality, dance, music and movement in joyous abandon, Bhagwan asked his sannyasins to be drunk with Life—to savor the sweetness and poetry in the wine of Life at any moment.

We began the journey through the chakras with Muladhara—now we are really arriving at Svadisthana, where we can start to express ourselves fully. We can choose to listen to Bhagwan's words and let ourselves be possessed by life in all its forms, dimensions and colors—by the whole rainbow, all the harmonies of music, deep meditation. In this way, we can live life "as it is."

Wearing distinctive orange clothing, sadhus and sannyasins gather at festivals in India to be cleansed and purified.

svadisthana yantra

Within Svadisthana is the white, shining, watery region of the shape of a half moon, stainless and white as the autumnal moon. He who meditates upon this stainless Lotus is free immediately from all his enemies (Kama—lust, Krodha—anger, Lobha—greed, Moha—delusion, Matsaryya—envy).

Sat Cakra Nirupana

description of the yantra

Number of petals Six.

Color Vermilion in the ancient texts, but more generally orange today.

Element Water, the essence of life.

Crescent moon Regeneration.

Makara Mythical fish-tailed alligator. Its serpentine movement reflects the sensuous aspects of someone dominated by their second chakra. The alligator is also associated with sexual power, as its fat was once used as an aid to male virility.

the bija mantra

Svadisthana's bija mantra (see pages 80–81) is VAM, which—when spoken—nourishes and purifies body fluids and brings alignment with the waters.

yantra meditation for color-breathing

1 Place the yantra in front of you.

2 Begin breathing gently.

3 Now start to "color-breathe" the orange hue of the six lotus petals. To do this, visualize the color intensely as you breathe in—let orange flow around the inside of your body as you hold your breath for a moment; let it remove toxins and blocks from your body as you breathe out.

4 After a minimum of ten minutes, begin to visualize the blue circle and the crescent moon at Svadisthana.

5 Again continue for some minutes, as the Water element within your body is stabilized and the chakra balanced.

6 When you are ready to finish, acknowledge the assistance you may have received from unseen realms and return to normal breathing.

7 To prevent feeling "spaced out" after a meditation, place a grounding stone under each foot during a meditation. When you finish, put both hands flat on the floor for a moment. Finally, relax and drink a glass of pure spring water.

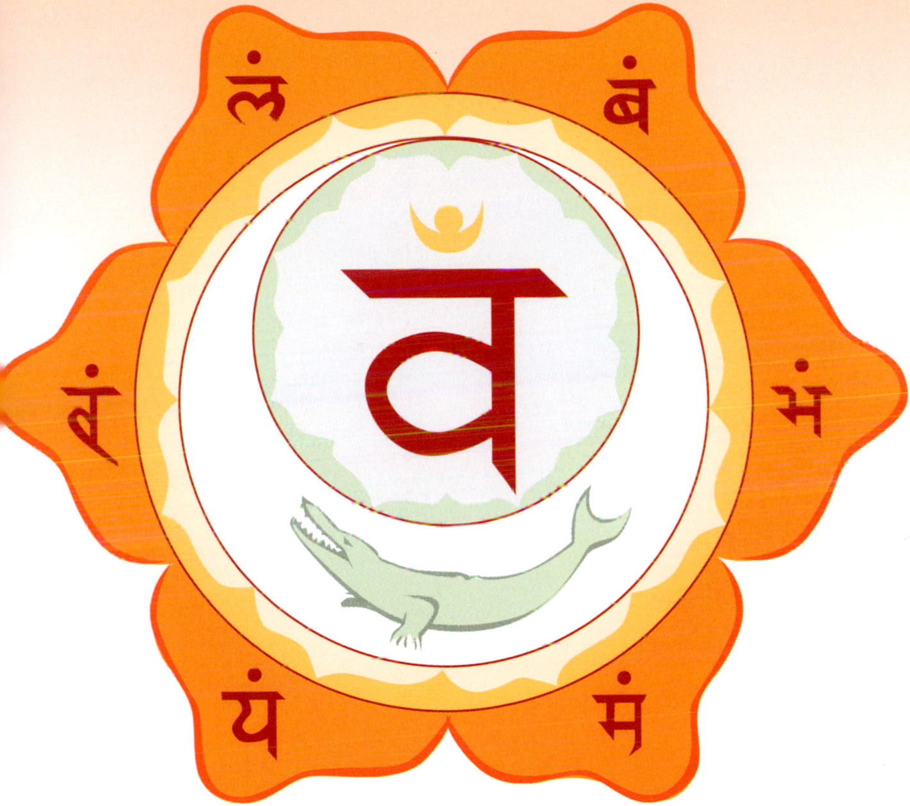
लं
बं
वं
व
भं
यं
मं

deities associated with svadisthana

vishnu

Vishnu is the preserver, who balances the creative energies of Brahma and the destructive energies of Shiva. He is associated with the second chakra, the seat of procreation, because he represents the preservation of the human race. Vishnu is depicted with blue skin and wearing a garland of forest flowers around his neck. Vishnu holds four key symbols in his hands:

- **A conch shell** reminding us of the importance of our listening skills; it also represents the pure sound that can bring enlightenment and liberation.
- **A disc** spinning on his index finger, which indicates the need for concentration or the wheel of time.
- **A mace or war club** reminds us that we may have to fight to subdue our ego.
- **A pink lotus**, symbol of spiritual enlightenment.

rakini

Rakini, the goddess who is associated with this chakra, is an aspect of Sarasvati, the wife of Brahma. She is linked with both art and music. She holds:

- **A trident** representing the unity of mind, body and spirit.
- **A battle axe**, which reminds us of the struggle to overcome negative attributes.
- **A two-ended drum** representing Time and the rhythm of physical life.

- **A lotus flower** showing us that spiritual development is possible for everyone. Her axe and trident are symbols of the fire god Agni. So although the primary element of Svadisthana Chakra is water, fire will transmute it into steam. These symbols mean that we too can achieve transmutation of consciousness on to a higher level.

crystals to activate svadisthana

The main gemstone crystals used to activate the Sacral Chakra are fire opal and carnelian. Other crystals that you could use are humble orange calcite and scintillating yellow topaz. Orange calcite works at a basic physical level. Its action is cleansing, and it is effective with energy imbalances that cause irritable bowel syndrome (IBS), by moving unwanted conditioning out through the Sacral Chakra. It also balances the emotions, inspiring confidence. Yellow topaz is a highly evolved vibrant gemstone that will cause the movement of energetic imbalances on elevated spiritual levels through this chakra, *after* using orange calcite for the physical levels.

fire opal

Like all opals, fire opal has a large water content, but sparkles with flashes of red "fire." It stimulates creativity. Psychologically, it is said to move emotional blockages because of its association with water. Conversely, in many ways its fiery nature is

Yellow topaz (left) helps overcome limitations. Orange calcite (right) balances emotions and overcomes fears.

quite apparent and intensifies the manifestation of our own inner fire: negatively as anger, or positively by moving the Sacral Chakra into enjoyment of our own sexuality, leading to enlightenment as radiance moves through the kundalini channel. Healers may choose fire opal for energetic imbalances of the kidneys and blood, aiding purification. It is beneficial for the eyes when used as a crystal essence/elixir. Opal has been gifted to us by the Earth in many different colors, each of which has specific healing properties.

carnelian

This gemstone varies in color from pink through to deep orange. It has a strong influence on the Sacral Chakra. For this reason it is recommended to energetically balance lower back problems, rheumatism and arthritis. It also assists the kidneys to regulate their water energies. Traditionally, carnelian is regarded as a protective stone, and in Celtic times it was part of the array of gemstones mounted in a warrior's breastplate or jewelery to accompany him into the afterlife.

Fire opal (top) or polished carnelian (above and above middle) are excellent to activate Svadishthana Chakra.

crystals to calm svadisthana

Emerald is regarded as "the stone of fulfilled love"; it encourages friendship, calms the emotions and brings wisdom. Emeralds were once worn to protect from epilepsy—a frightening condition when not understood. They were also believed to be an antidote to poison, an "occupational hazard" in medieval times, when kings would wear an emerald ring for this reason. The color and vibration of emerald are generally calming to Svadisthana.

You can obtain small pieces of uncut emerald, which are inexpensive, or a much pricier cut gem. Whether a crystal is large or small makes no difference to the *type* of energy it holds; it still has the same vibration whether it is one carat or ten. However, there will be *more* available energy if it is larger. Cut and polished gems transmit more light through them than uncut ones or less precious stones. Stones are considered precious because of their rarity, which is reflected in their price. Actually diamonds are not rare, but governments and multinationals control their price and availability.

using emerald to calm yourself

This exercise is more effective if you practice the relaxation technique shown on page 44, first. Make a small layout of crystals as follows over the sacral region.

1 Cleanse (see page 68) and dedicate all the crystals you will use.
2 Carefully place an emerald at the center of the Sacral Chakra, with six small, clear quartz points pointing inward in a circle around it (see right).
3 Wait in relaxed meditation mode for ten minutes for the chakra to become calmer, or until you are "told" to remove the crystals.
4 Come slowly back to everyday awareness.

Emerald is said to enhance psychic powers and clairvoyance.

If you cannot obtain emerald, then green-colored denser stones will be appropriate to calm an overenergized Svadisthana. Try using green aventurine, amazonite or green calcite, if the energy imbalance is connected with a physical body condition manifesting as disease or mental anguish. You will need to send a lot of unconditional love to begin to shift the problem. As a general rule, first begin to heal the physical body, then work at subtle levels of the aura and chakra system. *For this reason, crystals that operate at a vibrational level should not be used as a replacement for medical attention.*

You do not have to be undressed for crystals to be effective, but it helps to be wearing white natural cotton when you undergo a crystal healing.

crystals to balance svadisthana

Moonstone and aquamarine are ideal for using at the Sacral Chakra because of their associations with the element of Water. Moonstone has traditionally been valued to ease insomnia and develop psychic abilities. It works particularly with the feminine energy impulse. Aquamarine is regarded as giving strength in adversity and was traditionally believed to protect against the forces of evil. From a spiritual healing perspective, it aligns our physical body with the whole of our subtle-energy field. Energetically, it works to cleanse the kidneys and genitourinary system.

Moonstone, called "Mother Stone" is used on all parts of the body that "breathe" in a cycle.

making a crystal essence by the direct method

A crystal essence (or gem elixir) affects the mind, body and spirit—as do flower essences and homeopathic remedies. However, crystal essences generally affect the physical body more effectively than flower essences, but less effectively than homeopathic remedies.

Any crystal that is hard enough to be tumble-polished can be used to make a crystal essence, but you must be sure it is not water-soluble and does not have any poisonous or metallic qualities. If in doubt, use clear quartz because it balances all the chakras. To balance feminine problems associated with energy imbalances in Svadisthana, such as painful or irregular periods, a moonstone is ideal; it is also recommended for ridding the body of toxins and the emotional anxieties associated with "mother issues."

1 Wash and psychically cleanse the moonstone in clear water (see page 68).
2 Be clear about what you want to achieve, then ask for guidance from the crystal and follow what you intuit is right.

Aquamarine, cut or natural, looks like frozen water, hence it is an ideal crystal to work with our "inner seas" emotions.

3 Place the crystal in a plain clear glass of distilled or pure spring water and cover it with a sheet of white paper or clear glass.

4 Leave in the sunshine (or daylight) for approximately three hours.

5 Remove the crystal and thank or bless it.

6 Slowly sip the water over the course of the day. It will have become encoded with beneficial vibrations from the crystal: this is an etheric imprint; nothing physical is transferred.

7 If you wish to keep the essence for a while, preserve it in pure brandy or vodka (50 percent water: 50 percent alcohol) and store it in a dark-colored bottle away from sunlight and heat (a blue bottle is ideal). Stored bottles should not touch each other, and you should always keep them away from strong perfumes or chemical pollutants.

breathing exercise

Pranayama is a yogic practice to control subtle energies with your breath. The following exercise is a simple way to prepare yourself. Be aware that some of the more intense methods of breathing work should only be learned under the supervision of a teacher.

Eastern traditions that work with subtle energies have always encouraged practitioners to "breathe with their belly"; they may refer to this as "energizing the Hara." The Hara is located in a similar region of the body to that associated with the Sacral Chakra—that is, the lower abdomen. A young baby often uses this type of belly-breathing when in a deep sleep. It is the most natural way to breathe, although if you smoke you may find that your lung capacity is limited. The aim is to energize the lungs completely with prana. Because belly-breathing also benefits most of the physical body and the main chakras, it is greatly valued for its therapeutic properties. It has been developed into pranayama practice—the complete yogic breath.

pranayama practice

This is performed with full, deep yogic breath taken in through your nose. At this stage in learning it, allow your abdomen to rise as the lowest part of your lungs fills with a slow intake of air. Now, in the same breath, fill the middle part of your lungs, expanding your ribcage. Finally, still on the same in-breath, fill the very top and back of your lungs with air. Hold your breath for a moment or two, being aware of its effect on your belly/Sacral Chakra. Now *very slowly* release your breath through your mouth. With practice this becomes one smooth breath.

1 Stand with your feet shoulder-width apart and your knees slightly bent, but your spine straight.

2 Take a deep breath as described above, then raise both arms until they are above your head, with the fingers touching one another. Say to yourself or out loud, "Let pranic energy flow into me."

3 Slowly exhale and lower your arms, passing your hands over each of the seven chakras in turn. Say, "May this energy balance my chakras" as you pass each one. Notice any sensations in your hands or in the different chakra areas.

Do this breathing seven times at the minimum, or ideally three times seven times—with a short break for normal breathing between each set of seven.

Note: It is important not to strain your breathing beyond what you can comfortably manage.

aromatherapy and svadisthana

There are numerous herbs, plants and flower essences that will benefit Svadisthana. Red clover, currant, fennel, grapefruit and onion can all benefit the Sacral Chakra.

SACRAL CHAKRA ESSENTIAL OILS

The main essential oils that have a sympathetic resonance with Svadisthana are:

- **Sandalwood** This oil has a vibrational correspondence with Svadisthana. It comes from an evergreen tropical tree, and the essential oil is steam-distilled from the heartwood and roots. It is anti-depressant, anti-septic, anti-spasmodic, aphrodisiac, astringent, bactericide, expectorant and sedative.

- **Jasmine** This is a beautiful flowering shrub, whose strong perfume is produced by solvent extraction. It is analgesic, anti-depressant, anti-inflammatory, antiseptic, aphrodisiac, sedative and uterine.

- **Rose oil** This is obtained by solvent extraction or steam distillation. It takes around 30 perfect and specially cultivated rose blooms to make just one drop of essential oil. Its main use with the Sacral Chakra is as an aphrodisiac, although it is also regarded as anti-depressant, antiseptic, emmenagogic, hepatic, sedative and uterine.

- **Ylang-ylang**: These flowers come from a tropical tree called the cananga. It is a voluptuous, exotic perfume and is used as an aphrodisiac. It is also anti-depressant, antiseptic and sedative. Its use will help dispel anger held at the Sacral Chakra area.

- **Champaca**: This is a lesser-known exotic oil from India, which is obtained by solvent extraction. It is aphrodisiac, anti-depressant and stimulant.

aromatic bathing

It can be very enjoyable to explore sensuality with exotic oils. Warm bath water helps you to relax and absorb the oils, so it is excellent to bathe before going to bed. Any of the oils mentioned opposite are suitable.

1 Run a bath of warm (not hot) water and, when it is ready, add a maximum of five drops of essential oil (5 ml)—these can be a combination of oils.
2 Mix the water with your hands, then relax in it for as long as you wish.
3 Make your bath a special occasion and light candles associated with the color of the chakra (in this case, orange) and float flowers in the water too.

Cautions: Avoid getting the bath water in your eyes. Vary the essential oils you use, so that you do not risk a build-up of one type in your body. Consult an aromatherapist if you are pregnant. Do not use essential oils for children under 12 years of age, even in the bath, except with qualified supervision.

yoga asanas for svadisthana

active: parivrtta trikonasana (twisting triangle)

Parivrtta Trikonasana has the same effect on energy flows as the Base Chakra asanas (see pages 118–123), but the twisting movement helps to focus energy in the region of the Sacral Chakra. As you breathe into this asana, visualize orange-colored light coming into your lungs to help you.

1

1 Stand with your feet about 3 ft. (1 m) apart. Turn your right foot 90 degrees to the right, so that your body faces right, with your left foot only slightly turned to act as a strong base. Rotate your body toward your right leg, reaching down to the ankle or to the floor with your left hand beyond your right foot (for an advanced position).

2 Stretch your right arm straight up until it is in a direct line with the left arm. Repeat on the other side.

2

active: utthita parsvakonasana (extended lateral angle pose)

This asana stretches every part of the body, but especially the hamstrings and spine. The chest, hips and legs should be in a line in order to do this. The Svadisthana region becomes the center of balance, and so energy is focused there and can then flow uninterrupted through the spine and the associated nadis. The state of consciousness associated with the Sacral Chakra is pranamaya kosha (dream sleep), which is experienced on bio-energetic levels. As with other chakras, you can use the yantra or appropriate colored light as your focus.

1

1 Stand with your feet together and your arms stretched above your head. Jump your feet about 5 ft. (1.5 m) apart. Raise your arms sideways to shoulder level. Turn your left foot sideways 90 degrees to the left, keeping your right leg stretched and tight at the knee. Bend your left knee to form a 90-degree angle.

2 Place your left palm on the floor by your left foot. Stretch your right arm over your right ear. Look up to the ceiling. Stretch your spine and the side of your body. Repeat on the other side.

2

passive: natarajasana (pose of shiva)

"Nataraj" means "King of Dancers" (Sanskrit nata = dance; raja = king) and is the dancing form of Lord Shiva, a symbolic synthesis of the most important aspects of Hinduism and the Vedas. Natarajasana is performed most beautifully by ballerinas and ice-dancers. It makes your legs strong and supple. It requires the utmost concentration to perform it for some minutes, and during this concentration the focus should be on the Sacral Chakra region. It is this area that will begin to ground you again (energetically speaking) after your yoga practice. You may use the yantra illustration, placed a little distance away on the floor in front of you. If you are practicing outdoors, your gaze in this asana would normally be toward the level of the horizon.

162

1

1 Stand and balance on your left foot, while simultaneously raising your left arm above your head. Bend your right knee and lift it behind you, until your right hand can hold the right foot. Relax and maintain your balance.

2 Lift your right foot higher and stretch your left arm forward. Relax and maintain your balance. Repeat with the other leg.

yoga asanas for svadisthana

2

Chapter 4

THE SOLAR PLEXUS CHAKRA: MANIPURA

manipura chakra

The Solar Plexus Chakra, or Manipura, is also called, manipuraka, dashapatra, dashadala padma, dashapatrambuja, dashachchada, nabhi, nabhipadma and nabhipankaja. This chakra is traditionally located at the navel (hence the alternative name of the nabhi or navel chakra) because traditionalists believe the Solar Plexus refers to a distinct minor chakra.

In the Indian Tantric tradition, Manipura—"place of gems" or "shining like a pearl"—has ten red petals, with a downward-pointing triangle, representing the element of Fire at the center; however, in most modern chakra layouts it is placed at the Solar Plexus as a major chakra, with its ten petals shown in gold or yellow.

the functions of manipura

Diverse cultures throughout the world have revered the energy symbolized by the Sun. Solar deities, usually masculine in nature, include Ra (Egyptian), Inti (Inca), Tonatiuih (Aztec), Ku-kuul-kaan (Maya), Mithras/Sol (European) and Vishnu/Indra (Hindu). Manipura's element, not surprisingly, is Fire. In Hindu tradition Agni is associated with fire and lightning together with the fearful goddess Kali, who often has tongues of flame coming from her mouth. Think of Manipura as the Sun in your body. It draws in solar radiance as a type of prana and transduces it into a form that enables the flow of vital energies throughout the physical body to be regulated. It is a gathering point for lines of subtle energy, the nadis, which control all bodily functions, as well as being a powerful physical nerve plexus. The great Indian sage Patanjali says that through control of Manipura full knowledge and mastery of the body are achieved.

The meanings of the ten petals are: spiritual ignorance; thirst; jealousy; treachery; shame; fear; disgust; delusion; foolishness; and sadness. All these are aspects to overcome at this chakra level before proceeding to work on purifying the Heart Chakra. It is important to note that the three major chakras below the heart are principally concerned with the physical body and the world we perceive with our senses, whereas those above the heart are of a more spiritual nature.

MAIN CHARACTERISTICS AT A GLANCE

Color	Yellow
Key issues	Power, fear, anxiety, introversion
Physical location	Between the navel and the bottom of the sternum
Associated spinal area	Seventh and eighth thoracic vertebrae
Physiological system	Metabolic/digestive
Endocrine gland	Islets of Langerhans (groups of cells in the pancreas)
Nerve plexus	Solar plexus
Inner aspect	Opinion and personal power
Physical action	Digestion
Mental action	Power
Emotional action	Expansiveness
Spiritual action	Growth

manipura chakra

health issues and manipura

Digestive problems, diabetes and cancer are associated with Manipura. but above all the Solar Plexus Chakra is associated with stress.

associated body system

Manipura is positioned over one of the main regions of the body that reacts to stress. This plexus of nerves can often be felt as a tight knot if you press the area just below the sternum. If you feel discomfort, there is some stress or blockage. To heal this, you might try to remove yourself from the source of stress; improve your health; begin a routine of meditation and chakra "nourishment"; or seek the help of a healer.

associated endocrine gland

Manipura directs energy to the islets of Langerhans situated in the pancreas, which produce insulin to lower high blood-sugar levels, and also glucagons to raise low blood sugar.

STRESS AS THE EFFECT OF LIFESTYLE CHANGES

Four out of five people who experience various stressful changes in their lives at the same time will suffer from a major illness within two years. These major causes of stress have been identified by Dr. R. Rahe, who advises the U.S. Army Medical Corps on treatment for servicemen suffering from combat stress:

- Divorce
- Personal injury or illness
- Being fired at work or retirement
- Sex difficulties

- Gain or loss of a family member
- Change in responsibilities in work
- Change in work hours or conditions
- Outstanding personal achievement
- Moving house or abroad
- Change in sleeping habits
- Christmas
- Minor violations of the law

It is recommended that you do not make a number of lifestyle changes at the same time. If you must, a relaxation technique (see pages 44–45) may help.

168

the solar plexus chakra: manipura

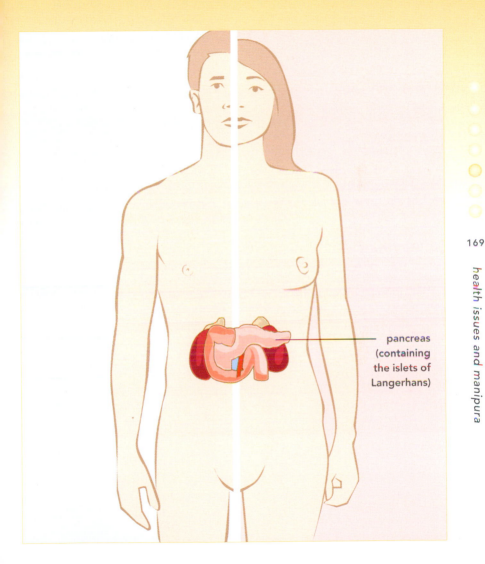

pancreas
(containing
the islets of
Langerhans)

the effects of stress and how to counteract them

Major everyday causes of stress include: "people poisoning" (pressures exerted by other people, from which there is no escape); unacceptable time pressures; sleep deprivation; and a high number of the lifestyle changes shown on the previous pages.

what you can do about stress

- Take action before you "crack up" or become ill. Recognize your tiredness and how much you can tolerate.
- Change your environment. Get away from the situation that causes the stress, if you can. It may save your life!
- Avoid alcoholic drink and drugs. Keep fit and eat healthily. Perhaps you can take up a discipline such as yoga, tai chi or some other Eastern practice that is based upon movement of subtle energies in your body.
- Learn a relaxation technique (see pages 44–45), how to breathe fully (see pages 154–155) and how to lower your muscle tension through massage (see page 117).
- Start to respect that you are a spiritual being of Light in a physical body. Begin to learn a meditation technique (see pages 276–277).
- Gain a good understanding of the reasons for stress and how it is related to emotional issues in your life.
- Take up hobbies and leisure activities.
- Treat yourself to a relaxing complementary health treatment, which will improve your energy levels, balance your chakras and alleviate physical symptoms.
- Walk, sing, chant or dance more often, and enjoy whatever is around you.
- Accept your feelings of stress and don't let them alarm you. When you have recovered, use the experience to deepen your understanding of other people.
- Be an example of how to handle stress *without* distress, because you are fortunate enough to have gained an understanding of the way pranic energy and chakras are central to the health of your body and mind.

Empower yourself each day by working on a physical or spiritual discipline.

MAJOR EFFECTS OF STRESS ON THE BODY

Check yourself out from the head down. Do you suffer from any of the following:

- Headaches, dizziness, insomnia, panic attacks
- Blurred vision
- Difficulty in swallowing
- Aching neck muscles
- Susceptibility to infections
- High blood pressure, cardiovascular disorders
- Over-breathing, asthma, palpitations
- Excessive sugar in the blood
- Nervous Indigestion, stomach ulcers
- Backache
- Nervous rashes and allergies
- Excessive sweating
- Mucous colitis, constipation, diarrhea
- Sexual difficulties, hormonal imbalances, inability to conceive

If so, then you are probably suffering from stress at some level.

the effects of stress and how to counteract them

emotional issues and manipura

From what you have just read about the effects of stress on your body, you can see that nothing exists in isolation: increased pranic energy expands your auric field and goes hand-in-hand with greater health in the physical body. In Manipura we experience the emotions of others by becoming a mirror to them. It is vital to keep this mirror bright, as you don't want to act like a sponge for anyone's anger or negativity.

expansiveness

As you begin to empower yourself, you start to open new doors in your life. You will find that you are more attractive to other people. Within your auric field, your Solar Plexus Chakra will give out a message of what a bright being you are. This in turn expands your auric field so that it is visible to those with clairvoyant sight. It will extend as light of finer and faster vibrations, beyond the usual distance around your body, to 33 ft. (10 m) or more.

Our vibrational field or aura is composed of less-visible and finer electrical vibrations as it ascends in speed (or frequency) and the farther it stretches from the body. As the field extends, so the color within it decreases

until eventually, in a highly spiritually evolved or enlightened person, all becomes clear white light, through which uninterrupted Divine Light can flow.

In Manipura we learn to assimilate wisdom in our unconscious mind. When we do this, greater spiritual energy becomes available to us. This enables us to heal our physical body and develop a right relationship with the wider world. It is sometimes called the body–mind connection.

However, the dark opposites of Manipura are power over others, contamination and contraction of our energy and arrogance. Those with an undeveloped Solar Plexus Chakra will dominate with their ego; they will not be happy with their situation in life, will shut down their inner fire, and their aura will not glow with bright light. They will have energetic blocks in the Manipura and also in adjacent chakras. To a lesser extent, the whole chakra system will be compromised.

The 13th-century Muslim poet and mystic Rumi said:

You cannot know fire from words alone. Enter the fire if you want to know the truth.

Leaving your worries aside, learn to meditate regularly.

emotional issues and manipura

increasing energy flow through the chakras

Begin this exercise to enhance the flow of energy throughout your entire chakra system by relaxing completely (see pages 44–45). Now you are going to journey through each chakra in turn, beginning at the Base Chakra. For every chakra, you must first visualize it and observe the type and strength of energy there (this is the check-out or inspection stage—it is not meant to be a detailed diagnosis). Then you focus on the chakras in sequence, as follows:

the solar plexus chakra: manipura

Relax and send increased subtle energy through your whole chakra system.

1 Be aware that through your feet and legs you are strongly rooted to the Earth. Visualize a deep, rich red earth color and feel it in your legs, flowing upward to your Base Chakra (Muladhara).

2 Focus on your second chakra, the Sacral (Svadisthana), and draw the healing power of Water into it. Visualize six orange petals around this chakra and a crescent moon reflecting into the water in the center.

3 Focus on your third chakra, the Solar Plexus (Manipura), and connect with positive solar energies and the Spirit behind and beyond the Sun. Feel its bright-yellow fire burning away any blockages at the chakra.

4 Focus on your fourth chakra, the Heart (Anahata), through which you experience the freedom of the element of Air. Imagine that you can fly like a bird and look down upon the green Earth.

5 Focus on your fifth chakra, the Throat (Vishuddha), and see it glowing with the protective, healing color of blue.

6 Turn your *closed* eyes inward and upward, toward the Brow Chakra (Ajna), and visualize it as a spinning silver disc.

7 Focus on the top of your head. Visualize your Crown Chakra (Sahasrara), there. Note how many petals you can see and let yourself be drawn into its center.

8 Now finish the meditation by taking a deep breath for each chakra in sequence, as you return downward to your Base Chakra and then to your feet.

increasing energy flow through the chakras

spiritual issues and manipura

Solar Plexus imbalances will leave you feeling extremely edgy and depleted in energy. You may become depressed, insecure and fearful. If this continues, the problems can become imprinted and habitual. However, when you overcome this—and your Solar Plexus starts to spin as intended in a balanced, focus way—depression turns into joy, insecurity turns into the experience of love, and fearfulness turns into confidence in any situation.

While all of these are admirable attributes, the real aim of chakra balancing is to fit the body to be a temple to Spirit. It is through the Solar Plexus that we connect with the meaning behind the Sun, as representative of the Light of Spirit on Earth. This is the reason that many early religions, including Christianity, revered the power of the Light of Spirit *behind and beyond* our star, the Sun.

growing into spirit

Energetically, the Solar Plexus Chakra stokes up the fuel reserves of our body. When its power is awakened, we feel fearless and any obstacles in our path are burned away. While it may be admirable if we know how to handle such power, for some people it results in dictatorial attitudes, manipulation and fame at the cost of others. In Manipura we translate our dreams into reality.

Fire is the element that is traditionally attributed to Manipura. It has three inner meanings at the same time: the Sun, our inner fire and Spirit. Today most people find it difficult to rise above this third chakra in order to experience these inner meanings as truths in their lives. It is part of society's conditioning—a kind of cultural hypnosis—which keeps us locked into our physicality by denying us a vibrant, personal link with Spirit. By gradually opening up to the possibility of our greater life of Spirit, we begin to balance Manipura, and it is only then that we may enter fully into the Heart, the next chakra. In Manipura the fire of our body (our internal fire) is consumed and turned to ashes by the power of the fire of the Sun as the Light of Spirit.

The Solar Plexus, as its name suggests, is our connection to the meaning behind the Sun. A balanced Solar Plexus will bring joy, love and confidence.

spiritual issues and manipura

manipura yantra

At the root of the navel is the shining lotus of ten petals, of the color of heavily laden rain clouds. Meditate there on the region of Fire, triangular in form and shining like the rising sun. Outside of it are three Svastika marks, and within, the seed-mantra Ram. By meditating in this manner upon the navel lotus, the power to create and destroy the world is acquired.

Sat Cakra Nirupana

description of the yantra
Number of petals Ten.
Color Golden yellow or greenish-blue.
Triangle Red downward-pointing triangle with T-shaped projections, which symbolize movement.
Ram Represents the strength and courage of who we are in the world. Some scholars believe the ram depicts the nature of a person dominated by Manipura—strong, but charges head-first.

the bija mantra
Manipura's bija mantra (see pages 80–81) is RAM. The speaking of this sound assists longevity and the rising of kundalini energy.

the three stages of meditation
According to ancient teachings, there are three stages of meditation and internal yoga (see pages 306–307), given the name of samyama. They blend into each other in a successive transformation as the mind is stilled and focused by the simplicity of the yantra symbol.

Centering, or dharana, is the sixth limb of Patanjali's yoga system and the first aspect of the internalization of yoga. Through the concentration induced by centering, every brief fluctuation of thought or experience ceases.

This takes one into meditation proper (dhyana, the seventh limb), when deep concentration can be sustained for long periods. The mind is held steady, focused solely on the subject of meditation.

The eighth limb of Patanjali's system is samadhi. It is the transcendental, super-conscious state of "no mind," when the mind is held so steady that it becomes united with the object of concentration.

manipura yantra

deities associated with manipura

rudra

Rudra is the god of fire and storms and the presiding god of Manipura. He is the destructive aspect of Shiva but can, however, also bestow blessings. Rudra reminds us that riding life's storms can strengthen us. Shiva is believed to have evolved from Rudra and they share a violent, unpredictable nature. Rudra is known as the Divine Archer, who shoots arrows of death and disease. He must be implored not to slay or injure in his wrath.

He is often depicted as:

- Red or white (representing life or death)
- Three-eyed
- Two-armed, showing the gestures of granting boons and dispelling fear
- Seated on a bull (called Nandi), as he is the Lord of Cattle.

When Rudra is white, it is because he is covered with ashes, affirming that he has overcome fears and ego, transmuting himself through fire into the worlds of Spirit.

lakini

Lakini is one of the seven shaktis associated with the metabolism of food in the human body. As Rudra's consort she is the goddess of fire. Lakini is shown as:

- Black or dark-blue, vermilion, pale red or deep red in color
- Three-eyed, or three-headed with three eyes in each face, inviting us to understand the physical, astral and celestial planes of existence
- Four-armed, holding a thunderbolt (which is symbolic of the electrical energy of fire, as well as the heat that emanates from her body) and a spear, shot from the bow of Kama, the Lord of Sex, and making the mudras (hand gestures) of granting boons and dispelling fear
- Dressed in yellow raiment (or sometimes white)
- Seated on a red lotus.

crystals to activate manipura

The gemstone crystals of topaz and yellow tourmaline are both recommended to activate Manipura.

topaz

Topaz is obtainable in a number of colors, but for Manipura choose clear, bright yellow. A small raw crystal works fine; it is not necessary to have an expensive cut or polished one. Topaz assists in the realignment of energies, and helps to bring a golden radiance into the auric field. Traditionally, it is a crystal of love and fortune. With such clear energetic properties, it is an excellent aid to the whole body metabolism, but especially to the liver, gall bladder and digestive processes. It not only helps with digesting food, but also with the digestion of ideas at the mental level.

yellow tourmaline

Like other tourmalines, this one is very focused in a directional manner, and has the ability to balance the two sides of our brain and our male/female energies. When using it with the Solar Plexus Chakra, instead of placing it on the chakra, use the crystal to draw out or cut away blockages. This enables proper activation of Manipura, to benefit issues such as stress, intolerance, deep sadness, hopelessness, grief and conditions of disease.

using crystals to boost energy flow

An excellent pick-me-up is to lie down (preferably on the floor in the relaxation posture, see pages 44–45, but in bed if necessary) and relax in the following way.

Activate Manipura by using topaz and tourmaline.

1 Obtain two clear quartz "points" about 2 in. (5 cm) long, plus one yellow stone or crystal: yellow topaz, yellow (not brown) citrine quartz or yellow tourmaline would be ideal. Cleanse them in the usual way (see page 68).

2 Ensure you are not going to be disturbed and switch off the telephone. If you wish, play some relaxing music to calm your mind.

3 Lie down, placing one quartz at your head and the other below your feet. *It is vital that the point of each crystal faces in toward your body, not away from it.*

4 Place your yellow crystal on your Manipura chakra. It is best if the stone is against your skin, but still works through clothing (especially white cotton clothing).

5 Take some deep breaths, relax, enjoy!

The effect of this session is to bring all the chakras into alignment through the central channel of the subtle-energy body. The yellow stone on Manipura helps it come into resonance with the others by clearing and purifying it.

183

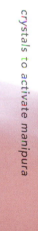

crystals to calm manipura

As already mentioned, most disease is associated with a lack of energy. Therefore we must be very clear as to why we might want to calm a particular chakra. In the case of Manipura, however, a calming/slowing down of energies passing in and out through the chakra will aid our general well-being and improve our concentration. This can enable us to study, work or meditate at deeper levels.

To discover if you are holding tension in your solar plexus, use your fingers to gently prod the area just below your sternum. Like as not you will find it sensitive or slightly sore

to the touch. This indicates some stored tension. When it is seriously tense, the discomfort will extend from front to back and will cause back pain, especially around the seventh or eighth thoracic vertebrae. When this condition worsens, it creates a horizontal band of tension—like a steel belt around the body. Of course you can imagine what this does to energy flows: they are locked into the lower chakras. Disease of the physical body will quickly result from such blockages.

Manipura is also closely related to our mental processes. The color yellow, with which this chakra resonates, encourages our thoughts and stimulates the brain. Yellow light used therapeutically by a color practitioner with a light instrument will improve calcium absorption into the body, dispel mental anxieties such as fear, clear the mind, treat digestive problems and disorders of the liver, spleen and pancreas.

Gemstone crystals to calm Manipura are emerald and sapphire.

Using emerald on the manipura chakra can calm imbalances associated with diabetes.

emerald

When used on Manipura, emerald will energetically calm imbalances associated with diabetes. It is also traditionally used for the liver, eyes and sinuses. But beware! It is said that if you always wear emerald as jewelery, you will experience negative emotions and if it changes color it may indicate unfaithfulness.

sapphire

This crystal is gifted to us by Mother Nature in many colors. For the purpose of Manipura calming, use blue sapphire. In common with other blue precious stones, it opens you up to higher spiritual realms by calming the physical body. In particular it brings deep wisdom and serenity. It should be placed on the chakra position or held within the aura at a comfortable level. Energetically it regulates the endocrine system and is excellent if you are undergoing deeply stressful events.

Blue sapphire cut and faceted or uncut, as above, is both protective and focusing.

crystals to balance manipura

Citrine is recommended as a good stone for general balancing of the Solar Plexus Chakra. It can be used in the form of a cluster, a point or a polished, tumbled stone. For the exercise below, a selection of tumbled stones of a good clear yellow will be best and should not be too expensive. Try to avoid getting citrine that is a dark treacle-brown in color, because it has been heat-treated and its power has changed.

Citrine has a sympathetic resonance with pranic energy coming from our Sun. It acts powerfully to cleanse, warm and energize. For this reason it balances our vibrational field so that we can walk consciously on Mother Earth, turning our eyes to the light that is manifesting through Father Sun.

We have seen that Manipura symbolizes the Sun in our bodies. From ancient times people have revered the power within and beyond the Sun. We all need sunshine to keep our bodies healthy, and an excellent way to activate the Solar Plexus chakra is to "breathe in" sunlight. Simply take deep breaths as you gaze at the Sun through half-closed eyes and visualize its energy focusing at the solar plexus and then filling your body. (Do not look directly at the Sun.)

Do not keep citrines like these in the sunshine as they will fade.

using citrine to balance yourself

Create a sacred space in your room; light a candle and some incense.

"Breathing in" sunlight is an excellent way to activate the Solar Plexus Chakra.

1 Lie on a blanket on the floor.
2 Place as many tumbled citrines as possible around the blanket in a circle (a minimum of six stones should suffice).
3 Lie down within the circle and relax.
4 If you wish, you can place another yellow stone on your Manipura point.

5 Affirm that you wish to balance your Solar Plexus Chakra, and ask for assistance from the hidden power of the citrine crystals.
6 Stay in the circle for up to 30 minutes.
7 Come back slowly to everyday awareness.

aromatherapy and manipura

The essential oil of sage (*Salvia officinalis*) is recommended for this chakra, but only for use in an oil diffuser (see pages 58–59) because of its strong properties. Other plants, herbs and flower essences for Manipura include blackberry, buckthorn, loosestrife, mango and peppermint. If you take both the plant (herb) and the flower essence of the same type within an hour of each other, the effect is deepened for the body (herb) and the energy field (flower essence). Blackberry assists the astral body; buckthorn strengthens the solar plexus; loosestrife promotes healing and flexibility and is sometimes used in athletes' massage cream; mango strengthens the Solar Plexus and Heart Chakras, and particularly the nadis (energy channels) in the chest; and peppermint calms down any digestive imbalances, especially those caused by stress held in Manipura.

the solar plexus chakra: manipura

The oil diffuser holds water and a few drops of essential oil.

SOLAR PLEXUS CHAKRA ESSENTIAL OILS

The main essential oils that have a sympathetic resonance with Manipura are:

- **Clary sage** This flowering plant is excellent to calm this chakra, although it should not be used if you have to drive afterward, are taking alcohol or are pregnant (except during the early stages of labor under medical supervision). It is the strongest relaxant known in aromatherapy and is capable of producing very euphoric states. It is anti-convulsive, anti-depressant, antiseptic, anti-spasmodic, emmenagogic and aphrodisiac.

- **Juniper** This is a small tree whose berries are crushed and the oil steam-distilled from them. It is the main purifying essential oil used for massage and is ideal to clear blockages from the Solar Plexus Chakra. Juniper really clears out the body (rather like a tonic) and helps digestion. It is the flavoring ingredient in gin, so perhaps the expression "gin and tonic" was an apt one! It is antiseptic, anti-spasmodic, emmenagogic and anti-toxic.

- **Geranium** The essential oil is made from the flowers, leaves and stalks. It is an adrenal-cortex stimulant and helps regulate hormone secretion throughout the endocrine system. An aromatherapist will also use it to detox the lymphatic system. It is an excellent oil to calm and balance Manipura, as it helps movement of pranic energy through the body. It is also anti-depressant, antiseptic, deodorant, diuretic and tonic, and excellent for treating PMS.

yoga asanas for manipura

active: gomukasana (cow pose)

This pose stimulates the kidneys and pancreas, helping diabetic conditions, which are associated with imbalances in the Solar Plexus Chakra. The crossed and locked knee position and the arm position cause vital energy to be focused at this chakra. This asana may be performed standing if your knees are painful. The state of consciousness you are seeking at the Solar Plexus Chakra is manomaya kosha (the waking state), which is experienced through your intellectual mind. Use a visualization of a bright-yellow flaming Sun to help you, and draw breath into your body as a bright-yellow light.

1

1 Kneel down and sit on your heels, or sit with your knees crossed over one another (this is the advanced position).
2 Raise your left arm over your head, bending it at the elbow and turning it down your back. Bend your right arm up behind your back to catch your left hand with your right. Lock your fingers together. Hold the position, then repeat on the other side.

2

ardha matsyendrasana 1 (sitting spinal twist)

This asana benefits the kidneys and pancreas in a similar way to Gomukasana. The intense twist of the spine works on the spinal nerves and, at a subtle level, improves energy flow through the ida and pingala nadis and the sushumna kundalini channel within the spine. However, the main focus is the massaging effect on the abdominal organs, which brings benefits to the Solar Plexus Chakra.

1 Sit on the floor. Bend your right knee and sit on the foot. Then bend your left knee and lift it over your right thigh, placing the foot flat on the floor.

2 Turn your body 90 degrees to the left and bring your right armpit over your left knee. Lock the arm over the knee, then move your left arm behind your waist, so that your left hand catches your right hand. Turn your neck to face left, looking over your left shoulder. Repeat on the other side.

1

simple version

1 Follow the steps opposite but turning to the other side.
2 Turning 90 degrees to the right, bring your left armpit over your right knee. Lock your arm over the knee.
3 Use your right arm to support and straighten your back. Repeat on the other side.

2

passive: ustrasana (camel pose)

The practice of this posture is recommended to keep your spine supple, work on the abdominal organs/muscles and the shoulder joints. During this intense stretch, focus on bringing a sparkling golden light into your Solar Plexus Chakra, where it will charge up and revitalize your whole body. If you have difficulty keeping your hips in line with your knees, place a cushion on top of your calves and tuck your toes under, to the ground, to raise your heels a bit. Only bend your back as far as feels comfortable.

1

1 Kneel on the floor with your buttocks raised off your feet. Gently lean backward, placing your right hand on your right heel and your left hand on your left heel.

2 Push on your feet with your hands and, taking your head back, curve your spine upward, pushing it up until your thighs are in line with your knees and the front of your body is straight. Relax into the position.

2

Chapter 5

THE HEART CHAKRA: ANAHATA

anahata chakra

The Heart Chakra or Anahata is also known as anahata-puri, padma-sundara, dwadasha, dwadashadala, suryasangkhyadala, hrit padma, hridaya chakra, dwadashara chakra and by various other names.

In Tantric teachings, Anahata (meaning "unstruck note") has 12 red or white petals, while the central part is a smoky-blue/black color symbolizing the element of Air. Anahata is positioned in the center of the chest and is connected to the Thymus Chakra (see pages 208–209).

the functions of anahata

The 12 petals of Anahata represent: lustfulness; fraudulence; indecision; repentance; hope; anxiety; longing; impartiality; arrogance; incompetence; discrimination; an attitude of defiance. It is associated with the element (or tattwa) of Air, and is the seat of the Divine Soul or Higher Self, the Jivatman, represented by the image of a motionless golden lamp-flame. It is linked to the ages of 22 to 28, when we are often forming deep relationships, hopefully based on reciprocal love. But the Heart Chakra is not primarily about falling in love; it is not a sentimental kind of love. Instead its fire is fueled by the love of creation—the same love that causes us to delight in the feel of soft rain or the scent of a flower.

Anahata is at the center of our luminous auric body. The color of light to balance it is a bright grass-green, and quite commonly the 12 petals are shown in this color. Anahata, midpoint in the seven chakras and midpoint in the body, is considered a gateway to higher consciousness.

In Tibetan Buddhism, the Heart Chakra is depicted as a white, eight-petalled heart center, the meeting place of the Red and White Drops, seat of the Very Subtle Mind and Very Subtle Wind, which are immortal and pass from lifetime to lifetime. In Taoism, this chakra is the House of Fire. It is located at the top of the central "Thrusting Channel," and is the counterbalance to the Lower Tan Tien, or House of Water.

MAIN CHARACTERISTICS AT A GLANCE

Color	Green and/or pink/red/white
Key issues	Passion, tenderness, inner-child issues and rejection
Physical location	At the center of the chest on the sternum
Associated spinal area	Fourth thoracic vertebra
Physiological system	Circulatory, lymphatic, Immune
Endocrine gland	Thymus
Nerve plexus	Heart
Inner aspect	Unconditional love and compassion
Physical action	Circulation
Mental action	Passion
Spiritual action	Devotion

health issues and anahata

Our heart forms part of the circulatory system. It is a hollow muscle that pumps oxygen-rich blood from the lungs to all parts of the body. By the time someone is in their seventies, their heart will have beaten some 3,000 million times! At a biological level, blood has three major functions: it conveys water, food, oxygen and all forms of prana; it removes waste products through the kidneys, liver and lungs; and it carries important parts of the immune system.

associated body system

Unfortunately, many people suffer from medically diagnosed heart disease, such as a disturbance of their heart rhythm, muscular, valvular and aortic disease and infections. Heart disease is a major cause of death in countries with an affluent Western-type lifestyle. However, doctors are beginning to acknowledge that heart disease is not just a physical issue. High blood pressure can be an initial sign of underlying mental strain, often caused by bottled-up stress, anger or frustration.

The health of the physical heart improves if we release past traumas and emotional pain and do not try to judge others. Sexual issues in particular need to be processed through the Base and Sacral Chakras. When they get mixed up with the heart center, which naturally gyrates toward unconditional love, great confusion occurs.

Alternative or complementary treatments can go a long way to balance the whole body–mind system and restore health. For example, if you consult a trained healer, he or she might detect that the Heart Chakra is seriously out of balance. The healer may find a predominance of red energy, indicating a predisposition to a physical heart problem that could be rectified *before* it manifests itself. Depending on the symptoms presenting at a physical level, a healer may be guided to rebalance Anahata using green light (either with an instrument or psychically). They might then move the red energy—symbolic of repressed anger—back down to the Base Chakra, where it could be worked with and eliminated.

associated endocrine gland

The endocrine gland associated with the heart is the thymus gland (linked to a separate small chakra, see pages 208–209), which initiates the movement of the body's defenses during illness and injury.

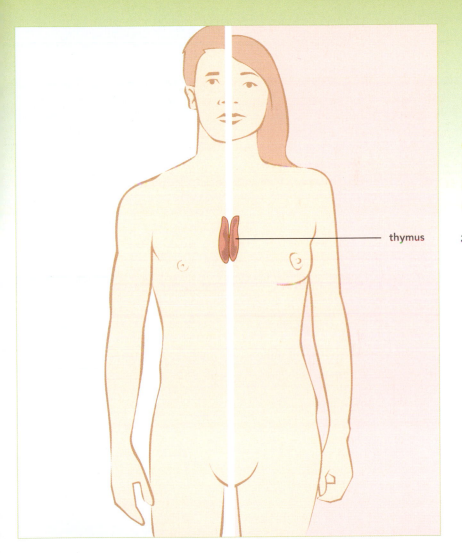

thymus

emotional issues and anahata

As we have seen, this chakra is associated with issues of the heart. All romantic love is motivated by our constant search for union with the source of love. The highest form of romantic love is given to us when we can give to others unconditionally. If we can learn to respect and understand another person's feelings, then we will also feel at peace within ourselves.

doubts and imbalances

If we are thwarted in love, and cannot make meaningful relationships with others or do not have friendships that last, we may begin to doubt ourselves. We may ask, "What is wrong with me? Why aren't I popular and loved like other people?" We may also question our ability to relate to others, and start to attract a dark cloud of doubt and confusion into our auric field.

Such feelings may grow until they are a real imbalance, preventing us appreciating others—or ourselves. If we don't deal with these types of feelings, we will begin to hold in our emotional pain. Then our whole chakra system starts to close in on itself and is no longer able to "feed" the physical body effectively. There is no input of love— and no output of love; the ability to love is dying in our physical body. Therefore we need to begin to *love* and *live*.

brightening up the aura and the chakras

If we, as individuals, can take the following steps, we will begin walking a path of increased awareness of our aura and our chakras, and will nourish our mental health and many other parts of ourselves, too. This is sometimes called the Path of Beauty.

- Take medical advice if you are suffering from great mental anguish.
- Begin a path of understanding about which types of therapy or counseling could help you. When we put out a message to the universe that we need help, then if it is part of the greater plan for creation, it must respond—that is the nature of universal love. We will always draw to ourselves the help we need.
- Start to practice some techniques that will increase your energy levels and self-esteem. Many great teachers have said, "if you cannot love yourself, you cannot love others."

*Respect for and understanding of
another's feelings leads us to feel
at peace with ourselves.*

203

attraction and compassion

Have you ever wondered why you are attracted to other people? Probably it's not simply because of the clothes they are wearing or their hairstyle. More likely it is because they have a special smile, a look, or something in their nature that attracts you. We all know that it is possible to fall in love across a crowded room, and we talk of people having a "magnetic attraction" to each other or being "blinded by love."

When you are in love, it is probable that you have found a person whose auric field complements your own. Earthly love is saying, "Yes, my aura finds yours attractive—let's merge and have a union." Initial responses are simply about vibrational attraction. Secondary responses are about who we want to spend our lives with; who would make a good father or mother for our children; who we can be with in our darkest hours; and to whom we can gift our love unconditionally. We are constantly searching for that perfect match, and along the way we are certain to meet many challenges.

the compassion of the buddha

As the source of spiritual fire, Anahata is sometimes referred to as the purging fire of the Creator's love. It is the sacred fire of devotion and spiritual inspiration. It is the fire that transforms our personal identity, our ego and our little lives into the greater life of Spirit. Our personal identity moves progressively from self, to others, to the Divine. When the Heart Chakra becomes fully open to love, it wants other beings to share in the love and peace of infinite awareness. This is an expression of the compassion of the Buddha. In this tradition the desire for this special kind of love is expressed by the vow, "I will not leave the Earth until *all* beings gain enlightenment."

Unconditional love flowing through the Heart Chakra neutralizes all negative energies. Just as in film romances "true love" always triumphs, so images of loving deities can transform us: their eyes meet ours and we are transported beyond the limitations of self. Enlightened beings—such as ascended masters Christ or Buddha—are mirrors of the loving, all-embracing spiritual potential in every one of us. When we look at them, they take us beyond ego into compassion and unconditionality.

The loving, spiritual potential in each of us is mirrored in the Buddha.

attraction and compassion

healing your heart chakra

To be fulfilled we all need the kind of love that is unconditional. As the central gateway to higher consciousness, the Heart Chakra needs to be nourished if we are to remain physically strong, capable of giving and receiving love and able to develop spiritually.

the power of touch

Our heart love is expressed through our hands: it is natural to pick up a child who is hurt and cradle him or her near your heart. It is natural to touch another person in compassion if they are sad. It is natural to hold hands with your lover, and to express your love for them with your hands.

The following touch-exercise can be done with a friend:

1 Sit next to them and close your eyes.
2 Gently, with a feather-soft movement, touch the tips of your friend's fingers with one hand. Notice what feelings this brings up for you.
3 Now use your thumb to press all over your friend's palm.
4 Then stroke the back of their hand. Each time notice what kind of touch you—and your friend—like best.
5 When you have finished, shake your hands toward the ground to release any unwanted energies and swap roles, with your friend now touching your hands.

For a long time, red roses have been regarded as a symbol of heart love.

nourishing your heart

One way in which you can nourish your own heart is to sit alone with a pink or red flower—a rose is ideal, because its wonderful perfume assists in balancing the heart. This exercise will calm your emotions, and prepare you for deeper visualization techniques.

1 Sit quietly for about ten minutes with your eyes closed as you do some deep breathing to release any stress in your body.
2 Now open your eyes and look at the beauty of the rose, revel in its perfume, touch it, enjoy the softness of its petals.
3 Shut your eyes again and try to re-create in your mind all those things you have learned about the rose. Developing love for the beauty of Nature is one of the best ways to "love the life you are living." Even if you live in a city, you will have the skies above you to marvel at.

the thymus chakra

The Thymus, in the center of the chest close to the heart, is emerging as a newly acknowledged chakra for our age. The way it serves to protect our bodies is vital, because increasingly we are subjected to all manner of pollutants in our food, water and air.

At one time doctors thought that the thymus gland (with which this chakra is associated) shrank to insignificant size and function once childhood was over. However, modern research is showing this not to be the case, and that it is a vital component in our bio-defense system and our immunity to disease in adult life. Clearly we need to care for our Thymus Chakra, as the thymus gland itself plays such an important protective role for our body, or the build-up of chemical toxins that are now being used indiscriminately may eventually compromise our immune system.

It was the second-century CE Greek doctor Galen, who gave the thymus gland its name, because it reminded him of a bunch of thyme flowers. *Thymos*, as it was called, was the main herb used as incense on altars to the deities, and the thymus was recognized as the place where we make our inner sacrifice in the altar of the heart within our physical chest. It was so revered that it was the source of inspiration, songs of love and praise, and was regarded as the "breath-soul" upon which human energy depended.

Thyme is an antiseptic and stimulates the immune system—however, use this herb in moderation.

MAIN CHARACTERISTICS AT A GLANCE

Color	Soft pink/blue
Key issues	Protection
Physical location	The center of the chest
Physical action	Appears to direct life-giving and healing body energies
Hormones	Produces thymosins
Major function	Produces special lymphocytes called T-cells that are vital to the immune system
Secondary functions	Regulates growth and muscular contractions
Lymphatic function	Connected with the flow of lymph through the body
Energetic action	Monitors energy flows
Spiritual action	The ancient concept of our "breath-soul" (see opposite)

We can help our Thymus Chakra in a number of ways:

- Giving love to others and ourselves
- Tapping our sternum a number of times each day
- Drinking thyme tea once a day (unless you have a diagnosed heart condition)
- Wearing protective turquoise crystals or thyme-colored sugulite over the Thymus Chakra
- Visualizing your breath as a blue-violet color
- Practicing yoga asanas that expand the chest, such as Bhungasana, the cobra.

anahata yantra

In the heart is the charming lotus of the color of the Bandhuka flower. It is like Kalpa-taru, the celestial wishing tree, bestowing even more than desire.

Sat Cakra Nirupana

description of the yantra

Number of petals Twelve.

Color Green or vermilion.

Element Air.

Star Two triangles superimposed on each other to form a star shape, representing balance and harmony.

Golden triangle Indicates the Divine light that can be revealed when this chakra is fully opened.

Crescent moon Represents the granthis of Vishnu, the psychic blocks that must be dissolved to achieve true enlightenment.

Antelope or deer Refers to the lightness and speed of the Air element. Avayu, the Vedic god of the winds, rode a deer.

the bija mantra

Anahata's bija mantra (see pages 80–81) is YAM, which upon sounding gives control over the breath and the dawn of true knowledge.

meditation to open the petals of the heart

This visualization will take you into great depths of stillness.

1 Sit upright with a straight spine, either in a yoga posture or on a chair.

2 Start to breathe deeply.

3 When you are completely relaxed, start to "color-breathe" green light, the shade of fresh leaves with the sunlight shining through them.

4 Focus your green breaths at the physical heart and the Heart Chakra, to bring yourself into a state of balance.

5 After a while begin to visualize your Heart Chakra as a beautiful pink rosebud with many petals closed in on itself.

6 Gradually uncurl each petal, releasing a wonderful fragrance. You may find some petals difficult to open, for they may hold unresolved pain that needs to be released. Each time you practice this visualization, try opening more petals. When they are all open, a brightly shining golden center will appear.

7 Hold this vision for as long as possible, then end your meditation and bring yourself back to everyday awareness.

deities associated with anahata

ishvara

The presiding god energy is Ishvara (or Isa), whose name means "lord" or "master." He is an aspect of Shiva and overlord of the three lower chakras. His absorption of passion helps us to remove any separation between us and the world around us. This deity is depicted with three eyes and two arms, and he makes the mudras (hand gestures) of dispelling fears and granting boons.

The best boon that Ishvara gives us is that of strengthening concentration. With concentration we are able to know that our soul dwells within us as the Eternal Self, as a spark of creation. Ishvara opens the delicate petals of the heart leading us out of confusion and into liberation.

Vagu, god of wind and Air, the element of this chakra, rides on a fleet of black antelope, which are said to pull the chariots of the Sun and Moon across the heavens.

kakini

The presiding goddess of Anahata is Kakini. She is the great and beautiful benefactor of devotion, who synchronizes the beat of our heart with the beat of the cosmos. She carries a noose in one hand, to remind us not to get caught up in spiritual expectation. In her other hand she holds a skull, which reminds us to maintain a pure mind. She makes the same mudra gestures as Isvara.

She is shown in enlightened and happy mood because she has drunk the Amrita, or precious nectar, that flows from the Soma chakra. The noose and the skull, far from being ominous symbols, encourage us to die to our self, to ignorance and to the ways of the world, so that we may dance the sacred dance of life.

crystals to activate anahata

When we talk of activating a chakra, we imply that it is lacking in energetic flow. However, you need to ascertain if this really is the case, by a diagnostic method; or, if you prefer to play safe, simply use one of the balancing crystals shown on the following pages. The main crystal used to activate Anahata is peridot.

peridot

Nature has given us the gift of this high-energy gemstone, which is also known as chrysolite and olivine. Its colors range from brownish-green to a bright clear green, and it is the latter that is used to activate the Heart Chakra.

Peridot activates Anahata in diverse ways: it is regarded as a cleansing stone, capable of clearing out toxins from the aura and physical body. On a psychological level, it assists negative emotions that may originate from the heart, such as jealousy, envy, hate and anger, and helps move these emotions out through the chakra. It can therefore be seen as "the stone of relationships"—easing away negative emotions that hold us back from truly loving, and replacing them with compassion, love and calmness.

Polished peridot (above) and sparkling precious faceted peridot crystals (right) have a resonant vibration with the heart.

using peridot to boost your energy vibrations

On a physical level peridot can assist the energetic vibrations of the heart and lungs. One way to use it is to leave a cleansed crystal in a glass of pure spring water overnight (preferably in moonlight) and then slowly sip the water in the morning—being careful to remove the small crystal first! Another way is simply to hold the crystal during meditation or tape it to the center of your chest, at the point where the spiralling energy of the chakra enters your body. Leave it on for no more than 12 hours at a time, then wash, cleanse and re-energize the crystal.

When using any crystal healing method, remember that disease has probably taken a long time to lodge itself in the physical body, having passed through all the levels of the aura to get there. You need to consciously ease the disease out again, dissolving any patterns or imprints that predispose you to it. This usually requires time and dedication. And of course you must follow any medical advice, and create the optimum conditions for your return to health, such as nutritious food, relaxation and a healthy lifestyle.

Sipping peridot-infused spring water can assist the vibrations of energy in the heart and lungs.

crystals to calm anahata

The most effective crystals for calming the energies of the Heart Chakra are blue sapphire (see page 185), pink topaz, pink kunzite and rhodonite.

pink topaz

This is a rare gemstone with a special correspondence to our heart and that of Mother Earth. As all crystals and stones come from below ground, they are often sensitive if placed in direct sunlight. Some of them—like amethyst and pink topaz—should not be left in sunshine, because they will actually fade over time.

In Native American traditions, rocks are regarded as Mother Earth's bones, rivers as her lymphatic system, oil as her blood, vegetation as her hair and the surface of Earth as her skin. Crystals—sometimes referred to as "frozen light"—are seen as the precious endocrine glands of her body. Therefore, when using pink topaz, we create an immediate synergy with the Thymus Chakra that is closely associated with the heart. Pink topaz disperses old patterns of disease that are held in the auric field relating to the heart; for a lung problem, green topaz is more appropriate.

Lavender kunzite (top) or pink kunzite (above) strengthen and protect the whole auric field.

pink or lavender kunzite

This is an excellent crystal to use at the Heart Chakra, and works with the human emotions at this time of human evolution on Earth. Pink or lavender kunzite especially helps to heal the pain of broken relationships or loss through death, when it assists the grieving process. Kunzite is always calming to the Heart Chakra, by bringing into the auric field increased levels of compassion. It is used to help lift depression arising from emotional turbulence, and to calm panic attacks.

An excellent Anahata remedy is a small quantity of pink kunzite crystal essence and five drops of rose essential oil poured into a warm bath. Light some pink candles and soak away your worries for a while. When you come out of the bath, take seven drops of the crystal essence and relax for as long as possible.

rhodonite

Rhodonite is used to clear out unwanted energies and to calm, and it is recommended that you use it for this purpose before placing any other crystal on the Heart Chakra. Because of its iron content (the black streaks), it grounds you

Rhodonite clears memories of emotional and physical wounds, in this or past lives.

and enables deeper work to take place toward the ideal of unconditional love. After using rhodonite to calm the Heart Chakra, you can then use rose quartz or rhodocrosite (see pages 218–219) to bring balance to Anahata.

Rhodonite is sometimes regarded as a "First aid" crystal for shock when it can be held, used in a healing method or be taken as a gem elixir (see page 71) over the course of a few days. It is also beneficial to have by you if your body suffers from a panic attack.

crystals to balance anahata

Watermelon tourmaline, green aventurine, rose quartz, rhodonite (see pages 216–217) and rhodocrosite may all be used to balance Anahata. They are best used as small, tumble-polished stones, with the exception of watermelon tourmaline, which is usually cut in "slices" to show off its naturally occurring pink heart in the midst of the green crystal.

watermelon tourmaline

This is the first choice to use in crystal healing for balancing the Heart Chakra. The green part brings life-force energy into the body, while the pink soothes and harmonizes. It helps to reconcile opposites and confusion about sexual roles. It can teach us to be self-contained, integrated and in loving harmony with all the different aspects of ourselves.

using green aventurine to balance heart energies

This crystal both calms Anahata and balances the energies of the heart and lungs. It is a sparkly green quartz with good all-around healing abilities. To balance your whole body, try the following exercise.

1 Place a cloth of bright green (silk is best, but cotton will do—do not use artificial fibers) on the floor.
2 Put as many tumbled green aventurine stones as you can find in a perfect circle around the cloth. (Cleanse all the crystals both before and after use, see page 68.)
3 Lie down on your back on the cloth, with your head to the north; in the center of your chest place another aventurine and four quartz points, equally spaced in the north, south, east and west directions, with the points facing inward toward the aventurine.
4 Relax for about half an hour.

Watermelon tourmaline calms the Heart Chakra and connects us to the source of unconditional love.

Green aventurine (left), rose quartz (below) and rhodocrosite (bottom) are all useful polished tumble stones for Anahata Chakra.

rose quartz

This stone will bring you friendship and love. It is an ideal crystal to give a friend, as it has gentle, caring energies. In meditation it will take you through opening the different levels of the Heart Chakra and find ways to connect you with your inner cosmic child. In the physical body, it can aid sexual and emotional imbalance and increase fertility. Hold a rose quartz in each hand while you meditate.

rhodocrosite

This is a good energy conductor, as it has a high copper content. It integrates physical, mental and emotional aspects at the heart level. It is an ideal crystal to give back to the Earth as an offering, if you are in a special place.

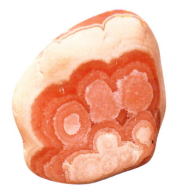

crystal massage

You can rebalance a friend's or lover's energy with a rose-quartz crystal massage. For this you will need to obtain a piece of smooth, tumble-polished rose quartz with a soft point (it must not be sharp), or one of the very delicate and rare natural rose quartz crystals. As usual, cleanse your crystal (see page 68) before use and have ready a pink candle, a comfortable place to lie down and a small quantity of aromatherapy carrier oil (5 ml), mixed with three drops of rose essential oil—only use pure essential oil, and not the type sold for aromatherapy burners.

This is going to be a very special crystal massage, given with unconditional love to a close friend or lover, who needs to be naked. It should be an enriching experience that enables both of you to take turns to share this loving time together.

1 Make a special ritual of lighting the candle together, expressing what you are feeling for each other in your heart.

2 Now start to anoint all of your partner's seven chakras with a small quantity of the oil on your finger. Proceed slowly and sensitively from crown to base, and then toward both feet.

3 At this point you should begin the Heart Chakra massage with the rose quartz. First, holding the rose quartz in your hand like a pendulum, find the direction of spiralling energy that is emanating from the chakra and let your hand softly follow it. *Very gently* spiral the rose quartz in and out over the skin at the center of the chest corresponding to Anahata. Take your time and enjoy this. Let the crystal work its magical frequencies of unconditional love.

4 Use more of the rose oil mix, if you need to. It should be a highly pleasurable experience.

5 End by gently massaging your friend's feet, then hold their feet firmly as you ask them gradually to be aware of your voice calling them back to everyday consciousness.

6 Drink some cool water and then swap roles.

Relax and be at peace as you enjoy giving or receiving this crystal massage.

aromatherapy and anahata

The scents of plants, trees and herbs benefit us in many ways: the scent exuding from the bark of birch enables us to find inner peace, while chamomile leaves and flowers give off a scent that has a strongly sedative effect, which opens the Heart Chakra and works on our

HEART CHAKRA ESSENTIAL OILS

The main essential oils that have a sympathetic resonance with Anahata are:

- **Rose** At the Heart Chakra this oil moves the energy of passion to that of unconditional love. When used with the energies of Anahata, it is also valuable as an anti-depressant following bereavement or the breakdown of a relationship with a loved one. It is antiseptic, emmenagogic, hepatic, sedative and uterine.

- **Melissa** This makes a good alternative to rose for massage to benefit the physical and etheric heart (or you can make a wonderful aromatherapy blend with the two), but take care when using it on those with sensitive skin. It has a slightly lemony perfume and enhances rose, lavender and geranium essential oils. Melissa is recommended for shock or grief and lowers high blood pressure. It has a sedative effect and strengthens Anahata. Like rose, it is extremely expensive and needs to be used sparingly. The wise Greek healer Paracelsus called melissa "the elixir of life." It is anti-depressant, antiseptic, anti-spasmodic, anti-viral, febrifuge, nervine and sedative.

- **Neroli** This is the number-one oil for stress or shock. It is made from the blossom of the bitter orange tree, has an extremely strong perfume and blends well with other oils. It is very beneficial for the skin, especially for rejuvenating dry or ageing skin. However, as a Heart Chakra oil, it is also superb, since it is anti-depressant, sedative and aphrodisiac.

emotional levels. Olive leaf taken as a herbal tincture strengthens the immune system, and pear-flower essence is recommended to inspire musicians. Strawberry and pomegranate eaten as fruits or taken as flower essences strengthen the Heart Chakra, while strongly smelling thyme, as a herb or flower essence, works on the physical heart/thymus connections.

massage and vaporization

A massage by a trained aromatherapist using a blend that includes any of the oils opposite, will be a really pleasurable experience. If you are unable to have a massage, perhaps the next best thing is to enjoy the perfumes and therapeutic properties of these oils, by using them in a bath or an oil diffuser (see pages 58–59).

Aromatherapy oils, used in a diffuser or massage, can benefit us in many ways.

yoga asanas for anahata

active: bhujangasana (cobra)

Physically, Bhujangasana works powerfully on the spine and, if performed under expert supervision, can realign it. The position should never be forced—only extend it within your own comfortable range. This asana opens and allows the beautiful symbolic lotus at the Heart Chakra to "flower." Visualize the flower opening, revealing golden stamens in the center like precious jewels. The state of consciousness you are seeking at the Heart Chakra is visnanamaya (awareness), your own personal experience of your wisdom body.

1 Lie flat on the floor, with your chin resting down. Place your hands flat on the floor under your shoulders, with your fingers pointing forward.

2 Gently raise your body to a comfortable height as you curve your back backward. Keep your pubis in contact with the floor—do not lift your body right off the floor. Your arms do not have to be straight; you may bend your elbows. Flexibility of your spine will develop with practice.

1

raised bhujangasana (raised cobra)

This is an advanced version of the previous asana. Proceed with caution.

Proceed as described above, then tuck your toes under and lift your whole trunk off the floor, keeping your back straight (this is like a push-up position). Your head should be looking straight forward. Hold the position.

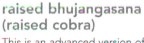

passive: janusirsasana (head-to-knee forward bend)

This asana stretches the backs of the leg muscles and loosens the hip joints, toning the abdominal organs and stretching the spine throughout its entire length. If you find sitting-forward bends difficult because your spine and hips are not very flexible, sit with your tailbone on the edge of a hard cushion to improve your flexibility from the hip joint. While bending forward, always endeavor to flatten your back as much as possible—this has the effect of opening the Heart Chakra. Remember that chakras open to the front and back (with the exception of the Base

1

and Crown Chakras), so focus on light coming into the center middle of your back. Use the yantra as a focus, or the color of a bright fresh green being drawn into your lungs and heart. This brings balance and harmony into the Heart Chakra as you relax into the posture. Only when you become extremely supple will you achieve the full asana shown in step 2.

1 Sit with both legs flat on the floor in front of you. Bend your right knee and move it to the right, tucking your right heel close to the crotch area. Catch your left big toe with both hands.

2 Lift your head, then on an out-breath bend forward over your left leg, to bring your face as close to your left knee as possible. Repeat with the other leg.

2

matsyasana (fish pose)

This asana strengthens the chest, neck and spine, as well as the respiratory system, and bending the body upward in this way benefits Anahata. There are two versions with different degrees of difficulty.

1 Easy posture: lie on the floor with your legs stretched straight out. Place your hands or elbows on the floor to support you, then arch your back and place the top of your head gently on the floor, keeping your chest raised.

2 Advanced posture: sit with your legs crossed in a full lotus position and, on an exhalation, lie backward, supporting yourself on your elbows, until the top of your head just rests on the floor. Bring your hands to rest on your feet.

Chapter 6

THE THROAT CHAKRA: VISHUDDHA

○ ○ ○ ○ ○ ○ ○

vishuddha chakra

The Throat Chakra or Vishuddha is known as kantha, kanthadesha, kanthapadma, kanthapankaja, shodasha, kanthambhoja, shodasha-dala, akasha, nirmala-padma, shodashara, dwyashtapatrambuja and by other names. The element associated with this chakra is ether/akasha, through which are transmitted the subtle vibrations of mantras, as used in Laya yoga.

Vishuddha means "to purify." In Tantric yoga, this chakra has 16 smoke-colored petals, each linked with one of the Sanskrit vowels, a mantra or a musical tone. The central chakra region is white, transparent, smoke or sky-blue in color, although modern interpretations of the Throat Chakra usually show the 16 petals in turquoise.

the functions of vishuddha

Vishuddha is regarded as an important bridge from the heart, in the raising of consciousness through the sequential activation of the chakras from the base to the crown of the head. In a sense it really is a bridge, because it takes us from one side of the river of life—our body—to the other side, into spiritual realms. Of the 16 petals, the first represents Pranava (the mantra OM/AUM); the next seven are mantras; and the last eight are associated with nectar and seven musical tones.

It is the place from where we can speak or sing our love: for our partner, our world, our god/s, our goddess. Conversely we can use our voice to hurt or slander, speaking bitter words that destroy and turn the energies of this chakra inward. Vishuddha will not continue to receive sustenance from the sacred ether unless we can speak and sing good words.

Energy imbalances in Vishuddha manifest as ear, nose, throat and respiratory problems in the physical body. So if there is discomfort or disease in these areas, the Throat Chakra will be the first one to give healing to. As it comes into balance, we learn to feel truly that we are "in our body" and can express the creative and life-affirming aspects of ourselves.

MAIN CHARACTERISTICS AT A GLANCE

Color	Turquoise
Key issues	Self-expression, communication and will
Physical location	Between the collar bone and larynx in the neck
Associated spinal area	Third cervical vertebra
Physiological system	Respiratory
Endocrine gland	Thyroid and parathyroids
Nerve plexus	Cervical ganglia
Inner aspect	Expression
Physical action	Communication
Mental action	Fluent thought
Emotional action	Independence
Spiritual action	Security

health issues and vishuddha

The Throat Chakra can help us to be powerful beyond words—an aspect shown by its traditional symbolic animal, an elephant.

associated body systems

Physically, Vishuddha is associated with the production of thyroid-balancing hormones. Interestingly, these are linked mainly to the way we develop: the Throat Chakra receives messages from higher chakras saying, "This is the rate at which your body will grow." Throughout our lives the thyroid and smaller parathyroid glands in the neck keep a variety of body functions going, including the repair of body cells, blood calcium and phosphate levels. Above the throat we are concerned with the higher processes of the mind and with development of our spiritual nature.

Imbalances that may benefit from Throat Chakra healing include:

- Graves disease
- Hypothyroidism and goiter
- Hyperthyroidism
- Hyperparathyroidism and hypoparathyroidism
- Exhaustion
- Digestive and weight problems
- Sore throats, neck pain and pain in the back of the head.

A deficiency of energy at this chakra (hypo-) can make us feel afraid, timid, manipulative and afraid of sex. An excess of energy (hyper) is an overstimulation that brings a dogmatic nature, arrogance or self-righteousness, or makes us excessive talkers. Such people are likely to be sexually dominant and forceful. A simple way to clear your Throat Chakra is to tap it three times with your fingertips. Remember to do this whenever you have difficulty expressing yourself.

When Vishuddha comes into balance, we can affirm life in the way we speak and express ourselves through song. It gives form to the feelings of our heart, and enables us to communicate telepathically, if this is our desire. When harmoniously balanced, the Throat Chakra enables us to develop an appreciation of global matters, so that we are no longer fixated on our group, nationality or birthplace. It brings us into resonance with all peoples and life.

associated endocrine glands

The thyroid produces thyroxine T4 and tri-iodothyronine T3 (promotes normal body and brain growth and repairs body cells), and parathyroids produce parathormone (calcium and phosphate metabolism).

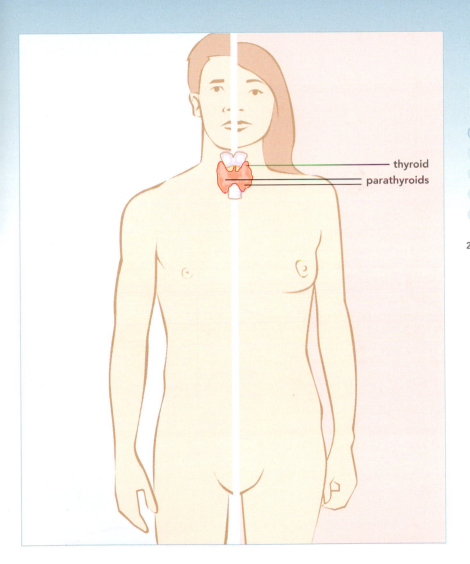

thyroid

parathyroids

prana: the breath of life

Respiratory problems arise because of a disassociation with the energy of ether (akasha), a specialized type of prana that passes through this chakra and is drawn into our body with every breath.

- We breathe—but don't think about the quality of our breathing.
- We take in air and oxygen—but don't think about the quality of that air.

It is not until we experience difficulties in breathing that we begin to really appreciate how precious the breath of life is. We can live for around 56 days without food, about 12 days without water, but air—including oxygen, prana and ether—we must have approximately every three minutes. Without air the electrical system that forms our fire energy, centered in our brain, quickly dies. Then we are termed brain-dead. But what if we only half-breathe all our lives—what does that do to us? Perhaps that is why yoga teaches specific breathing techniques, to increase the pranic flow through our subtle and physical body systems. The object of yoga is not to make the body better *per se*, but to make it a suitable "house" for our spirit.

exercise to control prana
In this exercise you should breathe only as deeply as is comfortable for you.

breathe in

1 Sit cross-legged in the lotus position
   on the floor, or in an upright chair
   with your feet flat on the floor. Ensure
   that your back is straight and your
   eyes closed.

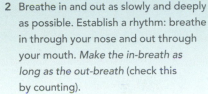

breathe out

2 Breathe in and out as slowly and deeply
   as possible. Establish a rhythm: breathe
   in through your nose and out through
   your mouth. *Make the in-breath as
   long as the out-breath* (check this
   by counting).

3 Hold the palms of your hands over your
   navel and feel the movement as you
   push air right down to the base of your
   lungs, making your abdomen rise. With
   each in-breath, continue filling your
   lungs, expanding your ribs.

4 Slowly exhale. Remember that you are
   still trying to keep the rhythm and the
   same duration of in- and out-breaths.

5 Spend ten minutes on this exercise to
   begin with. Then, over the course of
   a year, work up to one hour.

prana: the breath of life

emotional issues and vishuddha

We project an image of ourselves through our voice, or the absence of it. Clearly the way we communicate changes as we grow from baby to adult. On a physical level, you would not expect a man's voice to sound the same at seven years of age as it does at the age of seventy. In the same way, what he communicates through his voice will be different, depending on age and life experience.

freeing up channels of communication

The Throat Chakra is closely connected with this progression of communication as we proceed through life. A fluid auric field will assist it to function and will feed our communication processes. If it is blocked, this can result in depression and suicidal tendencies. At times when we cannot cope, or express ourselves, it may help to discuss problems with a qualified counselor. When we talk things over, a burden is shared and self-expression through this chakra is encouraged. Professional counseling can be backed up with other therapies: light treatment with turquoise light, crystal healing, wearing a turquoise necklace, a visit to a spiritual healer or regular chakra

visualizations using the color turquoise. Most people use their voice every day solely to express the emotional needs of their lower chakras. If this is your pattern, you should question it.

To a trained sound therapist, our voice indicates our strengths and weaknesses,

depending on the dominant or missing notes in our speech, which link to the health and wellness of our physical body. Even a listener who has developed a few skills can pick up information about someone by the way they express themselves: their emotions and mental state usually come across clearly in the voice.

the importance of listening

Our voice has the power to transform our lives, but often we forget how effective we can be when we communicate clearly. *Listening* is the real secret of communication. When we listen we hear what another person is really saying, and we can sort out the different layers within and behind their words. For example, we may say, "Yes, I am okay," but really mean "No, actually I am not at all okay." This is part of the mask we wear on the stage called "life," an outdated program stemming from the Victorian ethos of "children should be seen but not heard."

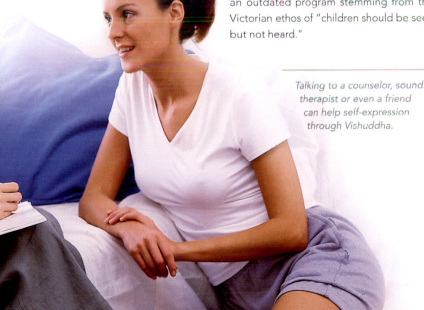

Talking to a counselor, sound therapist or even a friend can help self-expression through Vishuddha.

spiritual issues and vishuddha

Vishuddha channels akasha—the ether—into our bodies, and symbolically represents the source of all sounds and vibrations. It is said that when we master and fully activate this chakra, we develop the ability to hear all sounds and understand other languages through clairaudience (hearing sounds beyond the range of normal hearing) and extra-sensory perception (ESP). It is even said that we can understand the languages of birds and animals and those of spirit beings such as goddesses and gods, devas and elementals of Nature. In the Indian tradition, when we have learned Satya, truthfulness of speech, we can speak our deepest desires and have them come true.

satya: truthfulness of speech

From a psychological perspective, when we face up to our own truth—no longer telling ourselves lies—we are stripped bare and vulnerable. We have dropped our mask of social conditioning, which becomes for many of us a kind of cultural hypnosis, keeping us from waking to our true human potential. In yoga this hypnosis is called maya, or illusion.

Vishuddha wishes us to use our abilities, our voice, to give praise. Prayer is more than simply a request for your god to fulfill. It is communication between your soul and the unified field of consciousness that includes every other human, animal and the planet itself. Prayers are thought-forms that convey information to presences in Nature and other worlds. When the Throat Chakra is active and we express ourselves through it in prayer, word or song, we are naturally in praise of all the forces of creation.

We can all be drawn down into a state of inertia by our everyday lives. But the teachings of Vishuddha urge us to let our light shine, our voices ring out with Truth and Love, for when we have integrated these teachings into our lives we have only two more major chakras to integrate.

An affirmation is a repeated sentence that reminds us of our spiritual path. The Vishuddha affirmation is:

I will express my higher wisdom to others.

When Vishuddha is fully activated, the elementals of Nature can be understood.

vishuddha yantra

*In the throat is the Lotus called
Vishuddha, which is pure. This is the
gateway of great liberation for him
who desires the wealth of Yoga and
whose senses are pure and controlled.
He sees past, present and future and
becomes the benefactor of all, free
from disease and sorrow and
long-lived.*

Sat Cakra Nirupana

description of the yantra
Number of petals Sixteen.
Color Blue-gray.
Silver crescent Symbol of the cosmic sound, nadam, which represents purity.
Triangle a downward-pointing triangle, or akasamandala.
White circle represents full Moon, our psychic powers and the element Ether.
White elephant The animal guardian, AIravata, who carries the sound mantra. Associated with the god Indra. Airavata has no restraining collar—he is servitude transformed into service.

the bija mantra
Inside the akasamandala is a white circle containing the bija mantra (see pages 80–81), HAM. When this is sounded, it vibrates and energizes the brain and throat, bringing sweetness and harmony to the voice.

yantra meditation to explore desire
A fitting focus for a meditation on this yantra, to assist you to move from the state of maya/illusion (see pages 240–241), is "desire"—exploring not only *why* you may want something, but the whole concept of desire itself. There are no specific instructions other than to meditate in *stillness*. The whole point of yantras is to make the mind completely still: to have no dialogue with yourself, no thoughts, only concentration on the symbol itself (not even on the meaning of the symbol). It is pure meditation and not a kind of visualization. You can only experience meditation and stillness.

deities associated with vishuddha

sadasiva

In Hindu teachings Sadasiva is half-woman, half-man: Sakti and Shiva combined. Sadasiva represents the reconciliation of masculine and feminine aspects of our nature in order to evolve. Sadasiva has five faces, representing the five senses, each with three eyes. This god makes the fear-dispelling mudra (hand gesture) and carries nine symbolic items:

- **The noose** representing the danger of being caught up in spiritual pride

- **The goad** (a sharp, pointed stick) signifying the need to make further effort
- **The great snake** signifying wisdom
- **A trident** representing unity of the physical, etheric and causal bodies
- **A flame** for the fires of kundalini energy
- **A bell** for the quality of inner healing
- **A diamond sceptre** for indestructibility
- **A sword**: for need to learn discrimination
- **A battleaxe** for cutting away old aspects of the self.

sakini

Sadasiva's female aspect and consort is the goddess Sakini, who is described as Light itself. This goddess is an aspect of Gauri, the mother of the universe. She has the power to bestow psychic powers and can communicate with us through the medium of our dreams. She is usually depicted seated on a red lotus flower dressed in yellow. She has five faces, each with two eyes plus an awakened Third Eye Chakra.

She has four arms and carries a book for wisdom, a goad for control and a noose for intellectual power. Her fourth hand makes the sacred Inana-mudra over her heart.

crystals to activate vishuddha

Recommended gemstone crystals for activating the Throat Chakra are blue and yellow topaz, each of which are used in slightly different ways for activation.

blue topaz

This is an excellent crystal to use when you are ready to activate Vishuddha for deeper spiritual work, or for activation before sacred singing or performing with the voice. Its main purpose is to direct energy, thus aligning the body's meridians. For this reason you can use it sensitively when channeling beneficial entities or Nature spirits, or when you are passing Reiki energy (see pages 60–63) through the body during initiations. It can either be held or worn as jewelery close to the neck.

yellow topaz

Use this crystal to activate Vishuddha at a physical level. The energy imbalance that causes hypothyroidism can be "kick-started" into balance by yellow topaz. It is said to strengthen our nervous system and, through working intensely with Vishuddha, will aid our entire metabolism.

Blue topaz (left) and yellow topaz (above) activate Vishuddha in different ways.

using topaz to activate vishuddha

You can use either blue or yellow topaz for this exercise. You will need three small uncut topazes and two quartz crystal "points," 1–2 in. (2.5–5 cm) in length.

1 Cleanse the crystals (see page 68) and prepare your healing space by burning some incense or joss-sticks. You can use a special feather fan if you wish to move the smoke into all corners of the room, then let the smoke drift out of an open window. When you cleanse a room in this way, the smoke bonds with the positive ions in the air that are harmful to us, leaving behind beneficial negative ions. Native Americans developed this cleansing—sometimes called "smudging"—using sage, cedarwood or sweet scented grass. Those with psychic vision can see that a person's aura is cleared when using fragrant smoke. For auric clearing it is recommended that you start at the head and sweep unwanted energies down the body with the smoke, enabling them to be grounded into Mother Earth.

Using quartz crystals with topaz can help to activate Vishuddha.

2 Now lie down on the floor and hold the quartz crystals, one in the center of each palm, with the points pointing up your arm.

3 Place the three topazes as follows: one in the central notch on your collar bone and one on either side of your neck, pointing inward.

4 Relax for 30 minutes and enjoy your healing session with these crystals.

crystals to calm vishuddha

Sapphire and emerald are excellent gemstones to calm any of the chakras. All semi-precious gemstones give a high-quality healing vibration that is concentrated and more powerful than that of less precious stones. This is the reason why crystal healers choose to use them rather than the more common tumble-polished stones.

If you study a crystal by holding it up to the light, you may see many hidden colors. When the crystal is placed on the body, the colors draw to themselves that which is no longer needed and give the body the vibration it requires, because of the interference pattern that is made by the crystalline structural matrix over the body's field. This is true both of opaque colored stones and of clear crystals.

Although mineralogists will affirm that there are many reasons for a stone to appear colored, we can generally assume that its color is a reflection of the mineral content within its structure, or the way light passes through its crystalline matrix. This color is perceived as a vibrational message by our subtle color awareness at the deepest cellular level. This message enables the release and rebalancing of the whole body.

the throat chakra: vishuddha

Many prefer to use natural uncut crystals like this sapphire (left) and emerald (above).

A clear quartz "point" for healing and a rose quartz tumble-polished stone.

quartz

With quartz the situation is rather different, for the quartz crystal is constantly passing light through it, bending the light at 90 degrees as it exits the crystal. This allows full-spectrum light to be transmitted to the body area on which it is placed, enabling the body to draw from it the specific frequencies and harmonics that it requires. For this reason many crystal healers use only clear quartz. Quartz also displays rainbows of colored light within it if its structure allows the rays of light to be diffracted by imperfections.

gem elixir to calm the throat chakra

An excellent way to calm Vishuddha is to make a gem elixir (see pages 152–153) from sapphire or emerald. To potentize it still further, place a number of quartz points around the container, pointing inward. If you are unable to obtain sapphire or emerald, then the energies of rose quartz will assist in bringing loving energies and calmness into any chakra.

crystals to balance vishuddha

For thousands of years Native American peoples, particularly those of the south-west states where the Hopi people live, have revered crystals. They have a particular affinity with turquoise and instinctively fashioned this soft, easily carved stone into amazing jewelery. They found that when they combined it with silver, lunar energies were increased; when they used it with gold, solar energies were conducted and directed.

turquoise, gem silica and chrysocolla

Turquoise is regarded as the "stone of the sky"; it is not really a crystal, but is more amorphous in nature. It offers the wearer protection from radiation, particularly when worn around the throat. Amazingly, many Native Americans instinctively knew that the effects of high background radiation from uranium deposits under their lands would be neutralized in their bodies by wearing turquoise stones against the skin.

Today gem silica and chrysocolla are taking the place of turquoise. You can use chrysocolla for dispelling fears, and gem silica makes an excellent calming and balancing stone for Vishuddha. All three stones are very soft and must not be used for making gem elixirs—far better to enjoy them as jewelery, or as healing stones in their own right.

The amazing clarity of intention with which turquoise stones have evolved helps us to visualize the color turquoise, which we

Try to obtain natural (not reconstituted powder) turquoise in either polished or rough form as shown here.

Chrysocolla aligns and balances the chakras and helps to dispel fears.

should see as a clear light bathing us from above being drawn into our Throat Chakra, both at the front and back of the neck. The technique for doing this is called color breathing.

color breathing

This technique is really very simple. You only have to visualize an appropriate color for each chakra—in this case turquoise for the throat—and feel that you can saturate your breath with that color. Imagine it being drawn in through your nostrils, passing down your neck and throat into your lungs and chest. When you release your breath, imagine the color taking away with it any unwanted stagnant energies that cause disease.

The color blue, when given as light therapy, has been proven to be antiseptic and analgesic in nature. It reduces inflammation and helps congeal the blood. The blue/green color of turquoise, when given as light therapy, is most appropriate to calm throat and heart conditions.

aromatherapy and vishuddha

Of the many plants, herbs and flower essences suitable for use on Vishuddha, chickweed and cleavers are best used as the dried or fresh herb or in tinctures—they are generally cleansing to the body. Grapefruit as an extract helps weight loss, strengthens the immune system and is a cleansing tonic after illness. Magnolia-bark

THROAT CHAKRA ESSENTIAL OILS

The main essential oils that have a sympathetic resonance with Vishuddha are:

- **Lavender** This is one of the safest and most versatile essential oils. It is excellent in the bath (use 5 drops), in a vaporizer (burner), or as 2 drops on a handkerchief. It is the number-one choice in a home first-aid kit for insect bites, migraine, nausea, minor burns, stings, sunburn, small cuts, chilblains, eczema and panic attacks. Lavender is analgesic, anti-depressant, antiseptic, anti-viral, decongestant, deodorant, emmenagogic and sedative.

- **Chamomile** This refers to Roman chamomile (*Anthemis nobilis*), not

German chamomile. It is the best essential oil to calm the Throat Chakra, but do not use it if you need to drive a car afterward, for it can make you feel very "spaced out." For most uses, mix 2 drops of the essential oil with 5 ml of base oil. In a vaporizer, chamomile is excellent to ease headaches caused by overwork or stress. It is analgesic, antiseptic, anti-spasmodic, carminative, digestive, diuretic, emmenagogic and sedative.

- **Rosemary/thyme/sage** These three herbs, alone or in combination, make good steam inhalations. However, they are not recommended for use in home aromatherapy blends, and should not be used at all if you are pregnant.

tea can assist meditation on past lives, as well as harmonizing the Heart and Throat Chakras. Marshmallow softens negative traits associated with Vishuddha. And willow flower enables the release of old pains and sadness.

Fresh herbs, such as lavender (below, left), chamomile (below, center) and rosemary (below, right), make excellent hot tea infusions or inhalations.

making a steam inhalation

This type of inhalation is excellent for nasal blockages, sinus infections, coughs, colds and sore throats, all of which demonstrate that the Throat Chakra is struggling to keep minor infections at bay.

1 Boil 1¾ pint (1 liter) of water and pour it into a bowl.
2 Add 10 drops of essential oil (or the fresh herb steeped in water).
3 Put a towel over your head, close your eyes and inhale the vapor for a few minutes at a time, for up to 10 minutes.

253

aromatherapy and vishuddha

sound and vishuddha

The Throat Chakra is associated very powerfully with sound: the vibrations of our voices cause its molecular structures to change and rearrange themselves into patterns of harmony.

toning

Toning is a new technique, but the concept is as old as humanity. When we enter fully into toning, it is actually the sound of our soul listening to the music of the Celestial Spheres. Toning helps to balance health, chakras and energy fields—for you, animals, plants, groups as well as organizations. It enables a natural flow of prana through the body, stimulating cells and removing obstructions within acupuncture meridians and chakra systems. It brings the body into wholeness and is valuable to shift old patterns held at cellular levels, which are blocking spiritual growth.

Toning clears the energy field at many levels: on the physical level, in our cells and body organs; on the emotional level, where repetitive patterns disempower us; on the mental level, which can become polluted with dark clouds of negative energy; and on the spiritual level, which is striving to integrate higher dimensional energy.

how to tone

Toning is *not* chanting or singing, and does not have a coherent meaning, because you are randomly intuiting what sounds to make. It relies primarily on making vowel-like sounds with a nasal emphasis. First practice some deep breathing, then begin.

1 Sit comfortably on the floor or chair. Breathing out, push your tongue against the roof of your mouth, keeping it behind your front teeth.

2 Direct the outflow of breath through your nasal passages, and at the same time make a "mmmm" humming noise.

3 When you have got the hang of that, try making any of the vowel sounds—a, e, i, o, u—in turn, together with "mmmm."

4 Move your mouth into different exaggerated shapes and have fun.

5 Explore free expression, and don't let your mind tell you what you should be doing. Move your body and hands as you practice—don't become too rigid.

Regular toning releases tension in the throat and Throat Chakra. Musically speaking, the sounds that are produced are enriched with harmonics that are heard as several sounds at the same time, as multiples of the fundamental note. Sometimes they are high trilling notes and at other times very low notes, because of sound waves traveling at different frequencies and intensity.

mantras

A mantra is defined as poetic hymn, incantation or prayer repeated many times, either silently or out loud. More specifically, a mantra from a lineage such as Tibetan Buddhism or Zen consists of a few words that may or may not have a translatable meaning to the user, whereas a mantric chant is usually a repeated short phrase with a deep meaning. When used in spiritual ceremony or rituals (both personal and collective), mantras have the capacity to alter brainwave levels so that a person reaches into deep realizations and an altered state of consciousness.

using a mantra to benefit vishuddha

To chant a single-vowel mantra for the Throat Chakra, use "EYE," pronounced as in the English word "I." Modern single-vowel audible mantras (which are different from traditional bija mantras) for the other chakras are: Base: UH; Sacral: OOO; Solar Plexus: OH; Heart: AH; Brow: AYE; Crown: EEE.

1 Find a place where you will not be distracted by voices or other noises. Sit motionless and poised.
2 Breathe quietly and rhythmically through your nostrils, and send energy down into the abdomen (complete yogic breath).
3 Begin to tone a soft and gentle "EYE" *out loud*, benefiting the throat region and its chakra. Maintain a relaxed and passive attitude toward anything that tries to distract you.

In Tibetan Buddhism, chanting a mantra can lead into an altered state of consciousness.

MANTRAS FROM DIFFERENT TRADITIONS

Source	Mantra	Meaning
Buddhist	Bhagavan Sarva Tathagartha Om Mani Padmi Hum	Blest be all ye Buddhas Hail to the jewel in the lotus
Sikh	Eck Ong Kar Sat Nam Siri Wha Guru	The supreme is one, his names are many
Hindu	Hare Rama Shanti Shanti Om Namah Sivaya Om	Hail to Rama Peace, peace Reverence to Shiva
Islamic	La Ilaha Illa'hah Ya—Salaam An—Nur	There is no god but one God God the source of peace God the light
Jewish	Ehyeh Asher Ehyeh Eli, Eli, Elu	I am that I am My God, my God, my God
Christian	Allelula Ave Maria En moi Christus	Praise the Lord Hail Mary Christ in me
Sai Baba	Satya Dharma Shanti Prema	Truth, the Path, Peace, Love
Sufi	Hu E—haiy Hu—La	God the Living The word is the mirror wherein the Divine reverberates outwardly

yoga asanas for vishuddha

active: dhanurasana or (bow pose)

Dhanurasana benefits the abdominal area, since in the completed full posture only the abdomen bears the weight of the body. It is also good for the back, bladder and prostate gland. Your breathing will be fast, and from an energetic-flow viewpoint this posture benefits the Throat Chakra. It is common for rising pranic energy to become blocked at the throat, and this asana opens Vishuddha, moving energy up from the abdominal region, thus allowing the release of toxins on all levels. The state of consciousness you are seeking is an objective mental state known as anandamayakosha (the Body of Bliss). Visualize your incoming and outgoing breath as a beautiful turquoise blue light. Picture 1 shows a beginners asana.

1

1 Lie on your front, with your face down. Reach back, bending your knees and holding your ankles. Keep your knees together throughout the asana.

2 Pulling on your ankles, slowly and cautiously raise your trunk and legs as high as possible. Stretch your neck. Hold the position.

2

active: simhasana 1 (lion pose)

Despite its strange appearance, this pose needs to be performed with enthusiasm, but without straining. It helps you to learn the three bandhas that control the flow of prana in the physical body, and your speech becomes clearer, too.

This asana is dedicated to Narasimha, the lion-man incarnation of Vishnu (Nara meaning man, and simha meaning lion). Narasimha was a fierce creature who, when called upon, burst out of a pillar in the palace of the evil demon king Hiranya Kasipu, and rescued his pious son Prahlado who was a strong devotee of Vishnu.

1 Either kneel normally or kneel with your knees crossed over (similar to Gomukasana, see page 190). Stretch your trunk forward, keep your chest open and your back erect. Place your right palm on the right knee and your left palm on the left knee, then straighten your arms and make your fingers into extended "claws."

2 Open your jaw wide and stretch your tongue as far as possible toward your chin. Roll your eyes up and gaze toward the center of your eyebrows. Stay in this posture for about 30 seconds, breathing through your mouth. Repeat with your knees crossed on the other side, if applicable.

yoga asanas for vishuddha

2

passive: paschimottanasana (sitting forward bend)

The physical benefits of this pose are similar to those of Janusirasana (see page 226): stretching the backs of the leg muscles and loosening the hip joints, toning the abdominal organs and stretching the spine throughout its entire length. Energy-wise, this asana encourages the upward and downward flow of prana throughout the chakra system toward the Throat Chakra. Visualize the appropriate yantra as you perform it.

1 Sit on the floor with your legs stretched straight. Place your palms on the floor by the side of your hips. Exhaling, stretch over your legs, bending from the pelvic region. Hold either your ankles or your big toes (whichever you can reach comfortably).

2 Aim to get the back flat but do not overdo the stretch. *When you are a beginner at yoga, it is far better to stretch in the general direction of any asana than force the position.*

3 With practice you may be able to stretch right over your legs and touch your knees with your nose!

1

2

3

Chapter 7

THE BROW CHAKRA: AJNA

● ● ● ● ● ● ●

ajna chakra

The Brow Chakra or Ajna is also known as the Third Eye Chakra, the Eye of Shiva, ajita-patra, ajna-pura, jnana-padma, dwidala, bhru chakra and bhruyugamadhyabila. It is linked externally to the physical body just between (and slightly above) the level of the eyebrows.

The word Ajna means "servant" or "command"—in the sense of the Guru's command of spiritual guidance. It is referred to as the "ocean of nectar," the life-sustaining liquid that arises in the mouth of a yogi when he reaches a state of enlightenment. Ajna is depicted with two petals, representing the two aspects of prana that meet here. Its element is Ether.

the functions of ajna

In Tantric yoga, the Brow Chakra is associated with "manas" or mind, which is beyond even the most subtle elements, although still part of our existence in an Earthly body. In recent Western occult and New Age thought, Ajna has been identified with the "Third Eye"—our eye of psychic vision, a concept not found in the original Tantric system. When we fully associate ourselves with the power contained within Ajna we are able to step beyond the mind, with all its desires and longings, and enter the realms of knowledge and wisdom. However, if this chakra is blocked, we will confuse information with knowledge; or get carried away with our own powers of insight and use them for our own means or spiritual arrogance.

additional chakras associated with ajna

Ajna is often described as having at least four distinct minor (but important) chakras in a vertical line above it: the Manas, Indu, Mahanada and Nirvana chakras, the last-named being at the top of the head. All combine their energies and resonate with one another to form the Ajna, "Third Eye" or Eye of Shiva. Another minor chakra, the Soma, contains a triangulation of energy coming from the three main nadis (sushumna, ida and pingala), which combine to make the trinity of Brahma the creator, Vishnu the preserver and Shiva the destroyer (see pages 82–83).

MAIN CHARACTERISTICS AT A GLANCE

Color	White or deep blue
Key issues	Balancing the higher/lower selves and trusting inner guidance
Physical location	The center of the brow
Associated spinal area	First cervical vertebra
Physiological system	Endocrine and nervous
Endocrine gland	Pineal and pituitary
Nerve plexus	Hypothalamus
Inner aspect	Intuition
Emotional action	Clarity
Spiritual action	Meditation

ajna chakra

health issues and ajna

Darwinian theorists claim that the Third Eye is a remainder from a reptilian stage of human evolution, but it may actually have been the primary "eye" to form within our brain and should in fact be called the First Eye!

associated body system

Physical issues associated with Ajna are headaches and problems within the skull generally, including the eyes and ears. If you are continually stressed or experiencing headaches, part of the solution is to give attention to the Brow Chakra. Perhaps you are not nourishing her enough with meditation and visualization in quiet times, and must learn, for the sake of your own health, to switch off completely from this noisy modern world. If you sit in front of a computer screen for too long, the photo-receptors in your eyes become stressed—and headaches result. To counter this, visualization with the color green (as the light seen through trees), or taking a regular break from your computer and simply looking at some grass or vegetation outside, will relax your eyes, helping to keep your energy levels up and your health good, since the world of Nature benefits your whole complex.

associated endocrine gland

Ajna is linked with the pituitary gland (see pages 270–271) and energetically with the pineal gland. The pineal resembles a tiny pine cone, in the center of the brain directly behind the eyes. Research indicates that the pineal may be photo-receptive and able to sense light directly, because scientists have realized that it has a similar structure to the retina of the eye. A number of reptiles (especially small lizards) have a pineal gland that receives information from a rudimentary Third Eye with a lens, and similar photo-receptors to eye retinas. It is believed this enables them to see in ranges of light that are not normally possible for humans—such as infrared and ultraviolet (UV).

The pineal gland also secretes melanin and seratonin, which come into play when visualizing or relaxing prior to meditation. Our pineal gland is stimulated by a whole range of electromagnetic energy around us; far from being a degenerate gland, as was once thought, it is self-activating as ultraviolet light radiation surges toward Earth in the cosmic winds. By penetrating the decreasing ozone layer around our planet, UV light is beginning to have a profound effect on the raising of human consciousness.

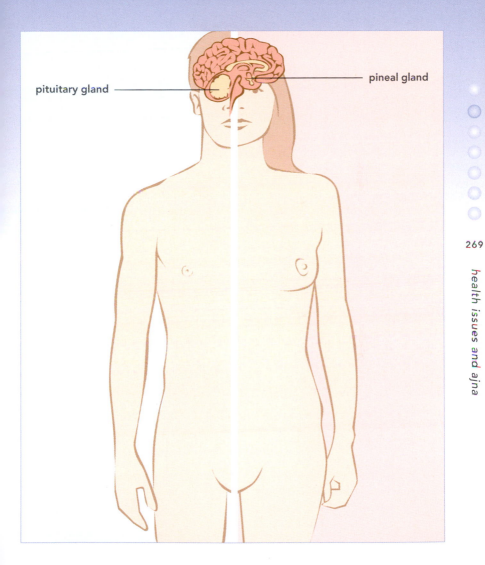

pituitary gland

pineal gland

endocrine imbalances associated with ajna

As we look deeper at endocrine system and hormonal functions from a metaphysical viewpoint, we first need to understand some basics. All the endocrine glands act together, usually orchestrated by the pituitary gland. And in general they malfunction in two different ways: either they produce too few hormones or too many. Balance can be restored by the pituitary gland, which is associated with the Brow Chakra.

Endocrine imbalances associated with maladjusted Ajna energies are:

- **Hyperthyroidism** (increased secretion of thyroxine) and **thyrotoxicosis** (usually caused by excessive amounts of a thyroid-stimulating hormone in the pituitary gland): Rest is prescribed and the condition of the thyroid is balanced with drugs. Natural remedies to take alongside medical supervision are the sea vegetable kelp, onion juice, cabbage, cress and spinach (note that these vegetables are of a balancing green color).

- **Hypothyroidism** (thyroid deficiency): This can stunt growth in babies and young children; myxoedema is thyroid deficiency in adults. In combination with medical treatment, kelp and a mineral supplement containing manganese should be taken. On an esoteric level, subtle energies should be improved around the throat and head in order to stimulate these higher chakras and thus the hormonal balance. This can be done with light or color treatments and crystals (if given by a trained healer).

- **Sleep disorders:** These are connected to melatonin/seratonin output and the way we respond to light. It is recommended that Ajna and Sahasrara (the Crown Chakra) are balanced by a healer, rather than attempting to do this yourself. You can go a long way to help yourself, though, by learning a relaxation technique such as that shown on pages 44–45. Deep relaxation for around an hour can be as beneficial to your body as a whole night of disturbed sleep.

seratonin

Seratonin levels affect the regulation of mood, sleep, sexuality, menstrual cycles and appetite, and play a role in many disorders, notably depression, anxiety and migraine. When natural light is diminished, your body converts the brain chemical seratonin into melatonin. It is detrimental to your body clock to sleep in a partially lit room, party the night away or frequently take long-haul flights. The extent to which you risk long-

Imbalances in Ajna energies can lead to seratonin depletion and sleep disorders.

term health problems is aggravated by living or working under artificial lights that do not have a full daylight spectrum. Winter depression, also known as Seasonal Affective Disorder (SAD), responds well to full-spectrum light treatment to boost seratonin levels.

psychic skills and ajna

Esotericists claim that, when activated with Divine Light, the pineal gland links to the pituitary gland, becoming a communication channel with the higher spiritual planes and enabling an exchange of information. They say that the Crown Chakra increases in size and strength, and the center point of its vortex of energy reaches down to the pineal gland. As this occurs, a burst of pure pranic energy is received. When the Crown Chakra is activated in this way, vibrationary levels throughout our auric fields become highly charged with Light. Some believe that if the Light vibrations of the astral body are speeded up sufficiently, it will be able to separate from the physical body, leading to astral travel.

To be able to astral travel, the Ajna (Third Eye), pineal and pituitary must first all be activated and vibrate in unison. This is done through deep meditation. This is the safest way to develop many special psychic abilities (sometimes called "occult"), including astral travel, extra-sensory perception, clairvoyance and clairaudience. It helps to develop skills with a group of people who will support your endeavors and enable you to share queries, although don't discuss of inner experiences, since they are for you alone to understand.

clairaudience

Clairaudience means hearing beyond your normal range, as your hearing becomes more acutely tuned. Did you know that you hear with the whole of your body as well as your ears? Play some enjoyable music and practice this: feel where—or which chakra—resonates with different beats or musical instruments. At times your hearing may pick up high frequencies from the world of animals and insects, or very low frequencies such as the deep Earth moan of a distant earthquake. The practice of "channeling" beneficent entities that may want to transmit a personal or global message is closely linked to clairaudience. In shamanic terms, these are a person's "guides."

When endeavoring to awaken spiritual skills, it is important not to rush the process. If you do not approach activation in the right way, powerful interacting forces within your head may give you headaches, earache, migraine or other deeply embedded problems of a mental nature. If you approach it in traditional ways—receiving

Society and culture benefit from development of positive psychic skills.

personal tuition from an enlightened being, a guru or teacher—the positive and negative forces interact together in a more focused manner. When combined into one "beam" of super-consciousness, they become strong enough to create a sublime experience of Divine Light in the head. With this Light you can project yourself away from your body, carry the Light with you and have the strength of Light to return to your physical body.

273

the power of the siddhis

There are many tantalizing powers, or siddhis, to be gained through yogic development. With practice you may even be able to learn how to separate from your physical form. But unless your life is dedicated to working with spiritual energy in a profound way, this should not be attempted. What *is* important is to develop your Third Eye in the realm of dreams, imagination and visualization. This is a vital step on the path to enlightenment. Intuition, prophecy, precognition, the ability to receive channeled messages and express them through Vishuddha and Anahata are among the more accessible ways that you can learn to reach states of super-consciousness.

the power of the imagination

Learn to honor your intuition and respect any flashes of insight (sometimes termed "second sight") that you may be blessed with. Don't say, "I only imagined it." Your imagination is powerful; it can create worlds; as the old adage says, "As you think, so you become." Realize that unless you respect your intuition by dedication to your spiritual path, you will block the workings of Ajna, which in turn will block the entry of UV light and its counterpart, Divine Light. Not only will your own path be slow, but since all is connected, it will slow the progress of other sentient beings as we progress in our development on Earth into Beings of Light in physically visible bodies. We each make a difference to the Divine "plan."

From a yogic perspective, as the pineal gland starts to resonate with Divine Light, our kundalini serpent power begins its spiralling ascent from the base toward the head chakras. Spiritual science states that this Divine Light is gathered together at the top of our sutratma—a kind of light conduit, or "soul thread," which passes down from the highest (fastest vibrational) part of our auric field into our physical body.

It is when we do not honor our spiritual nature that problems arise, energy radiance becomes blocked and illness manifests in the physical body. In connection with Ajna, we could then expect eye, nose, ear or brain disorders. Frequent headaches or migraine, can be caused by energy blocking something you need to see or hear, or is important for your soul development.

This Indian goddess statue shows a developed Third Eye, which is vital to enlightenment.

candle meditation to awaken inner sight

the brow chakra: ajna

This is a yogic technique, primarily to open you to the radiance of the "Light in the head." Along the way you can use it as a preliminary discipline in order to develop astral travel and other occult abilities, such as seeing auric fields. Without straining the muscles of your eyes, you will activate the pineal gland and the Third Eye.

276

1 Place a lit candle approximately 3¼ ft. (1 m) in front of you. You need to be in a room that is as dark as possible.

2 Relax and sit comfortably, either in the lotus position on the floor or in a chair.

3 As with all deep meditation, begin to withdraw from the peripheral senses of sight, sound, touch, smell and physical consciousness. Draw your attention into the center of your head, which is the region of the pineal gland. Your deeper psychic perceptive faculties and point of spiritual realization are focused centrally in the area between the middle of your forehead and the pineal gland.

4 With your eyes open and a soft gaze, look straight at the candle flame. Keep your eyes focused upon it and blink only if necessary.

5 When you do need to close your eyes, turn them upward to the position of the Brow Chakra in the center. You will see an image of the flame there on your "inner screen," and probably many colors.

6 Visualize the flame very intently, drawing it back if it starts to fade. Try to hold the image for as long as possible, then breathe deeply, open your eyes and bring yourself back to everyday reality.

Note: Only advanced meditators, or those under guidance from a spiritual mentor, should attempt to separate the astral from the physical body.

candle meditation to awaken inner sight

sensing energies

The rocks and crystals that occur naturally in any area are what give that place its particular essence, affecting people, plants and animals. They are part of what is termed the Spirit of the Land—the energies we pick up when we get our first impressions of a place.

Throughout the ages such energies have been given form and have appeared as fairies, little people or landscape "devas" (spiritual Earth guardians). All these are connected with the element of Earth. The element of Water is the domain of spirits called undines; the element of Air of the sylphs; within Fire, the spirits are known as salamanders. These are all types of energy that you can train yourself to see. Often you do not spot the energy taking actual form— instead it is a quickly moving bright light, or you simply sense that something is there.

how to sense auras by dowsing

Practice the following aura sensing until you get consistent results. (It helps if you fully detach yourself and have no expectations.)

1 Make two L-shaped rods from a bent piece of metal wire about 12 in. (30 cm) long—wire from a coat hanger is ideal.

2 Hold one of these rods in each hand, by the shorter piece.
3 Ask a friend to stand in front of you, not less than 16 ft. (5 m) away. Say, "Show me the edge of my friend's auric field."
4 Walk slowly toward your friend, with the rods horizontal and pointing in your friend's direction. When you reach the edge of their auric field, the rods will react, moving in or out in some way.

how to send energy to a friend

This is a simple but powerful way to begin to feel subtle body energy.

1 Sit opposite a friend.
2 Hold the palms of your hands toward each other, about 4 in. (10 cm) apart.
3 Decide who will be the "giver" and who will be the "receiver." Both of you must then close your eyes and concentrate. If you are the giver, ask to send energy as a golden healing light from the Center Chakra in the palms of your hands into your friend's hands and body. They should be able to feel this as a movement of energy—perhaps a pushing, pulling or tingling.

4 Change over, so that your friend sends golden healing energy to you.

5 When you have finished, shake your hands and then wash them in cold water to remove each other's energy.

Dowsing rods held in your hands will react when they sense the edge of your friend's aura.

seeing energies

The exercise below is excellent training to enable you physically to see energies such as spinning chakras or auric emanations. You must have a firm belief in your abilities in order to do so—do not doubt them, or you will place blockages on yourself. If nothing is happening, don't say, "I can't do it," but "I will be able to do it another day." Remember that children, living in a play-world of fantasy, are much more accepting of other energies than most adults, so we need to take time in our busy lives to relax and play more. If you have children, encourage them to use their imagination— let them have imaginary friends and talk to fairies. You will often find that small children can naturally see auras or lights around people.

Although some people have had the ability to see energies since birth, others have to practice hard to develop it. Seeing and sensing energies form part of a professional spiritual healer's training, as well as a shamanic skill.

exercise to see the energies of a tree

Perhaps the simplest way to see energies initially is around a tree.

1   In natural surroundings, find a tree that is silhouetted against the sky, some distance away from you. You can do this during the daytime, in sunlight, in moonlight or at dusk.
2   Ask to see the tree's energies—this "asking" is important.
3   Look toward, but past, the tree into the far distance and eventually you will spot the tree's energy field. Sometimes a big old tree has a huge aura, which may be visible as a kind of vapor, as a movement of swirling light or as a glowing light around the tree's silhouette.

"Tune in" and ask to see the tree's energies— you might be pleasantly surprised!

the brow chakra: ajna

ajna yantra

Ajna is like the moon, beautifully white. It shines with the glory of meditation. Within this lotus dwells the subtle mind. When the yogi… becomes dissolved in this place, which is the abode of uninterrupted bliss, he then sees sparks of fire distinctly shining.

Sat Cakra Nirupana

description of the yantra

Number of petals Ninety-six—depicted as having two, which overlap forty-eight on either side. The two petals symbolize the meeting of the energies of the secondary ida and pingala nadis (see pages 22–23) before ascending to Sahasrara Chakra and represent the duality that is present in all things.

Color White or deep blue.

Mantras The mantra "Hang," representing Shiva, is on one side. "Ksham," representing Shakti, is on the other side. Together they form the phrase "I am that I am."

White circle Represents the void.

Downward-pointing triangle contains the mantra OM and a lingam.

Linga itara Residence of the granthis (or blocks) of Rudra, which must be dissolved if we are to sustain the insights that we have achieved so far through the rising of kundalini energy.

Quarter moon Shown on the yantra, this indicates a vortex of energy.

Bindu The dot symbolizes complete detachment from our female or male body. Showing control of the body, it has managed to rise above the triangle that represents sexual energy in an "impure" state.

the bija mantra

Ajna has no true bija mantra, but you may use OM/AUM (see pages 78–79), which is placed within the triangle in the center circle. The sounding of this connects us to the primal cosmic sound itself.

Intense concentration on Ajna yantra with OM will open the "Third Eye" and higher senses; physically the right and left hemispheres of the brain merge and symbolically the marriage of Sun and Moon, mind and body, takes place.

deities associated with ajna

shiva

Shiva is the destroyer (see also pages 80–81) and is represented at the center of Ajna by an inverted triangle, which is symbolic of the trinity of the godhead, and of the supreme level that we can attain in our lives on Earth. This trinity is Sat, Chit, Ananda—or reality, consciousness and joy. Shiva is sometimes shown symbolically as a white lingam (penis), within the golden triangle of the yoni (female sexuality), indicating divine sexual bliss. At other times he is depicted in the traditional lotus pose in his embodiment of Kameshvara, the most beautiful male, with snakes around his neck, his blue body resting on a staff and his Third Eye open.

Often as Kameshvara, he is shown embracing his beloved Kameshvari, the most beautiful goddess, who usually resides in the Base Chakra as kundalini energy, but has now risen through the chakras to meet him.

shakti hakini

Shakti Hakini is usually shown as moon-white or a mixture of white, black and red. She has numerous faces (sometimes as many as six), which are three-eyed. She normally has six arms and holds a book, a skull, a drum and a rudraksha rosary. The skull reminds us that we have many lives on Earth, but they all pass away and what we are left with is our Divine self. The small two-ended drum that she holds symbolizes Time. Shakti Hakini makes the gestures of granting boons and dispelling fear. Hakini is normally clad in red raiment with a white upper garment, and is seated on a white lotus. Her minds are purified by drinking the Divine "nectar."

crystals to activate ajna

Perhaps you would like to develop your intuitional powers, your insight, imagination and clairvoyance? Then Ajna is the chakra to work with—provided the lower chakras are already in balance. It really is not beneficial to have a highly developed Third Eye if you have not yet come to grips with the basic life functions that manifest through the Base Chakra, for example.

diamonds

These beautiful precious gemstones need no introduction. However, they assist us to move into deeper levels. They are one of the finest examples of the crystal world gifted to us from Mother Nature, displaying all her beauty and timelessness.

If we wear diamonds as jewelery, their power enlarges and strengthens our energy field—whether we are a calm, happy person or a sad one. Whatever our emotions, they will be amplified in the astral/emotional levels of the aura; and whatever our mental processes, they will be amplified in the mental level. When we choose to wear diamonds for meditation, we amplify our aura in the areas where potent spiritual essences lie, around our spiritual and causal bodies.

Diamonds, whether uncut (left) or cut and faceted (above), symbolize timeless beauty.

herkimer diamond

If you are unable to use diamonds for your healing work, then a lovely, naturally faceted crystal (a type of quartz) is Herkimer diamond. "Herkies" are clear and very hard—almost as hard as diamonds—and they are nearly always double-terminated (with points at both ends).

using a herkie for activation

Only attempt to activate the Brow Chakra on yourself—do not do this to others unless you are a trained healer.

1 Rub your Third Eye area briskly.
2 Lie down, placing a Herkie on the Third Eye and relax. If you are ready for it, the crystal may assist in bringing you visions or guidance.

For any deep spiritual work, it is always best to have a clear intention of what you are seeking, and to form that intention in your mind. When that intention is clear, bright and shining (just like a diamond), you may be rewarded with extraordinary levels of perception. This activation can be made more powerful by resting Herkies on either side of your head, level with your temples. The temples are minor chakras—indeed,

Herkimer protects from geopathic stress, balances energetic cellular disorders and helps to access past-life memories.

they function as temples in our head, standing one on each side of the skull ready to receive offerings, with Vishuddha calling from below and Sahasrara, the Crown Chakra, beckoning from above.

crystals to calm ajna

We need to look at why you might want to calm Ajna. Perhaps you have constant headaches brought on by a stressful lifestyle; or cannot come to terms with new ideas that throw your comfortable views of life into disarray. You might also have too much information of a psychic nature coming into your Brow Chakra and feel unable to handle it. Equally, your Ajna "letter box" may have its entry sealed with a "Not in use" sign.

However, calming does not necessarily mean suppressing anything of a spiritual nature, and perhaps you are meant to be opening up to bigger possibilities. Try to keep an open mind about people and events, and to place judgements on hold. Calming Ajna makes for a harmonious flow of radiance into *whatever* you choose to do that is of a higher nature.

Perhaps you cannot sleep well. Ask yourself how much sleep you really need. The problem could simply be a physical one (too much to eat or drink late at night), or perhaps you do not want to acknowledge your dream worlds. Denying our dreams makes us sterile, uninteresting individuals. We are unable to project a visionary passion about anything, and start to wither away because our imagination and insight atrophy. Our letter box has been sealed.

Sapphire and emerald are the calming stones for Ajna.

Cut and faceted emeralds and uncut cloudy pieces can help to calm Ajna while you sleep.

emerald

Emerald calms Ajna because of its color vibration. When you go to sleep, tape a small piece of emerald to your Third Eye to help settle issues that have been brought just below the surface in uncomfortable dreams. Use emerald for headaches too, making it into a gem elixir or holding the crystal during meditation. Migraine headaches can be assisted by means of pranayama breathing (see pages 154–155). Do this for ten minutes, then lie down in a darkened room and self-massage your Third Eye, the base of your neck (Alta Major chakra, see pages 30–31) and the temples (minor chakras). Next, hold an emerald to your Third Eye. Rest for a little longer and your migraine will start to clear.

sapphire

Using sapphire in the same way as emerald, by taping it to the Third Eye, brings deep insight into matters of a spiritual nature. Insights can then be processed by your whole body–mind–spirit complex, for in this incarnation you have been given the gift of having a physical body and a mind that responds to fantasy, suggestion and symbols.

Emeralds are very good for migraine while sapphires bring insight into spiritual matters.

crystals to calm ajna

crystals to balance ajna

Historically, Ajna has had a very special love affair with lapis lazuli. This crystal was used in a number of ancient cultures (including Atlantis) to balance a person's highest spiritual powers.

If we could part the mists of time and peer into the distant past, we would find that people were more spiritually developed then than they are today. They had bodies of a finer etheric substance, and it is said that in the times when beautiful temples were built, the gods and goddesses could enter into them in spirit and manifest visible bodies of Light. Everywhere people could communicate easily with animals, trees, flowers and crystals. As Rudolph Steiner (the 20th-century founder of anthroposophy) put it, "The intention of the Graeco-Roman race was to charm Spirit into Matter." Today the tables are turned and we have dense etheric bodies, but the reality is that we have to experience this densification before we can return our energy bodies to the Light.

lapis lazuli

Good-quality lapis lazuli is a deep blue stone, with little gold flecks of iron pyrites sparkling in it like stars, and is sometimes called the "night stone." It is found mainly in

Lapis Lazuli; an ideal crystal to use on the "eye of Shiva"—the Ajna chakra.

India and Afghanistan, both areas of rich cultural and spiritual heritage. It was used extensively in the tomb of Tutankhamun for decoration, and by ancient Egyptian women to make blue eye shadow.

Working strongly and energetically, lapis lazuli strengthens the thyroid and parathyroid glands and our skeletal system, in which the history of the body is locked. It is also said to benefit energy depletions that cause hearing loss, blood and nervous disorders. On a mental/emotional level, lapis lazuli is used at Ajna to access our deep cellular memory, our hurts and fears, and bring them into acceptance in our lives through the wisdom of higher consciousness. When this occurs, we are better able to cope with whatever life deals out to us.

One way to experience the stunning energies of lapis lazuli is to make a crystal essence using the indirect method (see pages 70–71). It is too soft a stone to put into water using the direct method, because it contains an unstable mixture of minerals.

how to use lapis lazuli

Lapis is a powerful healer and balancer for the energies of Ajna and it will benefit you to spend time getting to know its qualities.

1 Cleanse the lapis carefully, but not with water (as it is a "soft" stone), instead with your intention by holding it in the palm of you hand and breathing gently upon it. In this way the pranic energy in your breath does the cleansing.

2 Now hold it to your Third Eye and ask to understand the lapis. It may be that colors or pictures will come into your head or you may receive a message directly from the crystal. Whatever it is, thank the lapis before disconnecting your energy from it.

aromatherapy and ajna

Passion flower, papaya and tarragon are recommended for Ajna. Passion flower, either as a herbal preparation or as a flower essence, is used to alleviate neuralgia and insomnia. As a fruit, papaya settles digestive-system disturbances, while its flower essence reminds people of their karmic lessons. Tarragon, as a fresh herb, is diuretic and digestive as a hot tea infusion with a little honey; as a flower essence it stimulates this chakra and assists self-expression and insight.

Resinous grains of frankincense (left) and fresh basil leaf (above).

BROW CHAKRA ESSENTIAL OILS

The main essential oils that have a sympathetic resonance with Ajna are:

- **Frankincense** Also called olibanum, this has a wonderful spicy perfume extracted from the resinous gum of a small North African tree. It has been used for centuries as an embalming oil. Today its golden, gummy pieces still form the main ingredient of the incense burned in Christian churches. You can burn frankincense directly on special charcoal discs, or use the thick amber-colored essential oil in a vaporizer. Its properties assist deep meditation and focus on the Brow Chakra. Frankincense promotes a feeling of profound relaxation and deepens awareness of the breath, taking you into dream states where past memories may more easily be accessed. For the physical body, as well as benefiting respiratory infections and asthma, it helps to slow down and deepen the breathing and is best used as gentle chest massage, which also helps to open the often-constricted chest area. Frankincense promotes new skin and cells, is anti-inflammatory, antiseptic, astringent, carminative, digestive, diuretic, expectorant and sedative.

- **Basil and holy basil** An aromatic herb much used in Italian cooking, basil was once powdered and taken as snuff. As an essential oil, it is excellent in a vaporizer to clear the head and give strength, helping to balance Ajna, Vishuddha and the minor head chakras. Basil was valued in medieval times as part of a blend for anointing the heads of kings and queens during coronation ceremonies and was called the "royal herb." It is effective for nervous disorders, poor memory, lack of concentration and headaches caused by congestion. Basil tea is recommended to sober you up if you are drunk! As massage oil, it is best as a blend with lemon and geranium and should never be used excessively; it should not be used as bath oil as it may cause skin irritation; avoid any use of basil throughout pregnancy. Basil is antiseptic, anti-spasmodic, carminative, digestive, emmenagogic, febrifuge and a nerve tonic.

yoga asanas for ajna

active: adho mukha avanasana (dog face-down pose)

This asana is particularly useful to gently prepare you for headstands, because you get used to the extra blood flow to the head. Energy-wise, you should concentrate on the Third Eye while you hold the pose for as long as possible. Alternatively, visualize a deep-blue light.

1

1 Kneel on all fours, then walk your hands farther forward, with your palms flat on the floor.

2 Raise your trunk, straightening your legs and keeping your feet flat on the floor. Pull in your abdomen. Your head should relax down in line with your arms and body. The shape of this asana is an inverted V.

2

active: yoga mudra in padmasana

This advanced pose is traditionally performed in Padmasana (the lotus position), but if this is difficult you can use a simple crossed-leg position. You need to suspend your breathing while you are in the mudra (work toward one minute) and maintain your focus on Ajna, the Brow Chakra. Only perform this once in each yoga program. The purpose of this mudra is to cleanse the nadis to support the esoteric practices of Hatha yoga. By focusing on Ajna you render the entire energy field ready for concentration/meditation (dharana/dhyana). The state of consciousness you are seeking is the intuitive state, for your Soul Body is nourished by intuition.

1

1 Sit with your legs crossed in the full lotus posture. Clasp your hands behind your back, locking your fingers together.

2 On an exhalation, bend forward and touch the top of your head to the floor (or as near as possible). Simultaneously raise your arms straight up behind your back. Hold for as long as possible without breathing.

2

passive: halasana (plough pose)

The physical benefits of this asana are numerous: the bowels move freely, the spine becomes flexible, all the internal organs benefit, and increased blood flow at the neck improves thyroid and parathyroid hormone production. Halasana is therefore said to help control your weight, either helping you to thin down or put on weight, so that you attain your optimum healthy weight. From an energy-flow viewpoint, this asana is supreme, toning all the chakras at the same time. Once mastered, this is also one of the most relaxing asanas. It gives you plenty of time to focus on moving energy into your Brow Chakra, and visions may result. However, don't forget to move slowly out of the asana, and don't go to sleep! If this pose is new to you, you can support your back with your hands or rest your legs on a chair/stool positioned at the correct height and distance behind your head (the assistance of a friend or teacher is helpful).

1

1 Lie flat on your back, with your legs stretched out and tight at the knees. Supporting your back, bend your knees, raise your hips from the floor and lift your trunk up perpendicularly, supported by your hands, until your chest touches your chin. Move your hands to the middle of your spine. Your legs should be straight with your toes pointing up.

2 Release the chin lock and lower your trunk slightly. Stretch your arms out on the floor and simultaneously move your legs up over your head, resting your toes on the floor behind it. Your legs should be together throughout and kept straight. Remain in this asana from one to five minutes, breathing normally. To come out of the pose, support your back and lower your knees as you bring them over your head to the floor. It is important to follow this asana with a backward bend, such as Matsyasana (the fish pose, see pages 228–229).

2

Chapter 8

THE CROWN CHAKRA: SAHASRARA

sahasrara chakra

The Crown Chakra or Sahasrara is also known as the Thousand-petalled Lotus, akasha chakra, sahasrara padma, sahasrara mahapadma, sahasrara saroruha, sahasradala, sahasradala padma, pankaja, kamala, adhomukha mahapadma, wyomambhoja, shiras padma, amlana padma, dashashatadala padma, shuddha padma and shantyatita pada.

Sahasrara, which means "a thousand petals," is described in Indian traditions as being placed above the head, while more modern theosophical thinking locates it at the top of the head. Mystics describe its 1,000 white petals being arranged in 20 layers, each containing 50 petals with letters of the Sanskrit (an ancient holy language) alphabet written on them. The colors of these petals changes as a shimmering rainbow of colors passes through them, although in the seven-chakra system the Crown Chakra is assigned the color of violet.

the functions of sahasrara

Sahasrara is the place of pure consciousness. From subtle anatomy we know that it is at the end of the main sushumna nadi, where it combines with the energies of the pingala nadi (solar and masculine energy) and the ida nadi (lunar and feminine energy) that have conjoined at Ajna during the rising of kundalini. The Crown Chakra symbolizes the balance of duality within us and our ability to experience super-consciousness, and then the bliss of transcendental consciousness. Because this state is impossible to describe, it is sometimes called "the Void." Perhaps the best way to begin to understand it is to enter regularly into deep meditation, where you let go of everything and find that all is peace.

additional chakras in the tantric system

- The Forehead Chakra—also called Indu or Chandra (Moon)—has 16 petals, is white and blossoms when we achieve exemplary spiritual consciousness.
- The Tantric Lower Forehead Center is also known as the Manas (Mind) Chakra. It has six petals that are normally white, but assume other colors associated with the five senses, plus mind.

These chakras are located between Ajna and Sahasrara.

MAIN CHARACTERISTICS AT A GLANCE

Color	Violet
Key issues	Inner wisdom and death of the body
Physical location	Top of the head
Associated spinal area	None
Physiological system	Central nervous system and brain
Endocrine gland	Pineal and pituitary
Nerve plexus	Cerebral cortex
Inner aspect	Release of karma
Physical action	Meditation
Mental action	Universal consciousness
Emotional action	Beingness
Spiritual action	Unity through transcendental consciousness

health issues and sahasrara

The connection point for Sahasrara is regarded as the fontanelle "soft spot" on a newborn baby's head. When this spot closes up, the baby's awareness of the infinite universe and super-consciousness becomes locked in. Then, for most of us, personality and ego take over in the physical body and little thought is given to spiritual matters until we anticipate our death. The way the soul leaves a body at death is different for a yogi who has dedicated his or her life to spirit. Yogic adepts may choose the time of their death, and when they decide to leave through the Sahasrara they are freed from the repetitive karmic cycles of death and involuntary rebirth. This is called the Solar Path and the Path of the Sages.

associated body systems

Indian teachings indicate that all our physical diseases are a result of separation from the infinite universe. Our auric field and chakras are vital in keeping us healthy. Diseases connected with Sahasrara include:

- **Headaches** An overburdened mind due to suppression of thoughts or feelings, or an obsession
- **Epilepsy** A miscommunication between our physical, emotional and spiritual selves. Provided you have already taken medical advice, you may work on the energetic level of these diseases at Sahasrara using balancing techniques. If in doubt, seek professional advice.
- **Paralysis** Withdrawal of energy from a given area, due to deep trauma causing us to deny life
- **Parkinson's disease** Tremors that may indicate fear from the past, future or the way we move in our physical body
- **High blood pressure** Bottling up anger and emotions, also linked to the Heart Chakra.

associated endocrine glands

The pineal is considered the conductor of the orchestra of all the glands, while the pituitary is the lead musician—and both of these are associated with the Crown Chakra. Sahasrara, in combination with the endocrine glands, focuses energetic information coming through the auric field at the crown of the head. In recent years the study of psychoneuroendocrinology has begun to bring the truths of ancient yoga understandings and modern science disciplines together.

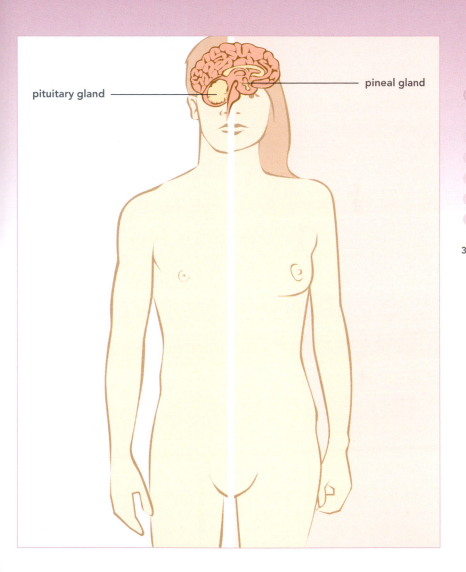

pituitary gland

pineal gland

unlocking your mind: the stages of meditation

In the Yoga Sutras of Patanjali (written advice for yoga practitioners), we read of the three stages for training the mind:

- **Concentration** Dharana, whose aim is to focus the inner experience
- **Meditation** Dhyana, whose aim is to expand the inner experience
- **Contemplation** Samadhi, whose aim is to deepen the inner experience.

dharana

The daily practice of concentration ideally comes after you have finished your yoga asanas. In the Raja system of yoga, which is regarded as one of the highest disciplines, it is usual to make specific times to practice it. Concentration of the mind might be on an abstract idea or an object. In concentration you try to *avoid* the chain association in your mind; for example, when you think of an orange, you may think of the tree—the sunshine that helped the tree grow—you wonder who picked the fruit. That is not dharana; in dharana you concentrate solely on the orange. The aim is to still the restless inner dialogue. Practicing at dawn can increase its effectiveness.

dhyana

When dhyana is reached, it is no longer necessary to practice concentration, because at this point on your spiritual journey, daily meditation replaces concentration. The term "meditation" can mean many things to many people. However, in the context of Patanjali's system and Raja yoga, dhyana means the following: whereas dharana contracts the mind, dhyana expands the mind around the subject. You enlarge the field of consciousness to take in the spiritual nature of (in this simple example) an orange. For most people, dhyana/contemplation is the final stage—samadhi is rarely reached.

samadhi

Of course, the practice of meditation does not normally use objects like an orange! To reach samadhi you are more likely to work with an abstract concept, such as unconditional love or a line from a sacred text.

Samadhi may be interpreted as uniting the lower consciousness or self with super-consciousness or the higher self. The highest principle, as Patanjali said, "is when the mind is so far concerned with the object alone, to a degree of one's seeming non-existence, that is Samadhi." However, not all meditation necessarily ends in the blissful state of samadhi. Experienced meditators say that samadhi comes when you least expect it, and you should not try to analyze the journey.

"Without leaving his house, one can know everything that is necessary. Without leaving himself one can grasp all wisdom."
Lao Tzu

using the power of light

Here are some different ways to increase light in your body.

mantras

The Ajapa Mantra is an unusual mantra, because ajapa means that it is not repeated verbally. It is not recited, but takes place continually—day and night. It is our breath!

Breath is a mantra because your out-breath has the sound of "ha" and your in-breath has the sound of "tha." Together they make "ha-tha"—and Hatha yoga is the yoga of bodily practices. With the breath comes prana, which is light. This light is encoded with life information, and it follows that if we increase our pranic levels, we can live life more fully. As we increase our light levels, we build our auric field; and the stronger that field, the easier it is for our spiritual light to shine out. Clairvoyants and those with psychic sight can perceive the aura, and in modern times scientists have tried numerous ways to record these light levels within our subtle bodies. Cutting-edge science now tells us that all matter is conscious energy, and that our bodies/minds are one. All things and all levels are folded together into an "implicate order."

vibrational healing

In the 1920s Royal R. Rife, an American researcher, made a polarized light microscope that showed the color, and subsequently the frequency vibration, of organisms. He developed a light Beam Ray that produced electromagnetic fields of the correct frequency to destroy viruses and bacteria. He went on to trial his methods at the University of Southern California, where he achieved a 90 percent success rate for curing all types of cancer. It is to be regretted that the medical authorities suppressed his work—like that of other medical pioneers, such as Dinshah Ghadiali and Wilhelm Reich, who were also developing vibrational types of healing.

light therapy

Today light therapy is available from many practitioners, and it is recommended that you undertake a course of treatment for any serious disorders. If you want to experience light therapy at home, a very simple way is to make solarized water: determine the chakra and the color you wish to use, then obtain a colored glass of the required hue. Fill the glass with pure spring water and leave it in the sunshine for up to 12 hours. The light

energy vibration of the colored glass will be transferred into the water, which you sip slowly throughout the next day.

For Sahasrara, use violet solarized water to increase spiritual growth, and bright-yellow solarized water to enhance mental abilities. To balance diseases of the head, eyes and throat, choose deep-blue solarized water. In fact, blue light is the prime choice for most healing work. Many people keep their drinking water in blue bottles, while others place a clear quartz crystal in their water bottle. If you wish your pets to have a loving, gentle nature, place a large chunk of rose quartz in their drinking bowl. Not surprisingly, the original intention behind British police forces using a blue light at the door of the police station was to calm people down!

using the power of light

Simple light therapy can be experienced by making solarized water.

cosmic light linking

This is a special meditation undertaken in a standing position, to link you to Earth through your feet and to the worldwide webs of Light and Life (the Earth's subtle energy grids).

1 Choose a quiet place outside. Stand with your bare feet on the earth or grass.

2 With your eyes closed, breathe into and activate all seven major chakras.

3 Send a strong "root" down from your feet to the center of Mother Earth (see pages 108–109).

4 Breathe in and raise your arms, then ask to be filled with the Divine Light of creation. As you breathe out and bring your arms down, imagine the light filling your central column of energy (the sushumna nadi).

5 Begin to see the light as a network of fine golden filaments spreading around you and even passing through you. Understand that these are part of the worldwide webs of Light and Life.

6 From your Heart Chakra, in the middle of your central energy column, visualize sending out the Divine Light through the golden filaments. See it passing through them to all the places around you that need clearing of negative energies.

7 Pass the light through all the golden filaments that are forming the energetic "net" or grid around Mother Earth. Everywhere the Divine Light touches is transformed from negativity into positive action.

8 Finally see the planet glowing with light; at this moment she can take her rightful place, as a blue/green jewel in the cosmos.

9 Feel joy, knowing that you have finished your "light work." Gradually release the light around you, shake your body and bring yourself back to everyday awareness.

"Grounding" through your feet helps link you to the Earth's energies.

sahasrara yantra

The lotus of the thousand petals, lustrous and whiter than the full moon, has its head turned downward. It charms. It sheds its rays in profusion and is moist and cool like nectar. That most excellent of men who has controlled his mind and known this place is never again born the Wandering, as there is nothing in the three worlds which binds him.

Sat Cakra Nirupana

description of the yantra
Number of petals A thousand.
Color Violet.

Form Bell-shaped, can be shown on a yogi's head. Associated with Divine knowledge and enlightenment; often shown as an open lotus.
Mandala Surya (Sun) and Chandra (Moon).
Triangle Within the Moon mandala.
Nirvana-kala Inside the triangle. Said to grant the power of Divine knowledge.
Supreme bindu Inside the Nirvana-kala. Stands for the silence led into by the sound of OM.

the bija mantra
The sound of Sahasrara is silence, and it has no true associated bija mantra, although OM (see pages 78–79) may be used, as the unmanifest sound of All or God.

THE LOTUS

The lotus is used as a symbol of the chakras because they look rather like flower blossoms within the auric field. The lotus flowers have been a potent emblem in India for thousands of years. The plant grows up from muddy waters to the surface of a lake and blossoms in the light, symbolizing human growth: we are often submerged in the muddy waters of our subconscious and may obstinately push our roots deeper into the mud, but this will eventually make us stronger. Once we break free, we grow upward, overcoming anything disturbing in our emotions (represented by water), and push the flower bud out of the water, thus nurturing our spiritual self in our journey toward the spiritual sun.

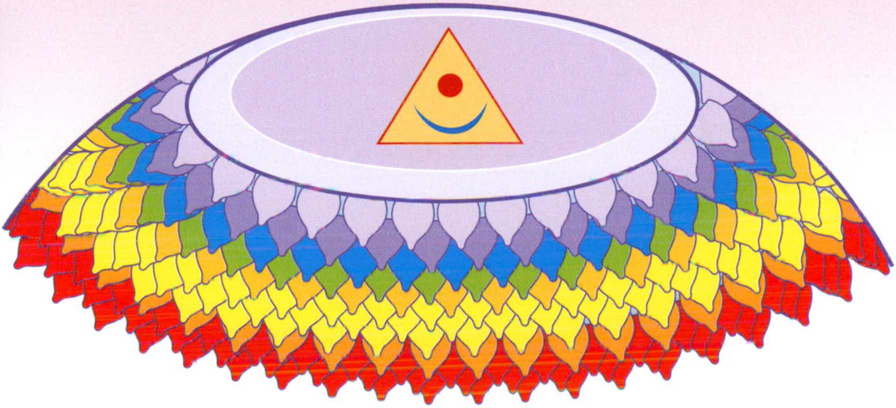

deities associated with sahasrara

shiva

This chakra is known as the "abode of Shiva." It is where the divisions between Shiva and Shakti are resolved, and where the goddess Dakini reaches the end of her journey, having been awoken from dormancy in the Base Chakra (see pages 106–107).

Lord Shiva, whose name means "Good," is the third person in the Hindu triad of gods (see pages 82–83), and is both the destroyer and regenerator of life. In this illustration Shiva is shown as being beyond the power of death, with cobras twisted around his neck. Cobras represent the mastery of kundalini, the serpent power. Shiva is seated on a tiger skin, because he has taken the creature's skin from Shakti, whose "vehicle" or totem animal it is. His hair is matted because he is Lord of the Wind, and he wears a diadem of the thin crescent moon. The trident of Shiva is symbolic of the three functions of the creator, the preserver and the destroyer.

shakti (parvati/durga)

Shakti is the female counterpart of the masculine energy that sustains the world, and is given many names, indicating her multidimensional qualities. She is primarily known as the Great Goddess—Devi or Mahadevi—although in her role as the consort of Shiva she is called Parvati or Durga. Throughout India she is worshipped every day by millions of people, perhaps being revered even more than Shiva himself.

She is variously known as:
- **Parvati** The mountain-girl
- **Gauri** Yellow-complexioned beauty
- **Himavati** Daughter of Himalaya
- **Jagatmata** The Mother of the World
- **Uma** The Light
- **Bhavani** The Goddess of the Universe

In her terrible wrathful forms she is Durga (the inaccessible); Kali (the black-complexioned goddess); Chandika, the Fearful One; and Bhairavi, the Terrible One.

crystals to activate sahasrara

The main crystals used to activate the Crown Chakra are celestite and blue sapphire.

celestite

Celestite is often called the "stone of heaven" and is a pale blue translucent crystal that works at a highly refined rate of vibration. It is the most powerfully beautiful expression of blue light known on the Earth. In the physical body it reduces stress by aiding relaxation into the realms of Divine Light. It will also work through additional chakras beyond the traditional seven to alter your physical rate of vibration and result in an "upgrading" of your web of life. A spiritually aware person will understand this as the true destiny for human beings, although others will subconsciously resist change.

Celestite is excellent made into a crystal essence by the indirect method (see pages 70–71). It can also be held during meditation or placed on an altar to focus the pure aqua ray of light into the Earth, where its peacefulness is currently much needed.

blue sapphire

The properties of this gemstone have already been discussed (see pages 184–185). It freely gives of its energies to activate all the higher chakras, and delights in its manifestation of an intense, focused blue light.

A heavenly blue celestite cluster (left) can reduce stress and sapphires (above) activate higher chakras.

quiet space indoors or in Nature. Ensure that you have cleansed and dedicated your crystals first—also always cleanse them after any healing work. Now you can begin.

1 Place a protective circle of light around yourself, by visualizing breathing pure white light into your body through your Crown Chakra, then passing from your hands (held in the prayer position) around your entire body.

2 Place the sapphire in your non-dominant hand, letting it nestle in the center of the palm, where there is a minor chakra. Hold the quartz in your other palm, ensuring that its point is directed toward your wrist, so that the energy will flow up your arm.

3 Now relax, breathe deeply and start to visualize the condition of your Throat Chakra, then of your Third Eye and finally of your Crown Chakra. Draw the pure blue light of the sapphire into each chakra in turn.

4 When you have finished, offer thanks for the healing gift and ensure that each chakra is balanced and that you have grounded yourself to the Earth (see page 108).

crystals to activate sahasrara

exercise to experience the energies of blue sapphire

You will need a small blue sapphire (uncut is fine) and a clear quartz point about 2 in. (5 cm) long. Ask the deva (the overlighting presence) of each crystal if you may use them to assist your spiritual growth.

If you have made an altar (see page 108–109), sit in front of it. Alternatively find a

crystals to calm sahasrara

Emerald (see pages 288–289) is recommended to calm the energies of Sahasrara, if you wish to switch your focus from spiritual matters to everyday ones.

charoite and sugilite/luvulite

These types of crystals can be used interchangeably as both have similar qualities to share with humans. It is only in recent years that these stones have been revealed to us by the Earth. They range in color from pale to deep violet, sometimes with the inclusion of darker minerals. Although they are not normally classed as gemstones, both are regarded as stones of transformation with particular affinities to Sahasrara. The crystalline worlds of these transformational stones are able to convert any negative energies coming into the chakra, in the form of psychic attacks that may manifest as nightmares.

Charoite encourages deep sleep and assists energetic disturbances of the brain, such as those resulting from autism and deep emotional problems. Sugilite/luvulite is excellent for learning difficulties as it is said to reorganize brain patterns. In this respect it will clear headaches, purify the blood and lymph, and is considered beneficial in easing the energetic

Sugilite/luvulite assists channeling. The best and rarest pieces are strong violet in color.

Polished charoite, recently discovered in Russia, aids spiritual transformation.

disturbances of epilepsy—all of these disorders have been associated with a malfunctioning and unbalanced Sahasrara.

crystal healing and acupuncture points

Clear quartz, diamond or other gemstones may be used effectively on acupuncture points or on the transient acupuncture Ah Shi points, which occur wherever there is a blockage or pain in the body. When the crystals are left in place for an appropriate time, these points come into balance or resonance through the vibrational rate of the crystals. Because crystals resonate at a very slow rate of one to three cycles per second (compared to normal human consciousness of 13–30 cycles of beta brainwave level per second while awake), the placing of them on or near the body allows an interdimensional exchange to take place. The matrix within the crystal structure becomes superimposed as an "interference" pattern over the treatment area of the body, and it is this "interference" pattern that leads to a reprogramming of the cells into a state of balance.

crystals to balance sahasrara

Clear quartz and amethyst, either alone or in combination, are excellent to balance the energies of Sahasrara.

clear quartz

This crystal exists in many forms and shapes. The quartz recommended for using with the chakras is a clear quartz "point" about 2 in. (5 cm) long. It can be single-terminated (with a point at one end) or double-terminated (a point at both ends). It can be shiny and polished or in its natural state. For some deep shamanic-type healing, the clearer the crystal, the better. If you wish to develop powers beyond the Crown Chakra, then clear quartz is the crystal to assist you.

quartz to protect your higher chakras

When working with your higher chakras, it is recommended that you wear a quartz point as a piece of jewelry hanging on your chest, with the point facing down toward the Earth. Place it in the position known to some Native American healers as "the spiritual grounding point": right at the end of the breastbone between the Heart Chakra and Solar Plexus Chakra. Doing this will always keep your electromagnetic field or aura perfectly clear. Anything negative coming near you will be repelled by light transmitted through the quartz. Always choose your crystal jewelry intuitively, and don't forget to cleanse it every night after you have worn it.

A perfect example of a naturally occurring clear quartz with double-terminated points.

Natural amethyst point (below). The best amethyst, like this geode (right), comes from Brazil.

amethyst

This is available as a geode (a hollow rock lined with crystals), a cluster or as single points that have been "extracted" from another mineral. Large geodes and clusters are good for placing in your healing space to maintain a high-frequency vibration, but keep them out of sunlight as they fade in strong light. Amethyst brings psychic gifts and is an excellent aid to meditation. It should *not* be used by anyone with mental disturbances such as schizophrenia, or with hyperactive children.

Violet light is known to reduce high blood pressure, reduce the appetite, calm shock and reconstruct the white blood corpuscles. Crystals of amethyst have a purifying, cleansing and antiseptic effect due to their color, which verges into the ultraviolet range of higher and faster vibration. They work directly on the Third Eye, the right brain (creative) area, the pineal and pituitary glands. When we cooperate with amethyst, it opens our body to the energy of three newly emerging, transpersonal chakras above the head, which we will study in the next part of this book.

aromatherapy and sahasrara

Various plants, herbs and flower essences are used for the Crown Chakra, including yam, witch hazel, comfrey, hawthorn and lavender. Lobelia now used sparingly as a herbal tincture was once smoked in Native American peace-pipe ceremonies. It is a "nervine" so acts as a tonic to stimulate and strengthen the nervous system.

Lime tree blossom makes a fragrant tea infusion to relieve headaches.

CROWN CHAKRA ESSENTIAL OILS

The following essential oils are used for their emotional-spiritual properties—not for physical ailments. The first three may be used as aphrodiasiac/moisturizing baths: put just two or three drops into a carrier oil or milk, then mix it into the warm water.

- **Ylang-ylang** This is a highly perfumed exotic flower that grows mainly in the Far East. In aromatherapy it aids relaxation, calmness and sensuality, although too high a concentration of ylang-ylang will bring on headaches. In cooperation with the unseen flower beings, whom we can petition through prayer, meditation or song, it will open us to Gaia Earth Mother.

- **Rosewood** This is sometimes replaced with other fragrances because the trees that grow in tropical Brazil and Peru are now an endangered species. However, it is possible to buy this essential oil from wood that has been cultivated in sustainable plantations. Rosewood connects and grounds the Base Chakra with the Crown. Again, seek the cooperation of the unseen worlds.

- **Linden or lime blossom** This comes not from the citrus fruit, but from the tree *Tilia vulgaris*, and is a highly concentrated perfume ideal for opening the channeling circuit that runs in a loop between the Brow, Alta Major and Throat Chakras. This creates the conditions of relaxation and concentration necessary for removing awareness of our everyday mind processes, in preparation for entering into an altered state of consciousness. When this occurs, some sensitive people are able to channel Beings of Light, including angels and ascended masters and those who guide us from other realms. Linden will also open us up to channel nature spirits and devas/angels of the landscape.

- **Lotus or water lily** This is an very rare essential oil. The properties gifted to us by the "flower beings" of lotus and water lily immediately open the Crown Chakra, bringing an almost hypnotic state of bliss. If you are unable to obtain the essential oil, lotus is sometimes available as an (unperfumed) flower essence.

yoga asanas for sahasrara

active: salamba sirhasana 1 (headstand)

If you have never done a headstand before, always prepare yourself first with asanas such as Halasana (see pages 298–299), Adho Mukha Avanasana (see pages 294–295) or Bakasana (see page 326–327) for a number of months until you are completely comfortable with them. Some teachers advise a year of regular yoga practice before attempting a full headstand. Do not do this asana if you have high or low blood pressure; instead begin very gently and slowly with Halasana (the plough). Once mastered, the headstand and its variations are regarded as the most beneficial asanas. Salamba

Sirhasana is known as the king of all asanas because it makes for healthy blood flow through the brain cells, thus increasing longevity and benefiting the pineal and pituitary glands, which act as a bridge to the higher chakras. So the Crown Chakra is particularly energized by this asana.

> **Caution:** This advanced asana is only for those who can balance safely. If you have a medical condition, do not attempt extreme asanas unless you have taken medical advice and are working with a qualified yoga teacher.

1

1 Fold up a blanket and place it in front of you, then kneel on all fours. Rest your forearms on the center of the blanket. Cup your fingers together and lock them, as they will be supporting your weight. Rest the crown of your head on the blanket, supported by your hands.

2 Raise your knees from the floor by moving your toes closer to your head. When you are ready, lift your trunk and bend your knees. Straighten your legs and balance.

2

active: bakasana (crane pose)

Bakasana helps you get a sense of balance and strengthens your arms, wrists and back, as well as supplying additional blood to the head, face and neck. It is this extra blood flow that carries the pranic energy flowing in and out of the Crown Chakra. Esoterically speaking, to place your head upon the Earth demonstrates humility and the willingness to learn and submit to the will of the Creator. Thus the Crown Chakra develops its "thousand petals" of light and union with all. The state of consciousness you are seeking at the Crown Chakra is cosmic super-consciousness. This leads to union (the true meaning of yoga) with the Divine source of creation—samadhi or nirvana.

Caution: This is an asana for beginners, but note the comments already given (see page 324) regarding existing medical conditions

1 Fold up a blanket and place it in front of you, then kneel on all fours. Place the *crown* of your head on the blanket about 6 in. (15 cm) in front of your hands, which should be flat and facing forward. Rest your head down and get used to having just a little weight on it. The position of your head and hands should make a triangle shape, for stability.

1

2 Now walk your feet toward your hands, straightening the spine. Bend your left knee and place it on the "shelf" of your left arm.

3 Do the same with the right knee. Bring your feet together and balance. If this is comfortable, hold the pose for one or two minutes.

passive: Salamba Sarvangasana 1 (shoulder stand)

If you move into this pose from Halasana (the plough), you can maintain the strong chin lock that is the main feature for subtle-energy control; this also facilitates comfort for the physical body. The inversion of the torso is reputed to assist numerous bodily functions. From a subtle-energy viewpoint, it allows the free flow of energies through the body until they reach the neck. At this point prana is able to flow into the brain, while there is a restriction of blood flow into it. When the posture is released, blood again flows freely to the brain. The Crown Chakra responds to energetic stimulation by an outpouring of sparkling golden white light. You may wish to concentrate on your Crown and visualize this as a fountain of light at the top of your head whenever you are in a Crown Chakra asana.

Caution: Only practice this pose under the guidance of a yoga teacher, since there are potential dangers associated with it if you suffer from high blood pressure, and during menstruation.

If you have a medical condition, do not attempt extreme asanas unless you have taken medical advice and are working with a qualified yoga teacher.

1 Lie flat on your back, with your legs stretched out and tight at the knees. Supporting your back, bend your knees.

1

2

2 Raise your hips from the floor and lift
   your trunk up perpendicularly,
   supported by your hands, until your
   chest touches your chin.

3 Move your hands to the middle of your
   spine. Your legs should be straight with
   your toes pointing up. Remain in this
   position for up to five minutes, breathing
   evenly. Aim to balance on your shoulders
   and be still—do not turn your head.

3

Chapter 9

THE NEW CHAKRAS

○ ○ ○ ○ ○ ○ ○

In this chapter of the book some exciting new chakra
discoveries are presented and explored in detail.

transpersonal chakras

We have seen how the chakras are energy centers correlating to areas and functions of the physical body that have been identified since Indian Vedic times. During the 19th and 20th centuries, followers of the school of Theosophy (see page 26–27) developed an esoteric philosophy linked to scientific progress. They assigned colors to each of the seven traditional chakras so that they matched the colors of the rainbow in the order in which they ascend through the body. They were updating ancient wisdom in the light of what they themselves perceived with their auric sight.

As we know, those who can see the auric field describe areas of swirling color, which are constantly moving and changing. Sometimes these colors are seen in particular "layers" that are described as the different "bodies" (see pages 14–15), or focus into specific vortices of energy, when they are known as chakras. However, now the energies coming to our world from the cosmos are changing.

into the future

On our small, fragile planet we are being saturated with increasingly potent and variable new energies from our solar system and from the galaxy. These energies, best described as high-frequency light, stimulate our evolutionary potential. When we look closely, using our higher consciousness, we begin to realize that the seven-chakra system (plus the other minor chakras that have already been mentioned) was appropriate for the last two millennia. But it is imperative that we build upon this "memory" in order to walk into the future. We can do this by connecting with the new energies. In the course of this great work our aura will expand and further major chakras will come into play.

newly discovered chakras

New transpersonal chakras, available to humanity at this time, in ascending order are: the Earth Star Chakra, the Hara/Navel Chakra, the Causal Chakra, the Soul Star and the Stellar Gateway. These chakras were first named by Katrina Raphaell in her book *The Crystalline Transmission* (1990), and many healers and crystal teachers are still working to deepen their understanding of these chakras. It has become clear that we are being given a new kind of personal spiritual empowerment that is not connected to any one religion.

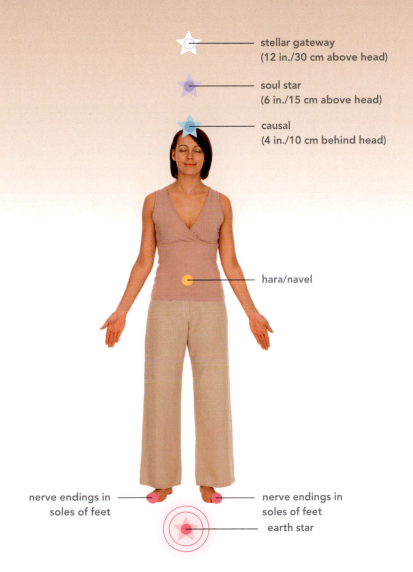

stellar gateway
(12 in./30 cm above head)

soul star
(6 in./15 cm above head)

causal
(4 in./10 cm behind head)

hara/navel

nerve endings in
soles of feet

nerve endings in
soles of feet

earth star

the earth star chakra

This chakra is like a "return to the future." We once walked the land as Beings of Light in past civilizations, such as Mu and Atlantis, and in those times knew we had come from the stars—and that to the stars we would return. But all things change, our bodies densified, and we were left with just our barely visible auric field. Ancient teachings tell us that we spiral around the universe, never quite coming back to the same place in space, and that we carry a little of the remembrance of past times encoded in our body cells.

awakening the earth star chakra

Wherever we walk, the Earth Star Chakra is below our feet and connected to us physically by nerve endings in the soles. The subtle energy connection is through the chakra reflexology points on the inner part of each foot as shown on pages 50–51. Today some of us are remembering our origins: recalling that wherever an Enlightened Being walks, the surrounding atmosphere is "lit up." For most people, the Earth Star Chakra is dark to black in color. But for Enlightened Beings, when their feet touch the ground, a beautiful magenta-colored glow goes with them— the awakened Earth Star Chakra, which becomes a part of their expanded auric field. This enhanced auric field combines its golden halo at the Crown Chakra with the glowing Light of three other major chakras above their head. At this point, while they are still in a physical body (albeit a highly refined one), they will have passed through the fourth and fifth dimensions and be preparing to ascend into the sixth dimension.

If you want to walk consciously, in touch with the ground, you should practice sending your "roots" down from your spine and the soles of your feet into the crystalline heart of Mother Earth (see page 108). This also connects you to the Earth Star Chakra and, together with crystal activations of a spiritual nature, is the first stage in your journey back to the stars.

MAIN CHARACTERISTICS AT A GLANCE

Color	Black, but magenta when activated
Key issues	Re-creation of matter
Physical location	Below the feet and spreading out in a circle
Associated physical areas	Nerve endings in the soles of the feet
Associated spinal area	Sushumna central nadi
Inner aspect	Restructuring of human DNA
Physical action	Awareness of Nature
Mental action	Overcoming polarity
Spiritual action	Preparation for Light Body ascension
Gemstone to activate	Clear quartz

the earth star chakra

crystals and the three celestial chakras

Before activation of the Earth Star Chakra takes place, another major chakra normally comes into play: the Hara/Navel Chakra, located just above the Sacral. The Hara is usually more developed in people who practice Eastern spiritual skills; Westerners usually have a more developed Sacral Chakra. The Hara is orange-yellow and works on our kidneys, digestion and the absorption of food. Because it gives us physical sustenance and strength (just as Eastern martial arts do), this is a key area in which to improve metabolism and weight loss in combination with the pursuit of Eastern practices. Crystals of tiger's eye and carnelian will help bring light into this chakra.

The three transpersonal and celestial chakras above our heads are the Causal Chakra, the Soul Star and the Stellar Gateway. They are located within and beyond our auric field, and can be seen as our personal relay stations to the stars; they transmit/receive a multiplicity of energies that get passed to all the other chakras.

Use tiger's eye (left) or carnelian (above) to balance the Hara/Navel chakra.

the causal chakra

This is located about 4 in. (10 cm) back from the Crown Chakra and lines up energetically with the Alta Major and the spinal column. While the Alta Major is concerned with distant memory, the Causal Chakra, when activated, is ready to guide our present lives—if we are on a path of exploration of Spirit. At such times it acts as a beneficial filter to "color" our intentions for the highest good of all humanity. From this you will understand that if we are bounded by our ego, then this chakra will not function.

Kyanite (top) directs energy while celestite (above left) and moonstone (above right) balance energies of the causal chakra.

The Causal Chakra enables us to consciously reprogram our lives through silent inner peace. It resonates with the crystals of kyanite, moonstone and celestite and with the color of aqua light. Activation of the Causal Chakra is assisted by focused attention from a skilled healer who, as a "Light worker," understands the part that Light plays in the raising of human consciousness.

the soul star

This chakra is located approximately 6 in. (15 cm) above the top of the head, in a direct line with (and merging into) the fountain-like golden-violet energies of the Crown Chakra below. It is our connection to the whole of our Milky Way Galaxy and pulses information from the galactic source to each awakened individual. In return, awakened souls transmit thought-forms back to the source while still in a physical body; but upon releasing the body at death, a seed of all that an Enlightened Being was remains in the Soul Star. This is why ancient peoples said that they became stars in the night sky and affirmed that, while their bodies may die, their souls never would. The Soul Star can be activated by a skilled healer with crystals using a selenite "rod" and is assigned the color of a delicate peach-pink light.

Crystals of selenite measuring up to 3 ft. (1 m) wide and 90 ft. (30 m) long have been found in Naica, Mexico.

Fragile, dark green moldavite has a special affinity with the Stellar Gateway.

the stellar gateway

This is the highest link we can make with creation at this time in the evolution of humanity. It is usually located 12 in. (30 cm) from the top of the head, but like the other two celestial chakras, its position varies enormously. Indeed, it is understood that this chakra of light, connecting us to the cosmos, is multidimensional, holographic, interstellar and timeless.

At this particular spiritual crossroads for humanity, creation is using the Stellar Gateway to call out to awakened humans, in order to illuminate them with the radiance of Divine Light of all creation. There is nothing that we can do personally to activate this chakra—activation will only occur when humanity is collectively ready.

However, we can do much to prepare ourselves by daily practicing acts of unconditional love, being non-judgmental, acting with compassion and grace toward all living beings.

meditating with moldavite

To assist awareness of the Stellar Gateway you may wish to meditate with moldavite—a powerful and rare, clear green crystal of extra-terrestrial origin. It is sufficient to hold moldavite during meditation and ask it to give you inner vision of an inter-dimensional starry kind—sometimes called "cosmovision." It assists clarity of higher purpose and intention, so that incoming energies of change may be anchored on the planet through *your* chakra system. Moldavite assists in clearing useless karmic patterns locked in any of your chakras, and brings clarity of purpose to the future.

the three celestial chakras

While many of us may only aspire to understand the three celestial chakras just mentioned, we will now revisit the seven major chakras in the light of a new awareness that tells us they process life-enhancing astrophysical properties. All seven chakras receive and transmit solar radiance. Our two temple chakras, our nipples/breasts and our genitals/ovaries receive and transmit lunar radiance. The remaining small and high-frequency minor chakras and the Alta Major, as well as numerous other energy nodes that are essential to the well-being of our soul–spirit–body connection, all receive and transmit cosmic radiance. Thus we are linked to the powers of Light and creation through these numerous chakras:

- Seven solar chakras
- Six lunar chakras
- Many hundreds of cosmic chakras.

the effects of moon and sun

We have long understood the influence that the Moon has on the tides of our oceans and

Our bodies have six chakras which are linked through the Moon to the power of light and creation.

on cycles in our bodies (especially women's menstrual cycles). In addition many ancient cultures worldwide gave special attention to the powers within and beyond the Sun. Wisdom teachings from the Maya of Central

America accorded great significance to the Sun, implying that a different type of solar energy occurs every single day, because of changing planetary positions as our solar system spirals toward the galactic center. Some individuals have even been able to ground specific star-system energy frequencies into their major chakras through intense work with crystals. When this is achieved and the chakra is active, it is as if they have a "stargate" within their energetic body field, resulting in an intense glow within their aura.

the light of creation

Humans cannot live without light and color. Light from distant stars can be analyzed by a scientific technique that splits the spectrum of starlight into its component parts, revealing the stars' composition by chemical elements. Crystal types are also identified in a similar process of spectrographic analysis. When we take into account that the beautiful crystals on

Mother Earth are similar in composition to the liquid crystalline structures within our body, we have a deep inner knowing that we are made of both the stars and the stones. This makes us truly cosmic Beings of Light in physical bodies, enabling us to identify ourselves with every starry point of light in the night sky.

Cultures worldwide have regarded the Sun as a symbol of creative energy.

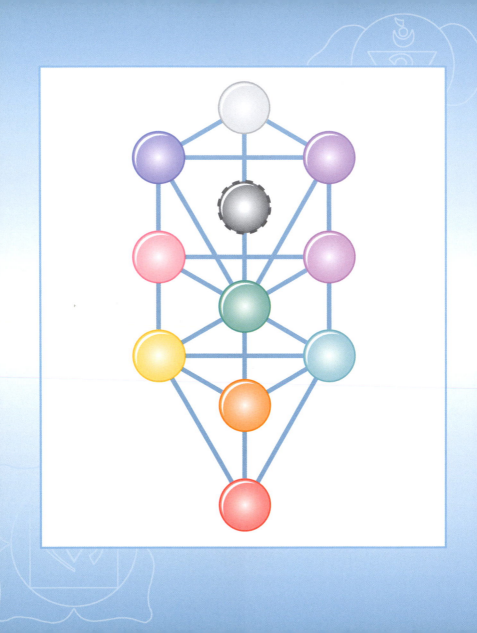

Chapter 10

CHAKRAS IN OTHER TRADITIONS

○ ○ ○ ○ ○ ○ ○

In Chapter 10 the chakras are placed within the
context of other traditions, such as Taoism, Kabbalah,
Sufism, Inca and Mayan teachings and shamanism.

taoism and the chakras

From around 3500 BCE Chinese people developed the principles of the "Way of Long Life," which included herbal diet, medicine, kung fu and therapeutic breathing—this was the beginning of Taoism. The first recorded Chinese doctor is said to have been Bian Que, who lived from 407 to 310 BCE and gave medical, acupuncture, gynecological and pediatric treatments. Dr. Zhang Zhongjing, who lived around 200 BCE, wrote extensively about disease, dividing it into six types following Yin and Yang principles, and has been credited with devising the first "map" of energy lines (meridians) used in acupuncture.

Taoism developed in three ways: reclusive study of the *Tao Te Ching* (the classic Chinese text, the *Book of the Way*), traditional shamanism, and the metaphysical and occult aspects that today are called inner Taoism. Because the last is a quest for immortality, it stands as the Chinese counterpart to Indian and Tibetan Tantra. Today there are several schools of Taoism. The basic teachings of esoteric Taoists are that we only have a limited store of life-force (ch'i or qi, equivalent to prana in yoga). In common with shamanic practices,

the belief that ch'i leaks away in everyday life leads to practices to increase ch'i, improve health and sexual enjoyment, and prolong quality of life. However the Eternal Tao is Infinite Wisdom, Infinite Love and Infinite Simplicity.

the microcosmic orbit

Inner Taoists control and manipulate ch'i by detailed exercises that channel energy through the body. The main method entails a circuit of energy called the Circulation of the Light or the Microcosmic Orbit. This orbit comprises two acupuncture meridians:

- The Governing Vessel, which runs from deep inside the lower abdomen up the center of the back to the root of the tongue
- The Conception Vessel, which runs from deep inside the lower abdomen up the back, over the head and finishes under the top lip.

Along these meridians are acupuncture points corresponding to chakra positions. Through both rhythmic breathing and visualization, the aim of an esoteric Taoist is to circulate the ch'i, balance Yin and Yang, attain cosmic consciousness, become an

immortal and return to the Tao. Sometimes these esoteric attainments are achieved through joyful and prolonged sex, with the aim of retaining semen. In old Chinese literature it is written that Emperor Huang Di (the Yellow Emperor) had inexhaustible sexual powers and became a god.

eastern energy techniques

Numerous energy techniques have developed in the East, among them tai chi, shiatsu, kung fu, qi gong, lok hup, ba fa and other internal martial arts. All these practices move and increase the power of the ch'i. A basic understanding of this energy is as follows:

- Masculine energy in the form of Heaven's Force is Yang in nature, contracting and centripetal in action and spirals into the top of the head—corresponding to the Crown Chakra. It then descends through the Brow, Throat, Heart, Stomach (Solar Plexus Chakra) and Tan Tien/Hara (Sacral Chakra) to the genitals (Base Chakra).

taoism and the chakras

A practitioner of Oriental arts focusing and holding energy.

- Meanwhile feminine energy in the form of Earth's Force ascends from the feet and genital region. This energy complements the male, because it is Yin in nature and is centrifugal and expanding in action. Entering the body, it ascends through the same organs/chakras until it reaches the Crown. At the chakras bio-electromagnetism flows out and ch'i/prana flows in to charge the body's internal functions. Excessive charge increases chakra function, while a decreased charge slows it down, predisposing the chakras to disease. So, as in yoga, an Oriental practitioner seeks harmony and balance in all things.

THE THREE TREASURES

- **Generative energy** or Ching (Jing) is stored in the lower Tan Tien, where it can be burned away when someone works to transform and release sexual desires. This is known as "lead flower emerging." This area corresponds to the Sacral Chakra (Hara). Ching generative energy travels down through the bones, having the qualities of Yin and water.

- **Vital energy** or ch'i (qi) is stored in the middle Tan Tien when a person is actively working on sexual desires or taming emotions. Then it is known as "silver flower emerging." This area is made up of the Solar Plexus, Heart and Throat Chakras. Ch'i travels up or down through the meridians, having the qualities of life and air.

- **Spirit energy** or shen is stored in the upper Tan Tien. When a person is highly developed emotionally and their thoughts are still, it is called "golden flower emerging." This area corresponds to the Brow and Crown Chakras. Shen travels up through the meridians, having the qualities of Yang and fire.

the kabbalah

The Kabbalah (also spelt Cabala, Cabbala, Cabalah and Qabala) is an ancient esoteric Jewish system dating from the 12th century. It contains secret knowledge of the unwritten Torah (divine revelation) that was given by God to Adam and Moses, dating back to the beginning of creation. In the first chapter of the Bible (Genesis), God creates the world in six days and rests on the seventh. The seven levels of the Kabbalah symbolize this.

An old Kabbalist holds the sephirothic tree in his hand.

chakras in other traditions

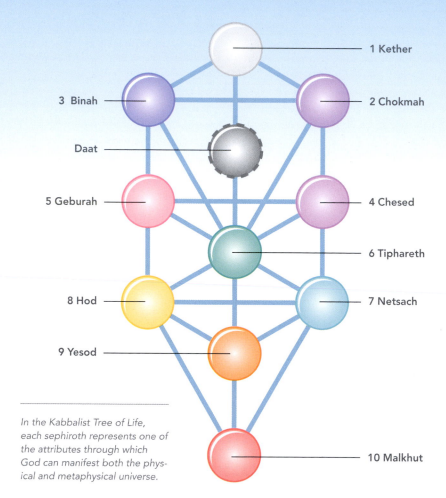

1 Kether

3 Binah

2 Chokmah

Daat

5 Geburah

4 Chesed

6 Tiphareth

8 Hod

7 Netsach

9 Yesod

10 Malkhut

In the Kabbalist Tree of Life, each sephiroth represents one of the attributes through which God can manifest both the physical and metaphysical universe.

The Kabbalah describes the path of descent from the Divine to the material realm, and the path of ascent to the highest level of spirituality. Through contemplation and meditation the goal of a Kabbalist is to ascend this symbolic "Tree of Life." Ten "sephiroth" make up the Tree of Life (this word has it roots in "cipher" or "number" and can also be translated as "sapphire") and have a direct correlation with the seven chakras.

When seen as an illustration, the Kabbalah also has three "pillars" or Powers: Primordial Will, Mercy and Justice. Primordial Will is perceived as holding the balance between Justice and Mercy, and the three pillars are held in a potent energetic arrangement, emanating a pattern of balance within the Tree of Life.

the meanings of the sephiroth

From a yogic perspective, as a spiritual seeker ascends the tree to the next sephiroth, kundalini rises to the next chakra. The numbers and basic meanings of the sephiroth are:

10 Malkhut or Kingdom This is the first sephiroth with which to work, and the aspirant then proceeds to ascend the Tree. It is a complement to Kether at the Crown, and is the garden paradise of the Divine kingdom of God on Earth. It corresponds to the Base Chakra.

9 Yesod or Foundation Referred to as the "mirror of mirrors," this is a composite energy of all the following sephiroth. Its functions are to do with rhythm, organic growth, the tides of the sea (and of life) and cyclical changes; it is central to the biological functions of life. Like the Sacral Chakra to which it corresponds, it is associated with the Moon.

8 Hod or Reverberation The sephiroth of learning, communication, trade, travel, commerce and the exchange of ideas. It is connected to the art of magic when the energies of will are controlled. It corresponds to the Yin aspects of the Solar Plexus Chakra.

7 Netsach or Eternity The sephiroth of relationships on many levels. It contains the qualities of impulsive or instinctive actions that occur after experiencing discipline, passion, understanding, wisdom or vision. It corresponds to the Yang aspects of the Solar Plexus Chakra.

6 **Tipareth or Beauty** This is attributed to Christ, the Sun, the heart of the tree or the central core of being. Tipareth represents all matters of healing, life, abundance and success. Like the Heart Chakra to which is corresponds, it harmonizes higher and lower forces.

5 **Geburah or Justice** This supports Mercy with qualities of discipline, discernment, rigor and judgment. It also represents conflict and violence and governs change, by overturning old systems of thinking with new ones. It corresponds to the Yin aspects of the Throat Chakra.

4 **Chesed or Mercy** Its virtue of obedience indicates cooperation with the rules of society. On an inner level, it leads to emotional awareness of the qualities of the heart/mind as expressed through the voice. This is reflected in human tendencies toward love, tolerance, learning and generosity. It corresponds to the Yang aspects of the Throat Chakra.

• **Daat or D'aath** The sephiroth of abstraction and the realm of the Holy Spirit. It symbolizes true knowledge or experience born of a combination of Understanding and Wisdom, when the left and right brain are united. Daat is not numbered and is hidden on the tree, being placed just below Wisdom and Understanding. It is not assigned a chakra.

3 **Binah or Understanding** The place where Divine revelation settles into our daily perceptions. It is representative of the intellect and is sometimes called the Great Mother of birth, as well as death. It corresponds to Yin aspects of the Brow Chakra.

2 **Chokmah or Wisdom** The contact point where the wheel turns between the Divine mind and human perception of the Divine mind. It is the place of visions and dreams. Within Chokmah, Light is perceived that brings about expansion of consciousness. It represents the Divine Father and Yang aspects of the Brow Chakra.

1 **Kether or Crown** The Virtue of Attainment. This represents the energy of Divine Light that enters the Kabbalistic tree pattern and flows downward through it as a "lightning flash." This is the place of beginning and ending. It corresponds to the Crown Chakra.

sufism and the seven lataif

Sufism is the practice of an esoteric and mystic branch of Islam. Mysticism enables a direct perception of reality, God or the Absolute without the need for an institution (such as a church or mosque) or discussion. For a Sufi, inner evolution is achieved through contemplation (muraqaba) and renunciation (fana). It is believed this not only benefits the individual, but also the wider world with which he or she comes into contact and the whole of society.

Abu Hashim of Kufa (8th century CE) was the first person to be called a Sufi. The word comes from an Arabic word meaning "wool" (usually woven into a warm cloak worn by followers of Sufism). Sufism spread throughout the Middle East from its origins in Iraq, and reached Persia, Pakistan, North Africa and Muslim Spain.

A woman, Rabi'a al-'Adawiyya (c. 717–801), from Basra in southern Iraq was one of the most famous Islamic mystics. St. Rabi'a had a profound influence on later Sufis, and her teachings deeply influenced the widespread European mystical love and troubadour traditions. She was known for her passion for God. Around the middle of the 9th century there was a division between asceticism and mysticism, and the Sufism movement appears to have developed further in Basra. At this time the idea was formulated that God was present in all and any part of his creation.

Sufis achieve inner evolution through contemplation and renunciation.

the lataif

The doctrine of Lataif (singular Latifa) was formulated by the 13th/14th-century Persian Sufi Alaoddawleh Semnani. Linking the seven prophets of the Koran with the mystical properties of seven Lataif, he named seven grades of being that comprise the ascent of the soul to the Godhead. Subsequently, in more modern teachings, reference is often made to a number of subtle organs or centers, called Lataif.

Generally it is believed that a Latifa has a wonderful subtle glow, like a halo of light, around it. We would do well to remember that these colors are vibrations of light, and not pigment (black or dark gray is a quantitive absence of light).

The meanings of the Lataif are complex and vary with different traditions and schools. They are considered to lie dormant in every person, and the help of a guide is necessary to activate the qualities within them.

Koranic verses also mention Lataif, known as Lataif-as-Sitta ('the six subtleties"). They are Nafsiyya, Qalbiyya, Sirriyya, Ruhiyya, Khafiya and Akhfa and are sometimes referred to as psychospiritual organs possessing super-sensory abilities. In addition Latifa qalibiyya corresponds to the Etheric Body. In many respects they are also similar to chakras. These six subtleties form the basis of orthodox Sufi philosophy.

They take the aspirant through stages of purification, cleansing, receptivity, illumination of the spirit, release of ego and remembrance of the qualities of God, respectively. Completion of the path occurs once the last two Lataif, Khafiya (secret) and Akhfa (most secret) are purified. This path is the inner Sufi way or "work" and upon completion the Sufi is named a Complete Man.

Latifa Akhfa—this Latifa symbolizes the deepest, hidden and most obscure Subtlety. Its position in the body alternates between deep inside the brain, thus association with the Crown Chakra, and the center of the chest, the Heart Chakra. It is called Nuqta-e-wahida (meaning point of unity) which is where the Tajalliat (or Beatific visions) of Allah are directly revealed to human beings. Entering deeply into its mysterious depths the adept may find information about the hidden knowledge of the universe. This center is so subtle that it needs the deep perception of a true sage to access it.

In summary, many of the basic Sufi understandings resemble the Kabbalah, the Indian chakra system and the eight yoga steps or stages of development as outlined by Patanjali (see page 99). We now recognize that at the core of all these paths to understanding are vibration and frequency.

THE SEVEN LATAIF

Latifa	Corresponding body part	Color	Named
Latifa qalibiyya	Etheric body	Black or dark gray	Adam of one's being
Latifa nafsiyya	Vital senses and animistic soul	Blue	Noah of one's being
Latifa qalbiyya	Spiritual heart	Red	Abraham of one's being
Latifa sirriyya	"The Secret" on the verge of super-consciousness	White	Moses of one's being
Latifa ruhiyya	Spirit, which is synonymous with God	Yellow	David of one's being
Latifa khafiya	Organ of spiritual inspiration	Luminous black	Jesus of one's being
Latifa akhfa	Divine Center or Eternal Seal	Sacred emerald-green (color of Islam)	Mohammed of one's being

THE WHIRLING DERVISHES

Some Sufi orders engage in ritualized ceremonies (dhikr), which may include recitation, singing, instrumental music, traditional costumes, meditation, trance ecstasy and dance. Sufi poetry is regarded as some of the most beautiful and poignant verse ever written. The Sufi dervishes of the Mevlevi order in Turkey are famous for their spinning dance: a type of meditation undertaken after fasting. When the dancers first enter they are wearing long black cloaks that represent the tomb. Then the dancers, wearing long white robes symbolizing the shroud, and a tall hat, begin to twirl rapidly on one spot. At the center is the Sheikh who represents the Sun; the dervishes represent the planets turning around him in the solar system of Mevlana. They start with their hands crossed on to their shoulders and move their arms so that the right arm is held high, palm upward, and the left arm low, palm downward. Energy from above enters the right palm into the body and is passed to the Earth through the left palm. Dancers who feel discomfort from whirling counter-clockwise can change to whirling clockwise. Eventually they fall to the floor and the process of unwinding quietly takes place. This occurs while the dancer presses his bare solar plexus and abdomen (hence the Solar Plexus and Sacral Chakras) against the ground. Whirling Dervishes can be seen performing near the Mevlevi Museum in Konya, Turkey.

Sometimes mystic Sufi songs or dances are performed as an appeal for the Presence of God, his prophets and angels. Qawwali is another form of devotional Sufi music common in Turkey, Pakistan, North India, Afganistan and Iran. Some of its modern-day masters have included Nusrat Fateh Ali Khan and the Sabri Brothers. In Uyghur culture "listening" refers to Sufi worship practices involving music and dance.

inca and mayan teachings

The Inca empire of South America, which developed from the 12th to the 16th centuries, became the largest empire in pre-Columbian America—and one of the greatest empires of the world before its last emperor was killed in 1533. Inca spiritual teaching from Peru suggests that we human beings form a bridge between Heaven and Earth (which is feminine in nature and is known as Pachamama). By making ourselves into "Saywachakuy," a pillar of light, we can connect the two realms. Inca shaman priests were believed to carry an incredible 100,000 years of spiritual teachings within them.

The Inca used an ancient, quite different and separate energy center system from yoga, in which the focus of a person's powers are seen in the auric field as "nawis" or eyes, each of which is associated with an element, a color and particular human qualities. You may like to think of the nawis as looking something like the pattern of "eyes" on the iridescent colored feathers of a peacock.

the seven powers
Esoteric teaching from the indigenous Maya people of Central America—rooted in a cultured Meso-American civilization that florished from 250 to 900 CE—called

Temple of Inscriptions, Nah Chan-Palenque, where Maya priests taught the secrets of the universe.

chakras in other traditions

chakras the "Seven Powers," and accorded each of them seven levels of vibration. These have been found, along with depictions of the aura, marked on numerous stone carvings of Mayan people and drawn in sacred books of theirs called "codices."

The Seven Powers are still taught today in Mayan esoteric studies and shamanic training. The first level that we need to balance is the physical level, our serpent power. The highest level is when we can fly to other dimensions like an eagle.

THE SEVEN NAWIS

Nawi	Element	Color	Qualities
Sacrum	Water	Black	Human impulses
Qosqo/navel	Earth	Red	Passions
Heart	Sun/Fire	Gold	Intuition/feeling
Throat	Wind	Silver	Thoughts/expansiveness
Forehead	Ether	Violet	Connection with the source
Left eye			
Right eye	The eyes give energetic information to the brain and head		

shamanism, power animals and the chakras

Shamanic practices are drawn from widely dispersed cultures and time periods. The term "shaman" is believed to have come from the Altai region of Siberia, although the word "x'man" (pronounced in the same way) is part of the Maya language of Central America. Modern usage of the word applies it loosely to anyone who draws power from Nature and focuses their psychic abilities in a good way to assist others in their group or tribe.

A power animal is an energy that takes the characteristics or shape of an animal to the observer. Typically power animals may appear in dreams or during shamanic "journeys," to give their power or "medicine" to help supplement the receiver's energies. Animal guides are rather different, since they are inner teachers who have chosen to instruct or protect the shaman.

medicine wheels

If you are familiar with shamanic teachings and use a medicine wheel as a map of consciousness, you can choose to work/meditate in appropriate quarters to illuminate specific chakras. Different tribes traditionally used their own colors for these quarters, but you may like to try the following suggestions:

Medicine wheels were built by the natives of North and Central America for spiritual and ritualistic purposes.

POWER ANIMALS LINKED TO THE CHAKRAS

The following power animals have traditionally been associated with the seven major chakras in the Native American and Indian traditions.

Chakra	Native American	Indian
Base Chakra	Snake/serpent	Elephant with seven trunks
Sacral Chakra	Dolphins	Makara (mythic crocodile)
Solar Plexus Chakra	Birds	Ram (male sheep)
Heart Chakra	All mammals	Antelope/deer
Throat Chakra	All humanity	White elephant
Brow Chakra	Spirit guides and ancestors	Garuda (eagle)
Crown Chakra	Kachina Universal Spirit	Enlightened human

- The East quarter is given the color red/element Fire; it is the place to come into resonance with your Base Chakra.
- The West quarter is given the color blue/element Water, and relates to your Sacral Chakra.
- The North quarter is given the color white/element Air, and relates to your Heart Chakra.

- The South quarter is given the color yellow/element Earth, and is your Earth–Sun consciousness at the Solar Plexus.

In the center of the medicine wheel you balance all these four elements with the color of the green light of Nature, and work with the energies of the higher chakras above the heart.

earth chakras

It may come as a surprise to learn that there are Planetary and Earth Chakras as well as our own body-energy chakras. However, our shining planet hurtling through space is a living body too, as Native American people have long affirmed.

You may like to discover the seven major Earth Chakras in your local area. These are associated with places where ley lines converge. Ley lines are energetic currents that flow above and/or below the ground. A good way to find them is to obtain old maps of the area and link together (using lines drawn on the map) significant points, such as old churches, crosses, the sources of springs, wells, ancient groves of trees, Neolithic earthworks, sites of old habitation, barrows and hills. Next, confirm your findings with a pendulum over the map, or visit the sites to sense their energies with dowsing rods.

sacred sites and the chakras

All over the world religious buildings have been built in places that were already considered sacred. Across Europe the first Christian churches were placed where there was an existing focus of belief, which throughout centuries of use had maintained a balance with the natural forces of the Earth. So you may find that under an old church there still exists underground water, which once came to the surface as a spring to bless "pagan" rites. You may sense that this point is the Sacral Chakra of the area. As you deepen your contact with the hidden forces of Mother Earth, you will come to see caves and chasms as the Base Chakra; places where ceremonial fires were traditionally lit as the Solar Plexus Chakra;

meeting places where the leaders addressed the people as the Throat Chakra; perhaps a hilltop overlooking a present-day city is the Brow Chakra. At this point you will be tuned into the Earth energies and will easily intuit the Heart Chakra, and then find the Crown Chakra, where the strongest flow of cosmic energy comes into the region.

Just like the flow of energy through the body's chakras, the Earth Chakras are calling out for balance. Groups of ordinary people are meeting to send positive thoughts and focus global meditations, often using a network of local ley lines and chakras as their starting point. When positive energy is once again pulsing through these places, they can function as intended: as the nerves, arteries and organs of Earth herself.

The Callanish stones in the Hebrides were placed there to focus Earth/cosmic energies.

planetary chakras

Where Earth Chakras are local energy "hotspots" associated with converging ley lines, Planetary Chakras are part of the whole global energy grid. The theory that the living matter of Earth functions like a single organism was propounded by research scientist James Lovelock in his Gaia hypothesis in the 1960s, and has since been backed up by other researchers and mystics.

the great earth serpent

This is an enduring rainbow of light that spirals around our blue-green planet linking the major Planetary Chakras together. It is a powerful energy current, comprising subtle-energy lines of light that, like kundalini, meet, cross and wrap

chakras in other traditions

Chakra flow around the planet forms major Earth energy lines.

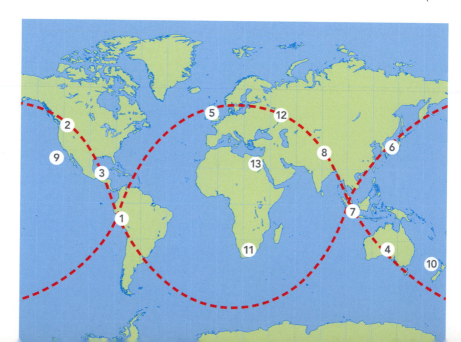

THE GLOBAL PLANETARY CHAKRAS

There are seven major Planetary Chakras, plus the Hara and three additional energy portals corresponding to the Causal Chakra, Soul Star and Stellar Gateway centers. The portal in Moscow is equivalent to the Earth Star, and the Great Pyramid in Egypt will only become energetically active when its "etheric capstone" is symbolically replaced.

1 **Root Chakra**: Lake Titicaca, Peru/Bolivia
2 **Sacral Chakra**: Mount Shasta, California, USA
3 **Hara Chakra**: Nah Chan (Palenque), Mexico
4 **Solar Plexus Chakra**: Uluru (Ayer's Rock), Australia
5 **Heart Chakra**: Aquarian triangle centered on Glastonbury, England
6 **Throat Chakra**: Mount Fuji, Japan
7 **Brow Chakra**: Gunung Agung, Bali
8 **Crown Chakra**: Mount Kailas, Tibet
9 **Causal Chakra**: Haleakala Crater, Maui, Hawaii
10 **Soul Star**: Lake Taupo, New Zealand
11 **Stellar Gateway**: Table Mountain, South Africa
12 **Earth Star energy portal**: Moscow, Russia (this portal opens only if the other 12 are balanced and open)
13 **Energy portal**: Great Pyramid, Egypt (this portal reopens only when its "etheric capstone" is replaced)

themselves about Gaia's sacred power places. The Earth Serpent winds itself around the turning sphere of Mother Earth in a loving embrace, seeking her heart. In this way the Planetary Chakras are synchronized and the harmonic balance of Earth is tenderly maintained.

The serpent features in Australian Aborigine stories of Kuniya and her nephew Liru, who meet at Uluru in the center of the continent. In Mexico, the great Rainbow-Feathered Serpent was known as Quetzalcoatl to the Aztecs/Toltecs and to the Maya as Ku'kuul'kaan. In China, the serpents take the form of elemental flying dragons breathing fire or water. And the mythology of Celtic Europe is replete with dragon stories.

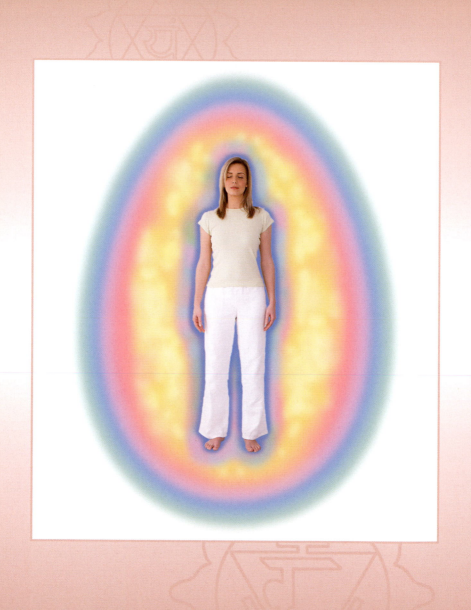

Chapter 11

CHAKRAS AND HEALING

○ ○ ○ ○ ○ ○ ○

This chapter of the book explains how to give
healing, whether or not the recipient of the healing
process is actually present.

healing with spirit

Modern research is confirming what mystics have been demonstrating through the centuries: that there is a universal healing force, which is an intrinsic part of our bodies. Scientists can measure bio-electromagnetic force fields being generated by the body; the heart has the strongest forcefield and has been measured 15 ft. (4.5 m) away. The combination of all the bio-magnetic fields from different organs, muscles and bones makes up our rainbow-like auric field.

bio-electromagnetic fields

It is a principle of magnetism that one force field interacts with another—this is called induction. That is what happens when a healer focuses a healing action. Our hands have a bio-electromagnetic field surrounding them. Measurements of a healer's hands have been recorded showing a field strength of 0.002 gauss, which is a thousand times stronger than any other forcefield emitted by the body. The field pulses out frequencies varying between 0.3 and 30 Hertz, with most of the energy being around 7–8 Hertz. This frequency is within the alpha brainwave level and, interestingly, our thalamus center within the brain controls brainwaves that are known to modulate the field's currents.

During stressed or disease conditions of the body, we experience unstable bio-electromagnetic fields. When healers transmit energy (usually through their hands), they maintain a stable field for their client, which for most people is preferable to an unstable one (as created by an alternating current). According to present scientific thinking, every time healers transmit energy into another person, the force fields produced affect charged particles ever so slightly, even in the farthest galaxies.

auric field

A study by Dr. Valerie Hunt at the University of California in 1977 showed that auric colors are produced in the range of 100–1,200 cycles per second (Hertz). This is similar to power and telephone frequencies, and a little above normal brainwave frequencies, which range from 0.5 to 35 cycles per second, and above frequencies recorded for muscles taken from electrodes on the surface of the skin. It is this energy that can be harnessed to help heal the chakras.

Healers transmit energy to help their clients maintain a stable bio-electromagnetic field.

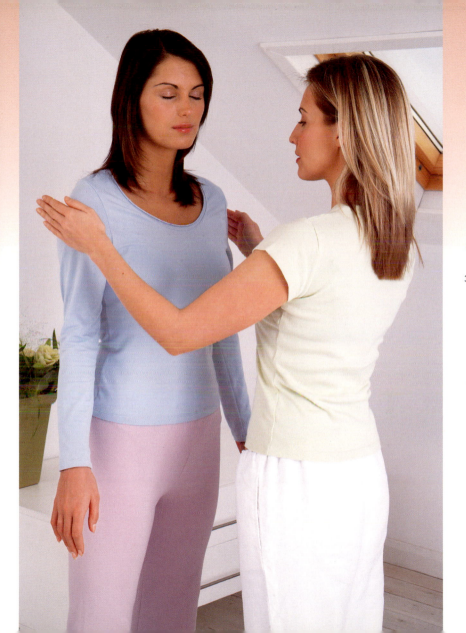

cleansing your healing space

Ceremony has been regarded as a vital part of life since the dawn of humanity and is a good method of invoking a powerful force in a way that is understood by people of all cultures, whether or not they speak the same language.

Energetically cleansing your space is an important part of a healing ceremony. First you must ensure that any crystals you intend to use have been cleansed (see page 68). Then you should clear your own aura (and that of your friend/s). A traditional way to do this is with smoke—as incense or joss-sticks, or in the Native American tradition with bundles of dried herbs called "smudge sticks." The herbs burned as cleansers are usually white sage, cedar and sweet grass (*Hierochloe odorata*).You will then be ready to dedicate your healing space, and may wish to say a prayer and ceremonially light a special candle before you begin your healing work.

MAKING YOUR OWN SMUDGE STICK

If you have a sage bush in your garden, it usually benefits from pruning. Save all the cuttings and dry them on a sunny windowsill until they are crisp (you can do the same with rosemary, thyme and cedar). When you have enough dried material, take twiggy pieces about 8–10 in. (20–25 cm) long with leaves attached, and bunch them together, with any loose leaves in the center. Traditionally the bundle is tightly tied with red cotton thread, but you can use any color. Trim all the stalks to the same length to create a handle, and your smudge stick is ready for lighting.

smudging yourself or another person

Smudging is more than just cleansing—it becomes a ceremony, too.

1 Open a window, or do this smudging ceremony outside.
2 Light your incense/smudge stick and have a large open shell or a fireproof dish with some earth or sand in it, in which to rest it.
3 Stand up and use a large feather to waft the smoke from head to feet. This clears the aura by taking harmful positive ions away from the bio-

electromagnetic auric field. They bond electrically with the fragrant smoke and drift away, being replaced with the beneficial negative ions needed.
4 Say some words or a prayer to indicate that you have finished. The aura will now be clearer to anyone who is clairvoyant, and the recipient should feel a little lighter in their body.
5 Extinguish the burning incense/smudge stick in the earth or sand.

preparing to give healing

The next stage is to align yourself with the healing energies. Ensure that you will not be disturbed, and have your healing space beautifully prepared: flowers and crystals are particularly appropriate.

Wash your hands, then relax completely using the breathing exercises given opposite. Ask for guidance from Beings of Light, angels of healing, Reiki masters or others who may inspire you. At this point you may like to say a prayer to align yourself with your own healing tradition. Finally, bring yourself fully into the presence of the person to whom you intend to channel healing.

breathing with your belly

This heightens your consciousness, and involves more of your body in breathing than simply your lungs. Basic yogic breathing teaches the importance of breathing in through the nostrils and then slowly and completely filling the lungs. The effect of this is a wave-like motion that first makes the abdomen (belly) rise and then subside, as more air goes into the lungs and top part of the chest. In this way you draw increased levels of oxygen into your body. The air is expelled slowly through the nostrils.

ETHICS

- A healer does not have to understand or know the name of a disease, but may help the client find the cause of their illness.
- A healer works with positive energy—not illness—and should explain from the outset that healing is a very different experience from a cure or remission.

- A healer does not use their own personal prana/energy, but asks to become a channel for healing energy.
- A client is advised to clear repetitive patterns of behavior and negative chakra imprints and to achieve high energy levels in their own body.
- The most important action for both healer and client is to send unconditional love to the seat of disease.

four-part breathing

Yoga also teaches that the breath is a key to relaxation and meditation—the very states you need to achieve to use crystals effectively and work on the chakras. Using the slow steady breath described opposite, begin to count silently as you: a) breathe in; b) hold your breath in; c) breathe out; d) hold your breath out. You can do this in a 2:1 ratio, counting ten for a, five for b, ten for c and five for d. Never force your breathing pattern, because this will negate any beneficial effects.

Candles, flowers and sacred objects attract healing energies into a room.

scanning the chakras
and channeling energy

Before healers lay hands on a client's body or work on their auric field, they may scan the body with their hands. This senses very small differences in the auric energy field. For example, there should be a feeling of flow, but instead there may be a hole, heat or coldness, or electrical activity indicating the degree to which the chakras are unbalanced or which part of the body needs healing.

acting as a clear channel

Healers talk of transmitting energy, running energy or channeling energy, all of which refer to the same process. It means that you do not use judgments during the healing session, but see yourself as a clear channel through which energy can flow. Envisage the channel like a jug that has milk poured into it, and from which you pour the healing milk out through your hands. Healers should feel energized after working (not drained), for a bit of the cream from the milk stays inside the jug!

When a healer starts to transmit pranic energy through the client's "wiring," it sets up both bio-electric and bio-electromagnetic fields. Scientific studies confirm that such force fields affect nearby electrons and physical body cells. In this way, the auric emanations of both healer and client are visibly enhanced. The ideal is for the healer to channel the specific "vibration" needed by the client. There are two main modes of healing:

- Offering the healing method up to creation (through masters, guides, angels, God)
- Channeling specific light/color/crystals/sound, or using other tools.

fine-tuning the technique

Practice makes perfect! In color healing, for instance, a new healer will try to visualize the color that is needed, but very often the color purple is the frequency they manifest. New healers who intend to channel color need to practice to identify the frequencies of a range of colors that are beneficial to clients; using crystals, light, silk cloth, sound frequencies or essential oils of the desired color can assist in this fine-tuning. Learning this can be difficult for many people, so instead some healers use clear white light as the channeling color. However, this may give an already energy-depleted body extra work to do, for you may mistakenly be giving a rainbow of colors instead; the client's body will then need to filter out the other constituent colors from the clear white-light spectrum.

By scanning a client's body, a healer can sense areas that need attention.

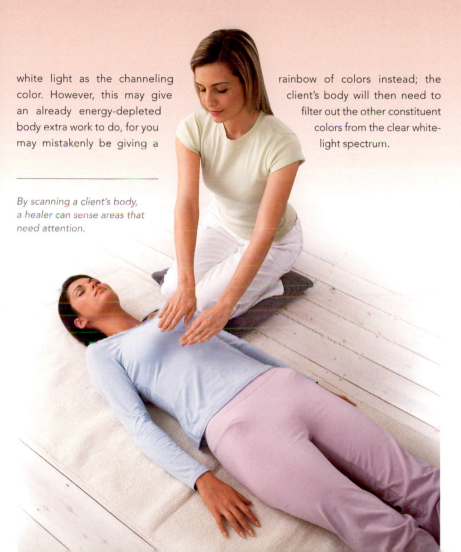

pendulum-dowsing the chakras

Using a crystal pendulum (dowsing) is a reliable way to ascertain the strengths and weaknesses of the chakras. First you need to build up an empathy with your pendulum (it is preferable not to let anyone else use it); if you have bought a new pendulum, treat it as you would any crystal by cleansing and dedicating it.

using a pendulum

The simplest way to use a pendulum is with Yes and No answers.

1 Find out which direction the pendulum moves in when you ask a question to which the answer is Yes. For example, "Is my name... [give your own name]?" Then bring the pendulum to a resting position.

Note: When you are using a crystal pendulum, never hold it right over a chakra, for it will not give a correct reading. This is because chakras immediately come into resonance with a pendulum's crystalline energies when they are stimulated by it.

2 In the same way find the pendulum's No response. Ask, "Is my hair blue?" (or anything else that is untrue). Practice the questions until the pendulum's responses are reliable.

3 Now, holding the pendulum in one hand, use your other hand to point a finger to a chakra position and ask questions such as "Is this chakra balanced?", "Is it underactive?" or "Is it overactive?" In this way you can build up a picture of your own energies by watching the pendulum's response. When you are confident with this technique, you can use it on other people.

checking chakra flow with a pendulum

If you are working with another person, ask them to lie down on their back. Use the middle finger of your non-dominant hand over the relevant chakra position, and keep your other hand (which is holding the pendulum) as far away as possible from the person's auric field. Relax and observe the pendulum as you receive answers to your silent questions. Remember that the front of a person's body is a softer, more vulnerable

aspect and will probably give a clearer reading than the chakras in their spinal region. Keep a record on a small chart of what you find out about each chakra. You are now ready to bring the chakras into balance (or perform whatever other healing is

When using a pendulum remain calm, with your mind unattached to the answers.

appropriate), but make sure that you only ever *work on one chakra at a time.* Check the results afterward with the pendulum.

giving chakra healing

Having ascertained the condition and energy flow of someone's chakras, you can move on to aura reading. Modern research confirms that the chakras usually exhibit the rainbow colors of red through to magenta, although occasionally they manifest other colors, particularly if there are major imbalances.

aura colors

For example, the Base Chakra is sometimes brown or dull; other chakras may be seen as small, uneven forms with a mixture of dull or dark primary colors; and some chakras may be barely visible. But after initial healing sessions, the auric field generally changes

and healers begin to see a range of brighter colors. Particular qualities are associated with specific auric colors:

- Anger or pain shows as red flashes in the aura
- Depression manifests as dull, dark colors—for instances, as a depressive cloud over the higher chakras
- Spiritual attainment shows as plumes of white light from above the head, or as a golden halo
- Healing usually manifests as blue, emanating from the healer's hands.

how to "read" the aura

To receive auric vision, do not limit yourself, for you *can* fall deeper into other worlds and rise to heights of "super-consciousness." Let go of all that is immediate; tune into the pulse of your life—breathe—hear the beat of your heart—breathe again. Look and you will begin to really see what is, and what is beyond.

Begin by making very gentle contact through the client's aura, so as not to startle him/her.

chakra healing technique

There are as many ways to give healing as there are people. One simple chakra healing technique follows.

1 Gently pass your hands through the client's auric field, and lightly contact the crown of their head with the palms of your hands.

2 Hold this position while you ask for energy to flow from the crown of your head into your hands and then into your client's head.

3 Rest your hands on their shoulders and wait until their breathing pattern stabilizes and deepens.

4 Now channel healing into the required chakras through your hands (or use crystals, color, and so on). See pages 382–383 for more advanced techniques.

5 Bring the client's energy field to a balanced level, sealing and protecting it.

6 Close the healing with your own personal prayer or words of thanks.

7 Assist the client to sit up, ground themselves and take a glass of water.

8 Wash your hands and cleanse your own auric field.

realigning displaced chakra energies

Remember that healing is not curing, and neither you nor the client should have specific expectations. It is not necessary to be medically trained to give healing, but a basic knowledge of anatomy and physiology helps. When working with chakras, you need to ascertain which ones to treat. You do this is by a combination of intuition, divine guidance and training. Normally it is best to begin by realigning the lowest imbalanced chakra first.

Many people suffer from a depletion of energy and dysfunction of the first chakra. It resonates with red light, so this is an appropriate color to channel through energy entry points in the feet, knees, hips, shoulders and coccyx. Another starting point is to understand typical negative and positive mental states, which are easily observed in someone's personality and body language. For you as a healer, the session starts as soon as your client enters the room and you begin picking up clues about their energy levels. But not every healer immediately sees technicolored auric fields!

chakras and healing

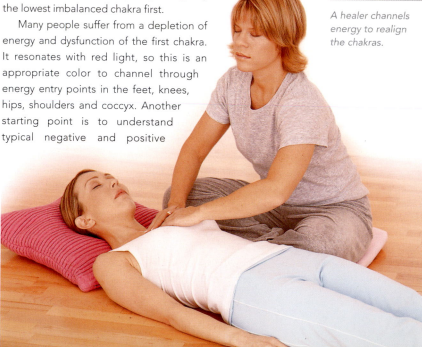

A healer channels energy to realign the chakras.

MENTAL STATES AND THE CHAKRAS

Base Chakra
Negative Typically coarse, violent, angry; greedy and self-centered; destructive, impatient, competitive
Positive Natural, bold, clear, courageous; direct, dynamic, spontaneous, self-reliant

Sacral Chakra
Negative Over-indulgent; materialistic, moody, possessive; lazy, jealous, envious
Positive Kind, receptive, tolerant, creative, respectful, tender and intimate, works positively

Solar Plexus Chakra
Negative Arrogant, hypocritical, incompetent, inflexible; concerned with power and fame; unable to finish things; underlyingly selfish
Positive Determined and intelligent; a leader showing warmth and humor, but cool, calm and assertive when required; positive self-esteem

Heart Chakra
Negative Emotionally unstable, self-indulgent and sentimental, jealous and lustful, procrastinating and indecisive
Positive Compassionate, open and cooperative, gives unconditional love leading to contentment, harmony, balance and grace

Throat Chakra
Negative Full of diffused energies; overoptimistic, exaggerating, uses words and actions to hurt others; poor communicator; depressed, joyless
Positive An educated adventurer who always succeeds; uses the voice to praise, sing and/or speak the truth

Brow Chakra
Negative Lacking concentration and imagination; fears the unknown; tense, cynical, harsh, sad; possibly phobic and detached from the world
Positive Authoritative, organizational, patient, shows integrity; reliable; clairvoyant

Crown Chakra
Negative Confused, depressed, alienated and fearful of death/suicidal
Positive Compassionate, gentle, inspired, intuitive; spiritual/mystic/psychic

healing with sound

Sound is a vibrational energy that passes through the medium of air, either from voice or instrument. It is not only received by the ear, but also penetrates the body and imprints our blood.

Specific instruments are particularly beneficial when giving sound in healing, such as the flute and harp when conveying the "inner nature" of sound vibration. "Tibetan" singing bowls are popular with sound-healing practitioners; indeed their use is so ancient that we know Japanese Bon shamans used them before Buddhism began.

tibetan singing bowls

Accomplished sound-healers may own and use a number of bowls, so first a few words about choosing one. Make sure you pick from a selection of bowls: the largest is not necessarily the best. Look carefully at the rim: if it's thin, it is Yin in nature (see pages 16–17); if it's fat, it is Yang. Are there any dents, marks or fill-ins? You also need a wand to "play" it with. Gently tap the rim with your wand and move it consistently around the rim at the same angle. A musical note should emerge. How do you "feel" about the sound? Try another, until you find the bowl that gives you the greatest satisfaction.

Don't overclean your bowl, but do care for it and get to know it well. Try half-filling it with water and holding the bowl in one hand, moving it gently as you play. The note may take on a haunting sound. Your bowl was originally crafted using differing amounts of seven metals, representing the inner planets, and it will have a musical note corresponding to (or near) one of the notes of a piano keyboard.

using a tibetan bowl

With your client laying down or sitting in a chair, gently take them into a relaxed state.

1 Gradually introduce the sound from your bowl—say, from 3 ft. (1 m) away.
2 While playing, let yourself be guided to bring the bowl to a part of the client's body or a specific chakra.
3 Keep a focus on this point. The bowl may be resting on their body or you may keep it in their auric field.
4 Gently withdraw the bowl when you sense its sound resonance has done its work.
5 Place the bowl silently aside and give thanks, knowing that its vibration continues to be absorbed for some time.

Using a Tibetan singing bowl does not require special mystical skills—just an ear for beautiful sounds.

advanced healing techniques

When you give healing, you are changing another person's body and auric field frequencies. It is likely that you will do this intuitively, or will be guided in diverse ways. You have read how you should protect your own auric field and set up a sacred space if you are giving healing. To assist the client, you may wish to consider using the following advanced stages and techniques during your healing session.

1 Ask for guidance and/or assess what is needed during the healing: for instance, aura reading, dowsing with a pendulum, muscle-testing, scanning, and so on.
2 Balance the chakra and ask to channel the healing.
3 Position crystals or other sacred objects, if these are being used.
4 Enlighten—drastically increase the healing vibration.
5 Move the energy as you are guided, drawing from the Earth and cosmic realms to benefit the client.
6 Allow—whatever needs to be.
7 Seal the encodements of the healing and protect the auric field of the client.
8 Acknowledge and thank both your own guidance and the crystals or other sacred objects you have used.
9 Stabilize the body energies and subtle-energy flows of both yourself and the client, then ensure that the chakras are balanced at an appropriate level.

Bear in mind that when you have finished the healing, you should ground both yourself and the client, by imagining roots going out through the soles of your feet into the center of the Earth (see page 108). You may wish to ask the client to visualize a healing protective blue cloak wrapped around them. Then it is essential that you take a moment to wash your hands in cold water, while the recipient of the healing is relaxing after the session. Both of you need to drink some pure water; this not only flushes toxins from the body, but also provides the medium for the living bioenergy and pranic energy to flow throughout the chakras and the whole mind–body–spirit complex.

The client almost always experiences profound relaxation during a healing session.

distant healing

*I am my own limitation—without my
own limitation, I am.*

Anon

Because "All is one," in order to give distant
healing (healing through the mind to
someone who is not physically present) you
should make preparations in the same way
as you would if the person were in front of
you. This means that you should cleanse
and prepare yourself, your room and any
crystals or sacred objects you will use.
Healers often use a "witness" for distant
healing—something that holds or
represents the person's energy field; it
might be a recent photograph (full-length,
with no one else in the picture), a few drops
of their blood, some hair, a signature or a
handwritten letter from the person.

It is both ethical and appropriate to ask
permission to do the healing and inform the
client of the time and day you will be
"transmitting," in order that they may sit
quietly to fully participate in their own
healing. It is recommended that you send
distant healing for a minimum of three days
in a row. *Never* give healing if you are
feeling upset or angry.

golden rules

Name, face and place are the three golden
rules for sending distant healing effectively:

- **Name** Preferably use the name they were
  given at birth.
- **Face** Look at a photograph or, in the
  absence of one, visualize the person
  looking well and happy.
- **Place** Visualize where they actually are at
  the time of the distant healing.

If you are using a photograph for distant
healing, you can easily place small crystals
on it in the appropriate chakra locations and
focus your healing intentions there.

other possibilities

In a similar way you can give distant healing
to yourself as a child; in the future or in the
present; to someone who is no longer in a
physical body; to the space between people
(their relationships); a place; a nation; a
personal or global situation; or a disaster.
With some of these examples you direct
healing energy to places or situations rather
than chakras.

Never underestimate the power of healing!

OM Shanti, Shanti, Shanti, OM.

A concentrated and
focused mind passes
across time and space
because we are part
of a unified, universal
energy field.

glossary

affirmation a sentence repeated silently to oneself that reminds us of our spiritual path.

akasha the ether or spiritual power that permeates the universe; in Yoga teaching, the fifth element that embraces the other four elements of Earth, Water, Fire and Air.

anti-seborrheic helping to control the production of sebum, the oily secretion from the sweat glands.

asanas the basic sitting, standing and reclining postures in Hatha yoga.

astringent constricting the body tissues and stopping the flow of blood or other secretions.

aura a rainbow of light; the body's external subtle-energy field.

bandha a body lock in yoga—a combination of particular muscles that are contracted and focused in order to alter subtle energy flows.

Bhagavad Gita an ancient Sanskrit text of 700 verses from the Mahabharata comprising Hindu philosophy and revered as sacred by most Hindus and especially by followers of Krishna.

Brahanas commentaries on the first four Hindu scriptures, the Vedas.

carminative helping to expel gas from the stomach and intestines.

chakra (lit. "wheels of light") pulsating focal centers of subtle energy in the luminous auric energy field.

ch'i (qi) a Chinese word referring to the energetic substance that flows from the environment into the body considered identical to Prana and Ki.

diuretic promoting the flow of urine from the body.

emmenagogic speeding up or inducing menstrual flow.

expectorant promoting the removal of mucus from the lungs.

febrifuge fever-reducing.

granthi in Yoga an energy block or psychic hurdle within the auric field; in Sikhism one who reads from a holy book.

gunas a quality, an ingredient or constituent of nature; the three qualities (tamas, rajas, sattvas) of food in Indian Ayurvedic practice .

Hatha yoga the system of yoga based upon Patanjali´s Eight Limbs (sutras), including physical postures, breathing exercises, cleansing, mindful awareness and meditation.

hepatic aids and stimulates the function of the liver.

karma the law of cause and effect; the total effect of a person's actions during the successive phases of their existence, regarded as determining their fate or destiny.

Ki a Japanese word for life-force energy, identical to prana and ch'i.

kinesiology, applied a method of diagnosing body health through muscle-testing.

Kirlian photography a form of photography whereby, when an object on a photographic plate is subjected to a strong electric field, an image is created on the plate.

kundalini energy the energy that was unleashed during the creation of the world; an energy, the full power of which, lies dormant at the Base Chakra, but can be increased through Tantric practices with the aim of union with the Divine source of creation.

mandala a circular symbol of the universe used as an aid in meditation; in Jungian psychology a symbol representing the self and inner harmony.

mantra a mystical syllable (such as OM) or chant; a poetic hymn, incantation or prayer repeated many times.

meridian a line of energy within and on the surface of the body, used therapeutically in acupuncture.

mudra a symbolic hand gesture used in Hindu dance and meditation.

nadi a channel for life-force or prana; there is one central nadi (the sushumna nadi) and two secondaries on either side: the ida nadi and the pingala nadi.

nervine stimulates and strengthens the nervous system.

prana an Sanskrit word referring to the energetic substance that flows from the environment into the body; the life-breath; bio-energy.

pranayama the control of energy (prana) through the breath. Developed as correct breathing combined with the application of bandhas and mudras in yoga practice.

radionics a method of diagnosis and treatment at a distance, using specially designed instruments with which a practitioner can determine the underlying causes of diseases in a living system.

reflexology an ancient Chinese healing technique using pressure-point massage (generally on the feet, but also on the hands and ears) to restore the flow of energy through the body.

Reiki a spiritual path; a form of spiritual healing, rediscovered in Japan that focuses Ki through the hands to benefit another person or life form.

samadhi a state of bliss, where the spirit is liberated and joins the Universal Spirit .

sannyasin a male or female monk who has renounced material possessions in order to walk a path of integration into the spiritual world.

Sanskrit the classical sacred and literary language of the Hindus of India.

Shaktism a denomination of Hinduism that worships Shakti/Devi Mata the Divine Great Mother in all her forms. Also the spiritual path that describes the seven major chakras we recognize today.

siddhis eight tantalizing paranormal powers that can be achieved through yogic development.

sruti knowledge that was revealed to the great seers; a term used to refer to the four collections that make up the Vedas.

Tantras ancient Hindu or Buddhist scriptures written in Sanskrit and concerned with ritual acts of body, speech and mind.

Tao Chinese philosophy of the Way of Long Life; Chinese character meaning "way," road or path; relates to Taoism.

Theosophy a school of mystical philosophy established by Madame Blatvatsky in 1875 incorporating Buddhist and Brahmanic teachings.

trimurti the Hindu trinity consisting of Brahma the creator, Vishnu the preserver and Shiva the destroyer, who represent the three forms of the supreme being.

Upanishads (lit. "those who sit near") sacred Hindu philosophical writings that elaborated on the earlier Vedas in the form of mystic or spiritual contemplations. Composed over several centuries from the 8th century BCE, there are 108 Upanishads, although only 13 are considered key texts.

uterine aids and stimulates the uterus.

Vajrayana Buddhism a form of Buddhism that aims to assist the student in the achievement of full enlightenment or Buddhahood in perhaps a single lifetime.

Vedas (lit. "knowledge") a collective term for the oldest and most authoritative Hindu scriptures, written in Sanskrit and comprising four collections: the Rig, Sama, Yajur and Atharva Vedas.

yantra a geometric design used as an aid in meditation; a visual symbol of complex spiritual concepts.

yoga one of the six classic systems of Indian philosophy concerned with the union of the individual with the universal consciousness; a system of bodily control leading to unity with a supreme being.

Yoga Sutras brief, but influential, ancient Indian texts, written in the Sanskrit by the sage Patanjali, which describe the philosophy and practices of yoga.

yogi a master of yoga who has achieved a high level of spiritual insight; a student of a guru.

index

index

index

acknowledgments

Author acknowledgments: I would like to thank all my teachers and students, who have added to my professional knowledge, and the Maya elders who have initiated me into ancient wisdom and unseen presences. In addition, all the editors and designers at Godsfield receive my grateful thanks. Lastly, but not least, my husband, a sound therapist, was my consultant on relevant sections of the book, as well as a patient researcher and reader of the manuscript—my loving thanks.

Executive Editor Sandra Rigby
Editor Lisa John
Executive Art Editor Sally Bond
Designer Annika Skoog for Cobalt ID
Illustrations KJA Artists
Production Controller Audrey Walter
Picture Researcher Sophie Delpech

Special Photography: © Octopus Publishing Group/Ruth Jenkinson.
Other Photography: Alamy 360-361; /Dinodia Images 84; /Mary Evans Picture Library 347; /mediacolor's 55; /WoodyStock 292 left; **ArkReligion.com**/Dinodia Photo Library 21; **Corbis UK Ltd** 17, 26, 56, 171; /Peter Adams 138-139; /Archivo Iconografico, S.A. 355; /Bettmann 25; /Radhika Chalasani 143; /Lindsay Hebberd 103; /KG-Photography/zefa 39; /Helen King 351; /SIE Productions/zefa 311; /Ted Streshinsky 83; /Robin Williams 208; **DigitalVision** 58; **Getty Images** 37, 86; /Kevin Cooley 96-97; /Elizabeth Simpson 18; **Image Source** 43, 131, 202-203, 205, 256; **Octopus Publishing Group Limited** 47, 79, 95, 110 centre, 110 bottom, 111 top, 111 centre, 111 bottom, 112, 113 top, 113 centre, 148 left, 148 right, 149 top, 149 centre, 149 bottom, 150, 152, 153 left, 153 right, 153 centre, 157, 177, 184, 185 top, 185 centre, 185 bottom, 186 left, 186 right, 206, 214 centre left, 214 bottom right, 214 bottom left, 216 top, 216 bottom, 217, 218, 219 top left, 219 centre right, 219 bottom right, 246, 248 left, 248 right, 249 left, 249 right, 250 centre left, 250 bottom right, 251, 286 left, 286 right, 287, 288 top, 288 centre, 288 bottom, 289 top, 289 centre, 289 bottom, 290 left, 290 right, 291, 316 left, 316 right, 318 left, 318 right, 319 left, 319 right, 320, 321, 321 left, 336 left, 336 right, 337 top, 337 centre left, 337 centre right, 338, 339; /Colin Bowling 253 right, 253 centre, 292 right, 322; /Stephen Conroy 253 left; /Frazer Cunningham 9, 15, 364, 367, 373; /Jerry Harpur 19; /Ruth Jenkinson 61, 64, 67, 80-81, 100-101, 115, 135, 276-277, 378; /Sandra Lane 49; /Peter Myers 63, 238-239; /Ian Parsons 46; /Mike Prior 69, 70, 117, 383; /Peter Pugh-Cook 223, 345; /Russell Sadur 44-45, 137, 174-175, 188, 215, 241, 271, 273, 307, 369, 371, 375, 376, 381, 385; /Unit Photographic 141; /Ian Wallace 48, 52, 59; **Photodisc** 10-11, 13, 187, 281, 340, 341, 356; **Science Photo Library**/Garion Hutchings 33; **TopFoto**/Dinodia 275.